THE MILITARY LAW DICTIONARY

RICHARD C. DAHL, B.L.S., LL.B.

Law Librarian

OFFICE OF THE JUDGE ADVOCATE GENERAL

U. S. DEPARTMENT OF THE NAVY

AND

JOHN F. WHELAN, B.A.

Reference Librarian

LAW SECTION, ARMY LIBRARY

U. S. DEPARTMENT OF THE ARMY

NEW YORK

OCEANA PUBLICATIONS, INC.

1960

For

MRS. J. R. SAUL

and

MRS. R. A. WHELAN

Library of Congress Catalog Number: 60-10208

PRINTED IN THE UNITED STATES OF AMERICA

Foreword

THIS VOLUME is intended to be a useful handbook for anyone interested in Military Law. We have tried to make it concise and practical. Military law, when broadly defined, encompasses so many fields that a multi-volumed dictionary could have been compiled. It is our opinion, however that a compact volume with short, clear definitions is more likely to answer the needs of the military lawyer. Thus the definitions selected were those the editors believed to be most useful.

These definitions were selected from a wide variety of sources. We have resisted the temptation to include definitions of our own. Our aim was to collect the important definitions currently used in military, legal, medical and allied fields. This dictionary was not intended to supplant the many fine dictionaries in these fields. Instead its purpose is to bring together all those definitions, and many of the abbreviations, most likely to be used by the military lawyer.

Some of our sources were the official dictionaries and publications of the Armed Services. Many definitions were found in leading legal treatises. Others came from various glossaries, dictionaries, articles, etc. Very often several sources would turn up the same or similar definitions, making our task of selection much easier.

As with most dictionaries there were far too many sources for individual acknowledgment. We have, therefore, included a list of references that indicate some of the works that were checked for terms. Works of this nature should be consulted for larger definitions and definitions of more obscure and less used words.

In the field of law, definitions are particularly important and require careful use. Entire books have been written about a single word or phrase such as "hearsay," "proximate cause," and "res ipsa loquitor." There are several important multi-volume dictionaries and one set of judicial definitions that runs to 60 volumes. THE MILITARY LAW DICTIONARY is designed to be a working tool that supplements and is in no way a substitute for those more ambitious works.

Like most dictionaries, ours was compiled on cards over a long period of time. This card file was kept, used, and tested in the Army Library and the Navy JAG Law Library. It has proven useful in these libraries and it is hoped that it will be equally useful in the field and elsewhere.

Richard C. Dahl
John F. Whelan

Table of Contents

A

ABANDON. To relinquish, give up, desert, or leave in disregard of a duty with respect thereto.

ABANDONMENT: The surrender, relinquishing, disclaimer, of property or of rights.

ABATE: To terminate; to decrease. Quash, beat down, or destroy.

ABATEMENT: Reduction or termination.

ABDUCTION: The taking away of a person surreptitiously by force. Commonly it means the act of taking away a woman against her will, or, if she is a minor, against the will of her parents or some other person having lawful control over her.

ABET: To encourage or set another on to comit a crime.

AB INITIO: From the beginning.

ABJURE: To renounce upon oath.

ABLE SEAMAN: A grade of merchant seamen.

ABORTIFACIENT: A chemical which will produce an abortion.

ABORTION: The premature expulsion of the foetus of a pregnant woman.

ABORTIONIST: One who criminally produces abortions.

ABROGATION: The destruction or annulling of a former law by an act of the legislative power, by constitutional authority, or by usage.

ABSCOND: Avoiding the process of the court by hiding or leaving the jurisdiction.

ABSENCE: Non-appearance, state of being absent or away from one's domicile, or usual place of residence.

ABSENCE WITHOUT LEAVE: Any member of the armed forces who, without proper authority (1) fails to go to his appointed place of duty at the time prescribed; or (2) goes from that place; or (3) absents himself or remains absent from his unit, organization, or other place of duty at which his required to be at the time prescribed, is absent without leave.

ABSENTE REA: In the absence of the defendant.

ABSOLVE: To set free, or release, as from obligation, debt, responsibility, or penalty.

ABSTRACT OF TITLE: Brief history of title to a piece of real estate.

ABUSE: To make excessive, ill-use, or improper use of a thing, or to employ it in a manner contrary to the natural or legal rules for its use.

ACCESSORIES AFTER THE FACT: An accessory after the fact is one who receives, relieves, comforts, or assists another personally, with knowledge that he has committed a felony. To constitute one an accessory after the fact—1. A felony must have been committed, and it must have been complete at the time of the relief or assistance. 2. The accused must know that the felony has been committed by the person received, relieved, or assisted. 3. The assistance must be rendered to the felon personally.

ACCESSORIES BEFORE THE FACT: An accessory before the fact is one who procures, commands, or counsels, the commission of a felony by another, but who is not present, either actually or constructively, when the felony is committed. To constitute one an accessory before the fact—1. There must be a guilty principal in the first degree. 2. The accessory must be neither actually nor constructively present when the offense is committed. 3. There must be some participation by way of procurement, command, or counsel. Mere knowledge that the offense is to be committed, or even mental approval, is not enough.

ACCOMPANYING: One may be considered to be "accompanying" an armed force although he is not directly employed by such force or by the Government but works for a contractor engaged on a military project or serves on a merchant ship carrying war supplies or troops.

ACCOMPLICE: Includes all "partners-in-crime" whether they are considered in strict legal propriety as principals in the first or second degree, or merely accessories before or after the fact.

ACCORD AND SATISFACTION: An accord consists of an agreement between contracting parties whereby one of them is to do something different from that called for by the contract. This accord is satisfied when the terms of the new agreement are fully performed. Both accord and satisfaction must take place before the old obligation is discharged, unless the new agreement expressly states that it is being substituted for the old.

ACCOUNTABILITY: The obligation imposed by law or lawful order or regulation on an officer or other person for keeping accurate record of property or funds. The person having this obligation may or may not have actual possession of the property or funds. Accountability is concerned primarily with records, while responsibility is concerned primarily with custody, care and safe keeping. **See Responsibility.**

ACCOUNTABLE: 1. Having accountability (individuals have accountability). 2. Requiring accountability (property or funds require accountability).

ACCOUNTABLE DISBURSING OFFICER: Any commissioned officer who receives and disburses public money in his own name. He is responsible for the funds so received and for their proper expenditure for the purposes specified by law and is required to account for them in accordance with law and regulations.

ACCOUNTABLE OFFICER: Individual required to maintain accounting, including records thereof, of property and funds, whether public or quasi public. The accountable officer may or may not have physical possession of the property or funds.

ACCOUNTABLE PROPERTY OFFICER'S BOND: A bond executed by an individual who is charged with the responsibility of protecting and maintaining Government property or keeping records for such property.

ACCRETION: Gradual and imperceptible accumulation of land by natural causes, as out of the sea or a river.

ACCUMULATED LEAVE: The earned leave credit of an officer, enlisted man, or civil service employee that may be carried over from one leave year to another.

ACCUSATION: The charge that one has been guilty of a crime or misdemeanor, made to a proper officer.

ACCUSE: Formally charging a person with the commission of a crime.

ACCUSED: The generic term for the defendant in a criminal case.

ACCUSER: Art. 1(11), UCMJ, provides that the term "accuser" shall be construed to refer: 1. To a person who signs and swears to charges, or 2. To any person who directs that charges nominally be signed or 3. To any other person who has an interest other than an official interest in the prosecution of the accused.

ACKNOWLEDGMENT: An "acknowledged" deed or other instrument is one to which is attached a certificate of a notary public, commissioner of deeds, or other officer designated by statute that the person purporting to have executed the said instrument appeared personally before the said officer and acknowledged that he executed it.

ACQUIESCENCE: Implies consent, and consent cures error.

ACQUITTAL: A person being duly charged with some crime and put upon trial and found not guilty.

ACQUITTANCE: An acquittance is, in general terms, a release or a discharge from obligation.

ACT: The common meaning of the word "act" is "that which is done or doing, a performance, a deed, a movement," as distinguished from remaining at rest. In the criminal law it is impossible to give an inclusive definition of the word in short space because, as is also true, in lesser degree, of intent, its character varies with each crime. Thus in homicide cases the act is the killing of a human being; in larceny, it is the taking and carrying away of personal property; in arson, it is the burning of a house; in rape, it is the having of sexual intercourse.

ACTING WITHIN THE SCOPE OF HIS OFFICE OR EMPLOYMENT: As applied to the members of the military or naval forces of the United States is "acting in the line of duty."

ACTION: A proceeding in court which if completed will result in a judgment.

ACTIONABLE: Furnishing legal ground for action.

ACTION IN REM: An action which has for its object a judgment against property to determine status.

ACTIVE DUTY: Refers to the status of being in the active Federal service of any of the armed forces under a competent appointment or enlistment or pursuant to a competent muster, order, call, or induction.

ACTIVE LIST: A list of all regular officers on active duty; A list of constituted units assigned to a major command for activation, and those which have been activated and are already serving in an active status.

ACTIVE SERVICE: Active duty; The status of a piece of equipment that is being used continuously.

ACTIVATE: To make a constituted or reconstituted unit active by assigning personnel to it.

ACTIVITY: 1. A unit, organizaion, or installation performing a function or mission, e.g., reception center, redistribution center, naval station, naval shipyard. 2. A function or mission, e.g., recruiting, schooling.

ACT OF GOD: Under the term "Act of God" are comprehended all misfortunes and accidents arising from inevitable necessity, which human prudence could not forsee or prevent.

ACTUAL KNOWLEDGE: When the order is conveyed directly to the accused.

ADAMISM: A form of exhibitionism in which the subject exhibits himself in the nude.

AD CURIAM: Before the court.

ADDENDA: Attachments.

ADDICT: "The term 'addict' means any person who habitually uses any habit-forming narcotic drug as defined in this chapter so as to endanger the public morals, health, safety, or welfare, or who is or has been so far addicted to the use of such habit-forming narcotic drugs as to have lost the power of self-control with reference to his addiction."—Section 221, Title 21, Foods and Drugs. The Code of Laws of the United States of America.

ADDITIONAL CHARGES: New and separate charges preferred after others have been preferred are known in military law as "additional charges."

ADDRESSEE: The individual or activity to whom a message is directed for information or action.

ADHESION: The entrance of another state into an existing treaty with respect to only specifically agreed parts.

AD HOC: For this special purpose.

AD ITERIM: In the meantime.

ADJECTIVE LAW: The law of procedure, and court organizations, as distinguished from substantive law, which determines rights and duties.

ADJOURNMENT: This halts the proceedings for overnight or longer than one day.

ADJUDICATE: To settle by a judicial action.

ADJUDICATION: The giving or pronouncing of a judgment or decree; also the judgment given.

ADJUTANT: A staff officer common to most staff organizations, charged with duties that vary from one command to another, but normally responsible to his commander for all official correspondence (except combat commanders), personnel and other records, standardization of forms, distribution of orders, and other specified administrative duties.

AD LITEM: While the action is pending.

ADMINISTRATIVE ADMONITION: An admonition given a person but not issued under the Uniform Code of Military Justice.

ADMINISTRATIVE DEMOTION: A nonpunitive demotion for inefficiency given an enlisted man by administrative action.

ADMINISTRATIVE DISCHARGE: A discharge given by administrative action, as distinguished from a discharge given as a result of a court-martial.

ADMINISTRATIVE LAW: The rules and regulations framed by an administrative body created by a state legislature or by Congress to carry out a specific statute.

ADMINISTRATIVE LEAVE: The status of an employee who is absent from his regular place of duty, but in attendance at a nonfederal meeting, such as that of a learned society, without, however, the benefit of per diem.

ADMINISTRATIVE OFFICER: An officer of the executive department of government.

ADMINISTRATIVE ORDER: One of the formal statements issued in connection with carrying out a specific combat operation or maneuver, which sets forth a plan for the logistical and administrative support of the operation; Loosely a routine order.

ADMINISTRATIVE REMEDY: A remedy that is not judicial, but provided by commission or board created by legislative power.

ADMINISTRATIVE REPRIMAND: A reprimand given a person but not issued under the UCMJ.

ADMINISTRATIVE RESTRICTION: A form of command restraint that a commanding officer may, within his discretion and without imposing arrest, restrict an accused person administratively to specified areas of a military command with the further provision that he will participate in all military duties and activities of his organization while under such restraint. Violations of such administrative restrictions are punishable as are breaches of punitive restriction.

ADMINISTRATIVE SEGREGATION: The close confinement of prisoners separate from the main prisoner group for purposes of control, safekeeping, prevention of injuries to the prisoners, or for other administrative purposes.

ADMINISTRATOR: Court appointed person who administers the estate of decedent.

ADMIRAL: A commissioned rank or person in the US Navy, corresponding to general; Used as a title for Navy officers above the rank of captain, or for Coast Guard officers above the rank of commodore.

ADMIRALTY: 1. A court which has jurisdiction of maritime causes, civil and criminal, controversies arising out of acts done upon or relating to the sea, or within tidal waters, and questions of prize. 2. The system of jurisprudence relating to the jurisdiction and practice of the admiralty courts.

ADMISSION: An admission is an utterance, express or implied, of any relevant and material fact, made by a party to the action, which utterance is adverse or inconsistent with his present claims. A party's admission need not have been against his interest at the time it was spoken. All that is required is that it be contrary to his present contention.

ADMISSABLE INFORMATION: That information offered to the court for its consideration which is both relevant and competent.

ADMISSIONS AGAINST INTEREST: Any voluntary statement by one accused of or suspected of crime, relating to some particular fact or circumstance and not the whole charge, which indicates a consciousness of guilt and tends to connect him with the crime charged and to incriminate him is admissible as an admission against interest.

ADMIT: To allow, take, or receive.

ADMIT TO PROBATE: To judge the validity of a will.

ADMONITION: An expression of official displeasure or censure, oral or written, addressed to an officer or enlisted man for a specific act.

ADOLESCENCE: The period commencing at 12 in females, and 14 in males, and ending at 21 years of age.

ADOPTION: 1. The act by which a person takes the child of another into his family and makes him, for all legal purposes, his own. Its force and validity depend upon the statutes of the several states. 2. The affirmation or acceptance of a contract which one is at liberty otherwise to repudiate.

AD REFERENDUM: For further consideration.

ADULTRY: Intercourse by a man, whether married or single, with another man's wife is adultry; but intercourse by a man, whether married or single, with an unmarried woman is only fornication.

AD VALOREM: According to the value.

ADVANCE PAYMENT: An advance of money, made by the Government to a contractor prior to, in anticipation of, and for the purpose of complete performance under a contract or contracts.

ADVERSE POSSESSION: A method of acquisition of title by possession for a statutory period under certain conditions.

ADVOCATE: An officer of the court who assists his clients and pleads their causes in court.

ADVOCATE-GENERAL: The adviser of the crown on questions of naval and military law. See also Judge Advocate.

AFFECT: The subjectively experienced feeling aspect of an emotion.

AFFIANT: One who makes oath to a statement.

AFFIDAVIT: An affidavit is a written declaration under oath, before a competent official, but it is made without notice to any adverse party. Because there has been no opportunity for cross-examination, affidavits are generally inadmissible as evidence on the grounds that they violate the Hearsay Rule. Certain exceptions to this are recognized in some states: affidavit of the loss of a document proved by copy; an affidavit of publication of a newspaper notice; affidavits used to obtain a provisional remedy as evidence in uncontested probate proceedings.

AFFINITY: Relationship by marriage between the husband and the blood relations of the husband.

AFFIRM: 1. To ratify or uphold. 2. To make a solemn religious assertion in the nature of an oath.

AFFIRMATION: An "affirmation" is a solemn and formal, external pledge, binding upon one's conscience, that the truth will be stated.

AFFRAY: At common law, an affray is the fighting of two or more persons in a public place, to the terror or alarm of the people. It is a misdemeanor. In some states the statutory definition is slightly different.

A FORTIORI: For stronger reasons.

AGENDA: Things to be done.

AGENT: A person authorized to create rights and obligations for another person, called the principal. The authority may be derived from contract made with the principal, or by appointment of the principal without contract, or may be inferred from the principal's conduct. The principal is liable not only on the contracts made for him by his agent but also for torts the agent may commit in the course of transacting the principal's business.

AGGRAVATED ARSON: The willful and malicious burning or setting on fire of an inhabited dwelling, or of any other structure, movable or immovable, wherein the knowledge the the offender there is at the time a human being.

AGGRAVATED ASSAULTS: An assault with intent to kill, to do great bodily harm, to rape, to rob, etc., is called an aggravated assault, as distinguished from a common assault, because the assault is aggravated by the concurrence of the felonious intent with which it is made. At common law aggravated assaults were punished more severely than common assaults, but they were not recognized as distinct technical offenses. All assaults were merely misdemeanors.

AGGRAVATION: That which increases the enormity of a crime or the injury of a wrong.

AIDER AND ABETTOR: One who shares the criminal intent or purpose of the perpetrator, and hence liable as a principal.

AIDING, OR ATTEMPTING TO AID, THE ENEMY: Aiding the enemy with arms, ammunition, supplies, money or other thing, or, without authority, harboring or protecting, or giving intelligence to, or communicating or correspondence with the enemy, either directly or indirectly, is punishable by death or as a court-martial or military commission may direct.

AIRCRAFT: Comprising generally the air-borne craft of the services, both heavier and lighter than air.

AIR FORCE: The Department of the Air Force at the seat of Government and all field headquarters, forces reserve components, installations, activities, and functions under the control or supervision of the Department of the Air Force.

AIR FORCE OF THE UNITED STATES: A designation for the overall USAF, sometimes used between 1947 and 1951 to distinguish the overall organization from its regular component which was ambiguously called the "United States Air Force."

AIR FORCE REPRESENTATIVE: A person, civilian or military, serving in a place outside AF jurisdiction, where he represents the views of, or acts for, the Air Force.

AIR JUDGE ADVOCATE: A judge advocate or staff judge advocate in the AF, as distinguished from one in the Army or Navy.

AIRMAN: An enlisted person of either sex in the USAF, as distinguished from an officer or warrant officer. Used as a word of common gender, as in regulations, where no distinction is being made between the sexes; An enlisted person of the male sex in the USAF, as distinguished from a WAF airman; An enlisted person of either sex below the rank of staff sergeant; one who flies, an aviator, an aircrew member, a pilot.

AIR POLICE: The organized police within the AF charged with maintaining law and order and security in the AF.

ALCOHOLIC PSYCHOSIS: Insanity due to alcohol.

ALCOHOLISM, ACUTE: Drunkenness; more specifically, drunkenness complicated by poisoning due to absorption of the alcohol.

ALCOHOLISM, CHRONIC: The habit of taking more alcohol than the person can handle; chronic poisoning because of absorption of excessive alcohol over long periods of time; or repeatedly demonstrated inability to absorb moderate quantities of alcohol without developing symptoms.

ALFA CODE: The following are the authorized code words for each letter of the alphabet: Alfa, Bravo, Charlie, Delta, Echo, Foxtrot, Golf, Hotel, India, Juliet, Kilo, Lima, Mike, November, Oscar, Papa, Quebec, Romeo, Sierra, Tango, Uniform, Victor, Whiskey, Xray, Yankee, Zulu.

ALGOLAGNIA: Synonymous with sado-masochism; active algolagnia being sadism; passive algolagnia being masochism.

ALIAS: Before; at another time; otherwise; the term is sometimes used to indicate an assumed name.

ALIBI: The plea of an alibi is a plea of not guilty, because at the instant of the crime, the accused was "elsewhere" than where it was committed. In theory this plea may be viewed from two standpoints. First, it may be regarded as a traverse of the crime alleged raising a clear and direct issue of the defendant's guilt on the whole case in the same manner as any defense involving the assertion of an independent and distinct fact, as, for example, the plea of insanity, or that the supposed victim of a homicide is alive. It may be regarded solely as traversing a single element in the criminal charge against the accused, i.e., his presence at the place and time of the offense.

ALIEN: Any person not a citizen or national of the United States.

ALIENATION: Transfer of property and land from one person to another. This term is often used for insanity; it, however, embraces besides insanity, imbecility and idiocy.

ALIEN ENEMY: A native, citizen, denizen, or subject of a hostile nation, of the age of 14 years and upward, not naturalized, and resident in the United States or in any territory in any way within the jurisdiction of the United States.

ALIENIST: Obsolete synonym for psychiatrist.

ALIMONY: The allowance made to a wife out of her husband's estate for her support, either during a matrimonial suit, or at its termination.

ALIMONY PENDENTE LITE: Alimony pendente lite is that ordered during the pendency of the suit.

ALLEGATION: A statement made by a party who claims it can be proved as fact.

ALLEGIANCE: Obedience due from the citizen to the government. It may be (a) natural, by birth; (b) acquired by naturalization, etc.; or (c) local, during residence in a country.

ALL FOURS: A case is said to be on "all fours" with another, when it agrees with it in the material points.

ALLISION: Running one vessel against another.

ALLOTMENT: 1. A portion of the pay of military personnel which is voluntarily authorized to be paid to another person or to an institution. 2. Action taken by an operating agency making funds allocated to it available to another office, generally one subordinate to it, for obligation by the latter. 3. Specific authorization of personnel by number to a command, organization, or unit. 4. The limitation on the number of personnel, that the Department of the Army places on each command, service, or other agency for the operation of installations and activities for which the allotment agency is responsible.

ALLOWANCE: 1. Money or something equivalent furnished in addition to the prescribed rates of pay. An allowance is given to provide for expenses for which a soldier's pay is considered inadequate, such as travel allowance, quarters allowance, clothing allowance, and subsistence allowance. 2. Prescribed amount of items of supply or equipment provided for an individual or organization.

ALL PRACTICABLE RELIEF AND ASSISTANCE: All relief and assistance which should be afforded within the limitations imposed upon one by reason of his own specific task or mission.

ALTERATION: Any change in the material terms of a negotiable instrument. Alteration is a real or absolute defense and may be pleaded even against a holder in due course.

ALTERATIONS EQUIVALENT TO REPAIRS: As applied to work on ships alterations consisting of (a) the use of different materials which have been approved for like or similar use and such materials are available from standard stock, (b) the replacement of worn-out or damaged parts requiring renewal by those of later and more efficient design previously approved by the bureau concerned, (c) the strengthening of parts which require repairs or replacement in order to improve reliability of the parts and of the unit, provided no other change in design is involved, (d) minor modifications involving no significant changes in design or functioning of equipment but considered essential to prevent unsatisfactory conditions.

AMBASSADOR: A public officer, clothed with high diplomatic powers, commissioned by a sovereign prince of state to transact the international business of his government at the court of the country to which he is sent.

AMBIGUOUS AND MISLEADING QUESTIONS: Questions which may lead the witness into making an unintentional misstatement or give a wrong impression to the court; included are those embodying two or more separate elements or questions and those assuming a fact to which the witness has not previously testified.

AMELIORATION: Betterment, improvement.

AMENDMENT: A modification or alteration to a law or treaty.

AMERICAN COMMON LAW: Consists of the common or unwritten law of England as it existed in 1607, when the colonists from England settled in America, or in some states at a later date, in so far as that law is applicable to the new surroundings and conditions and has not been abrogated by statute.

AMICUS CURIAE: A friend of the court; one who, for the assistance of the court, gives information of some matter of law in regard to which the court is doubtful or mistaken.

AMNESIA: The rejection of those exterior perceptions and sensations that are unpleasant to the ego and are refused entrance into the subconscious through consciousness which regulates them; loss of memory (antigrade and retrograde). It may be functional or organic.

AMNESTY: A pardon applied to a group of offenders, as, for instance, all who have violated a specific law

AMORTIZATION: The operation of paying off an indebtedness.

ANALGESIA: Insensibility to pain.

ANALYST: A practitioner who treats emotional disturbances by means of psychoanalysis. If the practitioner is a physician, then he is a psychiatrist as well as a psychoanalyst. If the practitioner is a psychologist or social worker, then he is a lay analyst.

ANAMNESIS: The history of a patient's disease.

ANCILLARY: Auxiliary.

ANEURIA: Diminished nervous energy.

ANILINGUS: The commission of a perverted sexual act by the use of the mouth on the anus. Individuals so indulging have regressed to the anal erotic level of development. It is essentially an infantile act.

ANIMADVERSION: The utterance of criticism or censure; a censorious comment or reflection.

ANIMUS: The intention with which an act is done.

ANIMUS FURANDI: The intention to steal.

ANLAGEN: Genetic predisposition.

ANNEXATION: The incorporation of newly acquired territory into the national domain.

ANNOTATION: An interpretive note or comment. In legal bibliography, frequently used to explain certain cases or statutes.

ANNUITY: A sum paid at intervals.

ANNUL: To cancel, make void, destroy.

ANNULMENT: Act of invalidating; act of making void retrospectively as well as prospectively.

ANOREXIA: Loss of appetite.

ANOREXIA NERVOSA: A hysterical loss of appetite, or a severe impairment of appetite due to emotional factors, usually leading to malnutrition or emaciation.

ANSWER: The formal written statement, under code state provisions, made by a defendant setting forth the grounds of his defense. It corresponds to what in actions under the common-law practice is called the "plea"; but as used in a statute providing that the defendant must appear and answer the petition (or declaration), "answer" refers to any sort of pleading filed by the defendant.

ANSWER MATERIAL TO THE ISSUE: A question calls for an answer material to the issue when the answer might be expected to have some bearing upon any subject of inquiry legitimately before the court, including the credibility of witnesses.

ANTE: Before, in time, order or position.

ANTECEDENT: Prior to; preceding.

ANTE LITEM MOTAM: Before suit was begun.

ANTE-MORTEM: Before death.

ANTE-NUPTIAL AGREEMENT: A contract made before marriage in contemplation of marriage.

ANTIDOTE: An agent which counteracts the action of a poison.

ANTISOCIAL REACTION: (Antisocial Personality). A personality disorder (not amouting to a psychosis or psychoneurosis) characterized by chronic antisocial behavior, unresponsiveness to punishment and inability to profit by experience.

ANXIETY: A sense of fear, poorly understood by the subject, which arises without apparent cause, or for which the apparent cause is trivial. This is in addition to the obvious dictionary definition of "anxiety." It has overtones of "impending" danger rather than present danger. It is often diffuse, poorly localized, and vague, but always distressing. In some patients anxiety is "converted" into a physical symptom which protects the patient from the source of future fear.

ANY OTHER PERSON: As used in UCMJ Article 121, any person (even a person who himself had stolen the property) who is an owner by virtue of his possession or right to possession thereof and who is other than the one who takes, obtains, or withholds the property.

ANY PERSON SUBJECT TO HIS ORDERS: As used in UCMJ Article 93 means not only those persons who by reason of some duty are required to obey the lawful orders of the accused, but extends to all persons who by reason of some duty are required to obey the lawful orders of the accused, whether he is in the direct chain of command over such person or not.

ANY PRISONER: Include a civilian or military prisoner.

APHESIA: Loss of speech.

APHRODISIAC: A drug which stimulates the sexual instinct.

APNEA: Transitory cessation of respiration.

APPEAL: An appeal is a proceeding by which a cause is brought from an inferior to a superior court for reexamination or review and reversal, retrial, or modification. Provision is made by the statutes of the United States and of the various states for taking appeals in criminal cases from the courts of original jurisdiction to a higher court for review. Thus, convicted persons are afforded every opportunity to rectify any errors that may have been made. The defense must file the application for appeal with reasons, within a short time after conviction.

APPELLATE DEFENSE COUNSEL: Represents the accused before the board of review or the Court of Military Appeals.

APPELLATE GOVERNMENT COUNSEL: Represents the United States before the boards of review or the Court of Military Appeals when directed to do so by the Judge Advocate General.

APPELLATE JURISDICTION: The jurisdiction which a superior court has to rehear causes which have been tried in inferior courts.

APPELLEE: A party against whom a cause is appealed from a lower to a higher court.

APPOINTING ORDER: Designates the kind of court, the place and time it is to meet, lists the members of the court, and when appropriate, the law officer and the members of the prosecution and defense.

APPORTIONMENT: An authorization by the Director of the Bureau of the Budget to a governmental agency making a designated portion of an appropriation (or contract authorization) available for obligation.

APPRAISAL: Estimating the value of property.

APPREHEND: To make an arrest on a charge of crime.

APPREHENSION: 1. Apprehension is the taking into custody of a person. 2. Any person authorized under regulations governing the armed forces to apprehend persons subject to this code or to trial thereunder may do so upon reasonable belief that an offense has been committed and that the person apprehended committed it.

APPROPRIATION: Authorization to make payments out of the Treasury for a designated purpose pursuant to an act of Congress. Appropriations are appropriately described as annual, continuing, multiple year, current, expired, lapsed, definite, indefinite, permanent, civil, etc.

APPROPRIATION LANGUAGE: Detailed description of the purposes for which funds may be used under a given appropriation title.

APPROPRIATION LIMITATION: An amount fixed by the Congress within an appropriation which cannot be exceeded for obligation or expenditure for certain objects or purposes.

APPROPRIATION RECEIPT: Collections, which pursuant to law, are deposited into the Treasury as receipts and appropriated for specific purposes.

APPURTENANCE: An adjunct; something belonging to another thing.

APRAXIA: Insane performance of preposterous acts.

APROSEXIA: Inability to fix the mind on any subject.

ARBITRATION: Arbitration involves an agreement between the disputants to submit their differences to some person or persons by whose decision they will abide.

ARMED FORCES: Construed to refer, severally, to the Army, the Navy, the Air Force, and except when operating as a part of the Navy, the Coast Guard.

ARMED FORCES OF THE UNITED STATES: A term used to denote collectively all components of the Army, Navy, Air Force, Marine Corps, and Coast Guard. See UNITED STATES ARMED FORCES.

ARMED SERVICES PROCUREMENT REGULATION: Uniform policies for the Departments of the Army, Navy, and Air Force relating to the procurement of supplies and services under the authority of Public Law 413, 80th Congress, or under other statutory authorization.

ARMISTICE: Is the cessation of active hostilities for a period agreed upon by the belligerents. It is not a partial or temporary peace; it is only the suspension of military operations to the extent agreed upon by the parties.

ARMS: Anything carried for defense, or used in anger to cast at, strike at, or inflict injury on another.

ARMY: 1. An inclusive term meaning the land military forces of a nation.
2. The Department of the Army at the seat of Government and all field headquarters, forces, reserve components, installations, activities, and functions under the control or supervision of the Department of the Army.

ARMY COMMITTMENT BOARD: Committee appointed to determine whether a person under investigation is insane, and if he is, whether he should be committed to an institution.

ARMY PROCUREMENT PROCEDURES: Implementation of the Armed Services Procurement Regulations and detailed procurement procedures for the Department of the Army.

ARMY, REGULAR: The permanent military establishment, which is maintained both in peace and war.

ARRAIGN: To call a prisoner to the bar of the court to answer indictment, complaint or information or for the purpose of sentence.

ARRAIGNMENT: The arraignment consists of reading the charges and specifications to the accused and asking him how he pleads. It takes place immediately after the disposition of challenges. However, if the convening authority has ordered any charges or specifications to be withdrawn, the arraignment will be preceded by the announcement of that fact by the trial counsel. When the trial counsel is ready to proceed with the arraignment, he will furnish each member of the court, the law officer, and the defense counsel with a copy of the charges and specifications upon which the accused is to be tried.

ARREARS: Money unpaid at the due date.

ARREST: Arrest may be defined as the taking or detainment of a person in custody by authority of law. In the common law, the power of arrest was almost equally invested in the police and the ordinary citizen. Arrests could be made on written orders of the court (warrants), by any person authorized to serve them. Arrests could be made without such warrants when a crime was known to have been committed, and when the crime was either committed, in the presence of the person making the arrest, or, in case the crime was a felony and was not committed in the presence of the arresting officer, he had good reason to suspect that. e.g. To suspect that such a crime had been committed.

ARSON: a. Any person subject to this code who willfully and maliciously burns or sets on fire an inhabited dwelling, or any other structure, movable or immovable, wherein to the knowledge of the offender there is at the time a human being, is guilty of aggravated arson and shall be punished as a court-martial may direct. b. Any person subject to this code who willfully and maliciously burns or sets fire to the property of another, except as provided in subdivision (a) of this article, is guilty of simple arson and shall be punished as a court-martical may direct.

ARTERIOSCLEROSIS: Hardening of the arterial walls.

ARTICLES FOR THE GOVERNMENT OF THE NAVY: The fundamental law of the Navy, approved by Congress, which was superceded by the Uniform Code of Military Justice. See Uniform Code of Military Justice.

ARTICLES OF WAR: A code of laws established for the government of the Army which was superceded by the Uniform Code of Military Justice. See Uniform Code of Military Justice.

ASEPSIS: An absence of pathogenic bacteria.

ASPHYXIA: Suffocation.

ASPORTATION: To take and carry away. If the defendant having taken possession of the goods, has not moved them, there is lacking the asportation necessary to constitute larceny.

ASPORTATION IN LARCENY: To constitute larceny there must be some asportation or carrying away of the property. But there is a sufficient asportation if the property be entirely removed from the place it occupied and be under the dominion and control of the trespasser, though only for an instant.

ASSASSINATION: A killing, or murdering, by surprise or secret assault; murder committed for hire.

ASSAULT: 1. Any person subject to this code who attempts or offers with unlawful force or violence to do bodily harm to another person, whether or not the attempt or offer is consummated, is guilty of assault and shall be punished as a court-martial may direct. 2. Any person subject to this code who—a. commits an assault with a dangerous weapon or other means or force likely to produce death or grievous bodily harm; or b. commits an assault and intentionally inflicts grievous bodily harm with or without a weapon; is guilty of aggravated assault and shall be punished as a court-martial may direct.

ASSAULTS, AGGRAVATED: Aggravated assaults, as distinguished from common or simple assaults, are those which are accompanied by circumstances of aggravation, such as assault with intent to kill, or rape, or to commit other serious crimes against the person. Specific intent is necessary to constitute aggravated assault.

ASSAULT: An assault has been defined as "any attempt or offer, with force or violence, to do a corporal hurt to another, whether wantonly or with a malicious intention, with such circumstances as denote an intention to do it at the time, coupled with the present ability to carry that intention into execution."

ASSAULT WITH A DEADLY WEAPON: In many states the statutes expressly punish as an aggravated assault an assault with a deadly or dangerous weapon. A deadly weapon is any weapon or instrument which is likely to cause death, when used as it is used in the particular case. A weapon capable of causing death is not necessarily deadly. When a weapon is clearly of such a character, or used in such a way as to be likely to cause death, the court will take judicial notice that it is a deadly weapon, as in the case of a loaded pistol or gun, an axe, a hoe, brass knuckles, a club, or a sledge hammer.

ASSAULT WITH INTENT TO COMMIT VOLUNTARY MANSLAUGHTER: This is an assault aggravated by the concurrence of a specific intent to kill in such circumstances that, should death ensue, the homicide would be voluntary manslaughter. It is an assault with the specific intent to take human life; committed in the heat of sudden passion caused by adequate provocation. There can be no assault with intent to commit involuntary manslaughter, for involuntary manslaughter cannot be intentionally committed.

ASSIGN: To place an individual or military unit under the control of a specific command, by orders which change the parent headquarters of the affected individual or military unit.

ASSIGNMENT: A transfer or making over to another of the whole of any property, real or personal, in possession or in action, or of any estate or right therein.

ASYLUM: Refuge; protection from the hand of justice.

ASYLUM STATE: A State in which a fugitive from justice from another state, which is demanding his return, is found .

ATAXIA: Failure of muscular coordination.

ATROPHY: A degenerative decrease in the size of tissues, organs, or parts of the body.

ATTACHMENT: A proceeding to take a defendant's property in legal custody to satisfy a plaintiff's legal demand. The object to hold the property to abide the order of the court for the payment of a judgment in the event a debt shall be established.

ATTEMPTING TO DESERT: An attempt to desert is an overt act beyond mere preparation toward accomplishing a purpose to desert. Once the attempt is made the fact that the person desists, either of his own accord or otherwise, does not cancel the offense. The offense of attempting to desert is complete, for example, if the person, intending to desert, hides himself in an empty freight car on a military reservation, intending to effect his escape by being taken away in the car, entering the car with the intent to desert is the overt act.

ATTEMPTS: An attempt to commit an offense is an act done with the specific intent to commit the particular offense which, except for the interference of some cause preventing the carrying out of the intent, apparently would result in the actual commission of the offense. To constitute an attempt there must be a specific intent to commit the particular offense accompanied by an overt act which directly tends to accomplish the unlawful purpose. The overt act must be more than mere preparation to commit the offense. The overt act required goes beyond preparatory steps and is a direct movement towards the commission of the offense. Soliciting another to commit an offense does not constitute an attempt.

ATTEMPTS TO COMMIT OFFENSES: Any act amounting to more than mere preparation, done with specific intent to commit an offense, and tending, but failing, to effect its commission, is an attempt to commit that offense. An attempt to commit an offense punishable by the UCMJ is punishable as a court-martial may direct, unless otherwise specifically prescribed. A person may be convicted of an attempt although it appears on trial that the offense was committed.

ATTESTATION: Evidence by witnesses to the execution of any instrument.

ATTESTATION CLAUSE: The sentence subscribed to a written instrument, signed by the witnesses to its execution, stating that they have witnessed it. They are then attesting witnesses.

ATTESTED AND UNATTESTED DOCUMENTS: With respect to the method of proving the genuineness of private writings, they may be divided into two classes: attested and unattested documents. An attested document is one which bears the signature of a person who subscribed his name thereto, at the request or with the assent of the party or parties to the instrument, as a witness of the fact of execution. An unattested document has no such signature.

ATTORNEY-AT-LAW: An officer in a court of justice who is employed by a party in a cause to manage the same for him.

ATTORNEY IN FACT: One who is appointed by another, with the authority to act for him in matters specified in the terms of the appointment.

AUTHENTICATE A DOCUMENT: To authenticate a document, the party offering it must show that the document is what it is claimed to be. 1. If offered as genuine, e.g., service record page, it must be proved to be genuine. 2. If offered as the forged check which accused cashed at the X bank, that the document is the specific check accused presented to the cashier.

AUTHENTICATION: A signature or seal that shows that a military document is genuine and official; A symbol or code in a message included as evidence of its authenticity and as a means of protecting the communications system against fraudulent transmissions.

AUTHORITIES: Legal references such as constitutions, treaties, statutes, regulations, cases, treatises, etc., that declare or deal with the law applicable to one's particular problem.

AUTHORITY: The power of a commander to command those subordinate to himself, or to take action within the scope of his command; By extension, this power, or a part thereof, delegated and used in the name of the commander; The commander who exercises this power, or the staff, office, or organization that acts for him; A law, regulation, order, letter, or the like, that serves as a basis for doing something.

AUTHORITY LIBRARY: A library that maintains a collection of laws, regulations, orders, letters, or the like.

AUTHORITY LINE: A line on a piece of military correspondence appearing just before the signature when signed by someone for the commander, showing its source of authority.

AUTHORIZATION: That which has been authorized; The instrument or document that grants a right, power, or thing.

AUTHORIZE: To grant by appropriate authority, a right, privilege, power, or thing to a person or organization.

AUTHORIZED: Granted, sanctioned, or approved by appropriate authority.

AUTHORIZED STOPPAGE: Deduction of a sum of money from a soldier's pay that is provided for in Army Regulations or other rules or policies. Authorized stoppages of pay are made to satisfy court martial fines, to meet debts owed to the Army or for which the Army serves as collecting agent, or to pay allotments, insurance premiums, etc.

AUTISTIC: Pertains to the schizoid temperament; living inside of oneself.

AUTISTIC THINKING: Fantasy-wishing, daydreaming, self-preoccupied thinking.

AUTO-EROTICISM: Sexual love or fixation on oneself.

AUTOPSY: The examination of a dead body to determine the cause of death.

AUTREFOIS ACQUIT: A former acquittal.

AVAILABILITY: As applied to work on naval ships the period of time assigned a ship by competent authority for the uninterrupted accomplishment of work at a repair activity.

AVIATION CADET: A person in training to become a commissioned AF officer with an aeronautical rating; The grade or status of such a person.

A VINCULO MATRIMONII: From the bonds of matrimony.

AWARD: A medal, ribbon, or letter of commendation given for meritorious or heroic service to the individuals country.

AXIOM: A self-evident or necessary truth.

B

BACTERIOLOGICAL WARFARE: Warfare conducted with bacteriological weapons, as by bombs filled with bacteria.

BAD CONDUCT DISCHARGE: A formal, punitive separation of an enlisted person from the military service under conditions other than honorable. Issued only pursuant to the approved sentence of general courts-martial, and of special courts-martial in certain circumstances. The offenses for which a bad conduct discharge may be adjudged are stated in the Manual for Courts-Marial, United States, 1951.

BAIL: A surety usually becomes responsible for accused' appearance —or accused himself puts up some security beyond his mere promise to appear at the time and place designated and submit himself to the jurisdiction of the court.

BAILEE: One who takes another's property into his care and custody.

BAILMENT: A delivery of personal property by one person to another, in trust for a specific purpose, to be returned when the trust is accomplished.

BALLISTICS: The science or art that deals with the motion, behavior, appearance, or modification of missiles acted upon by propellants, rifling, wind, gravity, temperature, or any other modifying substance, condition, or force; the art of designing missiles so as to give them efficient motion and flight behavior within the limitations set up by their purpose.

BANK DRAFT: A bank draft is a banker's check; that is, it is a check drawn by one bank on another bank, payable on demand.

BANKER'S ACCEPTANCE: A banker's acceptance is a draft accepted by a bank according to a previous arrangement made with the bank by a buyer of goods. The seller of goods often refuses to deliver goods to the buyer upon the buyer's credit alone.

BAR: A strip or strips of material usually metal indicating warrant or commissioned officer's rank up to and including captain in the AF and Army. A metal strip on which a decorative ribbon is mounted; the decoration represented by the ribbon so mounted; Short for 'overseas bar'.

BARBITURATES: A group of sleep producing drugs, such as veronal, luminal, and many others.

BAREBOAT CHARTER: When the charterer mans and operates the vessel himself.

BARRACK: Usually barracks, construed as a singular and plural. A building or set of buildings in which military personnel live or lodge.

BARRATRY: It is a misdemeanor, called "common barratry," or "barretry," frequently to excite and stir up suits and quarrels between individuals, either at law or otherwise. This is a common-law offense against public justice. It is defined in some states by statute as "the practice of exciting groundless judicial proceedings." At common law, there must be at least two of such acts, and perhaps three, to make one a common barrator. Some statutes expressly require at least three. The acts must be committed with a mean and selfish intent, and not for the bona fide purpose of promoting public justice, or enforcing private rights.

BASE: An air base or Air Force base; Short for 'base headquarters'; The housekeeping or other unit that operates a base, as distinguished from any other unit on the base, esp. in combinations, as base adjutant, base commander, base supply; Any area or installation from which operations are carried out. Often called a 'base of operations'; An area installation that supports an operation, as in 'supply base'; The bottom of a projectile.

BASE PAY: The pay of an enlisted man or officer according to his rank and longevity before additional pay is added for quarters, subsistence, flying status, overseas duty, etc.

BASIC AIRMAN: A person holding the lowest rank in the AF, normally one unskilled in an AF specialty or yet unassigned for on-the-job training; The rank of such a person.

BASIC ALLOWANCE FOR QUARTERS: An amount of money prescribed and limited by law which an officer or enlisted man receives to pay for quarters not provided by the government.

BASIC ALLOWANCE FOR SUBSISTENCE: A monetary allowance paid to all service personnel who are authorized to subsist themselves.

BASIC COMMUNICATION: The original letter, telegram, or other communication to which indorsements or inclosures are attached.

BASIC CORRESPONDENCE: The written correspondence on a subject, kept together and including the basic communication, inclosures, indorsements, etc.

BASIC CREW: The minimum authorized crew to man a specific aircraft on a given mission.

BASIC INTELLIGENCE: Intelligence of a general nature concerned with more or less permanent matters, for use in background evaluations.

BASIC LETTER: Any letter considered as introducing a new subject or a new phase of a subject, esp. such a letter when distinguished from its indorsements, inclosures, or other communications on the same subject.

BASIC LOAD: The load of an aircraft or structural member determined under a specified condition of static equilibrium; short for 'basic load of ammunition.'

BASIC MILITARY TRAINING: The military training given a person without previous or recent military training or exeprience.

BASIC PAY: Comprehends no element of pay other than the basic pay of the grade or class within grade as fixed by statute and does not include special pay for a special qualification such as that of a combat infantryman or diver, or incentive pay for the performance of hazardous duties such as flying, parachute jumping, or duty on board a submarine.

BASTARDY: The offense of begetting a bastard child.

BATTERY: Any unlawful injury whatsoever, however slight, actually done to the person of another, directly or indirectly, in an angry, revengeful, rude, or insolent manner, is a battery. Every battery includes an assault, so that on an indictment for assault and battery one may be convicted of an assault only.

BATTLE CASUALTY: Any person lost to his organization because of death, wound, missing, capture or internment provided such loss is incurred in action. "In action" characterizes the casualty status as having been the direct result of hostile action, sustained in combat and related thereto; or sustained going to or returning from a combat mission provided that the occurrence was directly related to hostile action. However, injuries due to the elements or self-inflicted wounds are NOT to be considered as sustained in action and are thereby NOT to be interpreted as battle casualties.

BAWDY-HOUSE: A house of ill fame; a house of prostitution; a brothel. A house maintained for illicit intercourse.

BEACH COMBER: An idle or vicious vagrant about wharves and beaches at seaports.

BEFORE THE ENEMY: If an organization is in position, ready to participate in either an offensive or defensive battle, and its weapons are capable of delivering fire on the enemy and are so situated that they are within effective range of enemy weapons, then that unit is before the enemy.

BELLIGERENCY: The status of de facto statehood attributed to a body of insurgents, by which their hostilities are legalized.

BENCH WARRANT: An order issued by or from a bench for the attachment or arrest of a person; it may issue either in case of a contempt, or where an indictment has been found.

BEQUEATH: To give property to another by will.

BEST EVIDENCE: The best evidence of which the nature of the case admits, not the highest or strongest evidence which the nature of the thing to be proved admits of. A copy of a deed is not the best evidence; the deed is better.

BEST EVIDENCE RULE: Rule Stated: A writing is the best evidence of its own contents, and must be introduced unless it has been lost or destroyed, or its absence is otherwise satisfactorily accounted for.

BESTIALITY: Sexual intercourse with animals.

BETTING: The act of making a wager; a species of gambling.

BIAS: A particular influential power which sways the judgment;

the inclination or propensity of the mind toward a particular object.

BIGAMY OR POLYGAMY: Bigamy or poligamy became a crime in England, by statute in 1604, and has been declared by statute in all of the United States. It is committed where one, being legally married, marries another person during the life of his or her wife or husband.

BILE DUCT: A tube or channel conveying the secretions of the gall bladder.

BILLET: 1. Shelter for troops consisting of private or nonmilitary public buildings. 2. To quarter troops in private or nonmilitary public buildings. 3. A personnel position or assignment which may be filled by one person.

BILL OF EXCEPTIONS: A written statement of objections to the decision of a court upon a point of law, made by a party to the cause, and properly certified by the judge or court who made the decision.

BILL OF LADING: A document prepared by the shipper of cargo giving the name and address of the shipper and the consignee and a list of the cargo with the weight and dimensions.

BILL OF PARTICULARS: If, after examining the indictment or information, you believe the location, date and nature of the crime is not set out in specific terms or the particular transactions of of which the accused is charged is not averred in the indictment or information with sufficient particularity to apprise the accused of the charges, then you should file a motion for a bill of particulars. The object of a bill of particulars is to notify the accused of the specific charges against him and to acquaint him with a particular transaction that the State will rely upon so that the accused may prepare his defense. The accused is not entitled to a general disclosure of the evidence of the State in advance of trial.

BILLS OF EXCHANGE: A bill of exchange as defined by the Uniform Negotiable Instrument Act is "an unconditional order in writing addressed by one person to another signed by the person giving it, requiring the person to whom it is addressed to pay on demand, or at a fixed or determinable future time, a sum certain in money to order or to bearer." This type of instrument has three parties: the party drawing the paper, the drawer; the party to whom the instrument is addressed, the drawee; and the party to whom payable, the payee. When the paper is accepted by the drawee, he then becomes the acceptor. The acceptor's liabilities are similar to the liabilities of a maker of a promissory note.

BINDER: A temporary policy of insurance.

BIOPSY: The removal and examination, usually microscopic, of tissue or other material from the human body, for purposes of diagnosis.

BIRTH: For purposes of homicide—The act of being wholly brought into the world; parturition. For purposes of inheritance: The conception of the foetus.

BISEXUALITY: Erotic inclinations or capacity to both sexes existing in one individual.

BIVOUAC: An assembly of troops on a piece of terrain, sometimes without shelter; a temporary encampment; the site of such an assembly or encampment.

BLACK BOOK: An AF publication, handled as secret, summarizing USAF aircraft characteristics.

BLACKMAIL: Blackmail is the extortion of money from a person by threats of public accusation, exposure, or censure. An example would be the blackmail of a merchant by threatening to expose alleged or actual fraud. Frequently, blackmail is committed by a woman with a male accomplice. The woman places her victim in a compromising position and the male accomplice then turns up to effect the squeeze.

BLASPHEMY: Blasphemy is the malicious reviling of God or the Christian religion. It is a misdemeanor at common law. If written or printed and published, the offense is called "blasphemous libel."

BLOCKADES: The obstruction of communication with a place in the possession of one of the belligerents by the armed forces of the other belligerent.

BOARD: A body of persons, either military or civilian, or both, appointed to act as a factfinding agency or as an advisory body to the appointing authority. A board may be authorized either to recommend or to take final action on such matters as may be placed before it.

BOARD FOR THE CORRECTION OF NAVAL RECORDS: Consisting of a board of civilian officers and employees of the Navy, it is authorized, by the Secretary of the Navy's precept, to review, upon its own motion, or upon request of the individual concerned, his next of kin, legal representative, or guardian, as applicable, petitions for the correction of Naval Records; the scope of its review is to determine whether an error has been made in a Naval record, or whether, under normal standards of Naval law, administration and practice, the petitioner has suffered a wrong as the result of an error of omission or commission in his record, or through some manifest injustice in the treatment accorded him.

BOARD OF MEDICAL EXAMINERS: Constituted to inquire into and report upon the physical qualifications of such candidates for appointment or promotion in the naval service as may be ordered to appear before them.

BOARD OF REVIEW, DISCHARGES, AND DISMISSALS: Authorized, by the Secretary's precept, to review upon its own motion, or upon request of an individual concerned, his next of kin, legal representative, or guardian, as applicable, the type and nature of discharges or dismissal certificate or other documentary evidence of discharge or dismissal of former members of the service, except a discharge or dismissal by reason of the sentence of a general court-martial; the scope of the review is to determine, whether, under reasonable standards of law and discipline, the nature of the discharge or dismissal should be changed, corrected or modified, and if so to decide what change, correction or modification should be made.

BOARD OF SURVEY: Officers appointed to investigate the circumstances of the loss or damage to, or destruction of, property and generally to fix the responsibility for the loss, damage, or destruction and to take such other action as may be required by law or regulations.

BOATS: Comprising generally water-borne craft suitable primarily for shipboard and similar use.

BONA FIDES: Good faith, honesty, as distinguished from mala fides (Bad Faith).

BOOK: Within the meaning of the copyright law a single page, if complete in itself, may constitute a book, even if the composition is written or typewritten rather than printed.

BOOKING: The complete processing and recording procedure by the desk section of the military police station for a person apprehended.

BOUNTY: An additonal benefit conferred upon or a compensation paid to a class of persons.

BOYCOTT: Generally involving refusal by nationals of one state to deal in any way with the nationals of another state, has sometimes been effective in bringing a state to settle differences which diplomacy did not speedily adjust.

BRAINWASH: To manipulate various psychological and morale factors so as to induce a person to reveal confidential information or to subscribe to false statements.

BRANCH: Any of the three military services of the United States.

BREACH: The violation of an obligation assumed.

BREACH OF ARREST: Committed when the person in arrest infringes the limits set by orders, and the intention or motive that actuated him is immaterial to the issue of guilt, although proof of inadvertence or bona fide mistake is admissible in extenuation.

BREACH OF THE PEACE: An unlawful disturbance of the peace by an outward demonstration of a violent or turbulent nature.

BREAKING: The word "breaking," as used in defining burglary, is employed technically rather than popularly. Any removing or putting aside of something material which is a part of the house and which is relied upon as security against intrusion would constitute breaking. Breaking requires some force, no matter how slight, to effect the entry, but it does not necessarily contemplate violence. Merely turning a key, lifting a latch, or pushing open a door might be sufficient.

BREVET: A commission conferring on an officer in the army a rank above that which he holds, without, however, giving him increased pay.

BRIBE: Money given or offered to a public officer in order to influence his official acts.

BRIBERY: The act or practice of giving or taking bribes or of influencing the action of another by corrupt inducements. Bribery of public officials is a crime both for the bribe-taker and the bribe-giver.

BRIEF: A written statement for the guidance of the court. A summary or abstract.

BRIEF ABSENCE: A period of less than 24 hours is a brief absence.

BRIG: Prison or place of confinement.

BRIGADIER GENERAL: A commissioned rank or person immediately above colonel in the Army and AF.

BROTHEL: A house kept for purposes of prostitution; a common habitation of prostitutes.

BUDGET DIRECTIVE: Directive of the Budget Officer for the Department of the Army to estimating agencies within the Department of the Army prescribing the time and manner in which estimates are to be presented to the Budget Officer. This directive also sets forth the basic assumptions to be considered in preparing the estimates.

BUGGERY: Insertion of the penis into the anus or rubbing it between folds of buttocks. When the penis is that of an adult, and the anus is that of a child, the perversion is called "pederasty."

BUILDING: Includes a room, shop, store, office or apartment in a building.

BURDEN OF PROOF: The Burden of Proof is a legal term used to describe the duty placed upon a party to establish his affirmative contentions. Some confusion has arisen in the use of this term. In fact, there are two doctrines upon the subject, one that the burden of proof shifts, the other that it does not. Those courts maintaining the latter doctrine hold that the burden of evidence or the burden of going forward with the evidence may shift from one party to the other, but that the burden of proof does not. This latter position seems more acceptable since whoever has the affirmative of the issue must, in the final analysis establish his assertions in order to succeed.

BURGLARY: Burglary is the breaking and entering the dwelling house of another in the nighttime with intent to commit therein murder, manslaughter, rape, carnal knowledge, larceny, wrongful appropriation, robbery, forgery, maiming, sodomy, arson, extortion, or assault. It is punishable as a court-martial may direct.

BUSINESS: Includes business, profession, occupation, and calling of every kind.

C

CADAVER: A corpse; body of a dead person.

CADET: As used in this UCMJ, the term "cadet" refers to a student in a service academy.

CADRE: A group of persons, normally composed of both officers and enlisted men, forming the core around which a new unit is to be developed.

CAIN COMPLEX: Rivalry between brothers and sisters over the family possessions or the affection of one or both of the parents.

CALENDAR: A list of causes arranged for trial in court.

CALL: Construed to mean an informal visit of courtesy requiring no special ceremonies.

CALUMNY: False accusation.

CAPITAL OFFENSES: An offense is capital when the maximum punishment which the court may adjudge includes the death penalty.

CAPITATION FEE: A fixed charge for persons within a certain class.

CAPITULATION: A capitulation is an agreement defining the conditions of surrender of military forces, places, or districts within the command of an officer. Such agreements are purely military and can have no political force.

CAPTAIN: 1. In the U. S. Navy, an officer senior to a commander and junior to a commodore. The commanding officer of any naval unit or activity. 2. A commissioned rank or person in the AF, Army or Marine Corps, immediately above first lieutenant; A name sometimes applied to an officer in charge of an aircraft or group of aircraft; an aircraft commander or pilot.

CAPTAIN'S MAST: A hearing where the commanding officer of a ship imposes punishment on violators of regulations or the discipline. According to the Uniform Code of Military Justice, such punishment is called non-judicial punishment.

CAPTION AND ASPORTATION: As a prerequisite to obtaining possession and appropriating the property, it is necessary, to constitute larceny, that there be an actual physical caption, or taking, and an asportation, or carrying away, thereof. The caption consists in securing dominion over the property; the asportation consists in removing it from the place which it formerly occupied.

CAPTURE: The seizure by force of a person, persons, thing or geographical location; Such seizure considered as a capability residing in a military force; Such seizure considered as a military objective.

CARCINOMA: A cancerous growth.

CARDIOGRAM: A tracing indicating force and form of the heart's movement.

CARDIOLOGIST: A physician specializing in the study and treatment of diseases of the heart.

CARGO: The entire load of a ship, steamboat, or other vessel, usually applied to goods only and not to passengers.

CARNAL KNOWLEDGE: The commission of an act of sexual intercourse under circumstances not amounting to rape, by a person with a female not his wife who has not attained the age of 16 years.

CARNALLY KNOW: Sexual bodily connection. Generally applied to the act of the male in sexual intercourse in violation of law.

CARRY ARMS OR WEAPONS: To bear, carry, or wear them on the person or in the clothing or in a pocket, or for the purpose of being armed and ready for offensive or defensive action in case of a conflict with another individual.

CARTELS: Cartels are agreements made to regulate intercourse during war. Such conventions may regulate postal and telegraphic communication, the reception of flags of truce, the exchange of prisoners, the care and treatment of the same and of the sick and wounded.

CASE: Is a general term for an action, cause, suit or controversy, law or in equity. Case at bar refers to the particular case which is before the court.

CASE LAW: A body of law created by judicial decisions, as distinguished from the law derived from statutory and other sources.

CASHIERED: Dismissal and cashiering were formally regarded as quite distinct in military law; the latter involving in addition to a dishonorable separation from the service a disability to hold military office; there is now no practical difference in the use of the terms.

CAST AWAY: To dispose of, throw aside, or discard without authority or justification.

CASTRATION: The removal of one or both testicles; female c., the removal of the ovaries.

CASUAL: A military person awaiting duty assignment or transportation from a station at which he is not assigned or attached.

CASUALTY: Any military person whose services are lost because of death, injury, capture, desertion, sickness, or interment; A person, military or otherwise, killed or injured.

CASUS BELLI: An occurrence held to warrant hostilities.

CATAPLEXY: A prostration or sinking to the floor due to sudden loss of muscle control.

CATHARSIS: In psychiatric usage, this indicates a "talking out" by the patient of his problems with resultant emotional relief. Operationally it is about the same as "abreaction."

CATHEXIS: The emotional "energy" attached to an idea or to an object; or the focussing of such energy upon some object or idea.

CAUSA: A cause, occasion or reason.

CAUSA CAUSANS: The immediate cause.

CAUSA MORTIS: In contemplation of approaching death.

CAUSE: A suit or action in court; any legal process by which one seeks a right.

CAUSE CELEBRE: Celebrated case (in law).

CAVEAT: A warning.

CAVEAT EMPTOR: Let the buyer beware.

CENSURE, LETTER OF: It ". . . is a separate written statement addressed to an officer" by his CO or a superior commander in the chain of military command for the sole purpose of punishing the officer for the commission of a minor offense or of adversely criticizing conduct or performance by the officer addressed in one or more specified situations, a copy of which is forwarded to headquarters. 1. Not proper if conduct of officer constitutes an offense not "minor." 2. Implication is that letter of censure may be imposed for conduct not constituting an offense under UCMJ.

CENTRAL INTELLIGENCE AGENCY: An organization under the National Security Council that coordinates the intelligence activities of government departments and agencies, correlates and evaluates intelligence relating to national security, and provides for disseminating this intelligence within the government.

CEREBELLUM: Main portion of the brain below and behind the cerebrum.

CEREBRUM: The brain. More specifiically cerebrum refers to the major frontal and upper parts of the brain.

CERTIFICATE OF CORRECTION: Used only to make the record correspond to that which actually occured at the trial.

CERTIFICATE OF DISCHARGE: Statement issued when one leaves military service. A certificate of discharge confirms the release of the soldier named in it, and states the character and record of his service.

CERTIFICATE OF HONORABLE SERVICE: Written statement to next of kin of personnel who die in the service denoting recognition of service.

CERTIFICATION: A formal attestation of a matter of fact.

CERTIFIED COPY: Is a copy to which is added a certificate under the hand and official seal of the public officer who is authorized to certify the same, stating that the said officer has compared the copy with the original document on file in his office and that the same is a correct transcript thereof and of the whole of the original.

CERTIORARI: A common-law writ issued from a superior court directed to one of inferior jurisdiction commanding the latter to certify and return to the former the record in the particular case.

CERTIORARI, WRIT OF: A writ commanding the return of the record of a cause pending before the court, so that the party may have a review of the proceedings.

CERVICAL: Pertaining to the neck.

CERVIX: The lower portion of the uterus.

CESSION: The transfer of territory by one state or government to another

CESTUI QUE TRUST: The beneficiary of a trust.

CHAIN OF COMMAND: The succession of commanding officers from a superior to a subordinate through which command is exercised. Also called command channel.

CHAIN OF TITLE: Successive conveyances of land arranged consecutively, from the government or original source of title down to the present holder.

CHALLENGE: 1. Any process carried out by one unit with the object of ascertaining the friendly or enemy character of the individuality of another. 2. Make formal objection to having a certain member on a military court. Either the accused or the trial person appointed as a member of the court or as the law officer should not be permitted to act as a court member or as law officer with respect to the proceedings in which the challenge is made.

CHALLENGE FOR CAUSE: An assertion by either the prosecution or the defense that because of the existence of certain facts a member of the court or the law officer should not be permitted to act as a court member or as law officer with respect to the proceedings in which the challenge is made.

CHAMPERTY: Is a bargain with a plaintiff or defendant to divide the land or other matter sued for between them if they prevail at law, whereupon the champertor is to carry on the party's suit at his own expense. An example of champerty is where an attorney agrees to carry on a suit, and take as compensation a part of what he may recover, or where one purchases and takes an assignment of a chose in action or right to sue in equity, or purchases land or personalty held adversely by another than the vendor at the time of the purchase.

CHANCE VERDICT: One determined by hazard or lot, and not the deliberate understanding and agreement of the jury. A verdict is not a "chance verdict" merely because, in arriving at the amount the jury took each juror's estimate of what should be assessed as the damages and divided the total by the number of jurors and afterward knowingly and understandingly agreed that such quotient should be the amount of the verdict.

CHANGE: A serially numbered modification, applicable to all copies of a publication. The term "change" includes those which may be printed, mimeographed, or duplicated by other means. A change is promulgated in the same manner as, and to the same holders of, the basic publication.

CHANGE ORDER: Written order making changes in a contract, which changes are authorized under the provisions thereof.

CHARACTER: The character of the accused means his reputation, i.e., the general consensus regarding him and his conduct based on his deportment and conduct, which is held by his neighbors, friends and acquaintances.

CHARGE: Indicates the article the accused is alleged to have violated.

CHARGE AND SPECIFICATION: 1. A description in writing of the offense which the accused is alleged to have committed. 2. The formal written accusation in court-martial practices consists of two parts, the technical charge and the specification.

CHARGE D'AFFAIRES: The title of diplomatic representative of inferior rank. He has not the title or dignity of a minister, though he may be charged with the functions and offices of the latter.

CHARGE OF QUARTERS: A noncommissioned officer responsible for the care and policing of a given area for a given period of time; the responsibility involved in this activity.

CHARGING LIEN: A lien which an attorney has on the judgment, decree or award obtained by him for his client, for his services rendered in procuring it.

CHATTELS: Personal property.

CHEATING AT COMMON LAW: A cheat at common law is the fraudulent obtaining of another's property by means of some false symbol or token, such as, when not false, is commonly accepted by the public for what it purports to represent.

CHECK: A negotiable instrument in the nature of a bill of exchange, drawn on a bank by one of its depositors which must be paid by the bank to the payee named in the check.

CHEATS AND FALSE PRETENSES: Cheating, as a common-law offense, is the fraudulent obtaining of the property of another by any deceitful and illegal practice or token, not amounting to a felony, which is of such a nature that it directly affects, or may directly affect, the public at large. Such a cheat is a misdemeanor at common law.

CHEVRON: A mark or insigne in the shape of a caret or V, worn to indicate rank, class or service.

CHIEF OF NAVAL OPERATIONS: The principal naval adviser to the President and to the Secretary of the Navy on the conduct of war, the principal naval advisor and naval executive to the Secretary of the Navy on the conduct of the Naval Establishment, and, ex-officio, a member of the Joint Chiefs of Staff.

CHIEF OF STAFF: Capitalized when used as a specific title; The senior or principal member or head of a staff; The principal assistant in a staff capacity to a commander, usually the head of a coordinating staff.

CHIEF PETTY OFFICER: Senior enlisted rate in the U. S. Navy.

CHOLINESTERASE: An enzyme which prevents the accumulation of acetylcholine at nerve ends and thus plays an important role in the chemical transmission of nerve impulses.

CIRCLE OF WILLIS: The arterial ring at the base of the brain.

CIRCUMSTANTIAI EVIDENCE: Evidence which tends directly to prove or disprove not a fact in issue, but a fact or circumstance from which, either alone or in connection with other facts, a court may, according to the common experience of mankind, reasonably infer the existence or nonexistence of another fact which is in issue.

CITATION: 1. Specific mention in orders or dispatches. 2. Written narrative statement of an act, deed or meritorious performance of duty or service for which an award is made. 3. Reference to legal or other authorities.

CITIZENSHIP: The status of a person owing permanent allegiance to a country and being entitled to the enjoyment of full civil rights.

CIVIL ACTION: An action to recover some civil right, or to redress some wrong, not being a crime or misdemeanor.

CIVIL AFFAIRS: Matters concerning the relationship between military forces located in a friendly country or area and the civil authorities and people of that country or area, usually involving performance by the military forces of certain functions or the exercise of certain authority normally the responsibility of the local government. This relationship may occur prior to, during, or subsequent to military action in time of hostilities or other emergency, and is normally covered by a treaty or other agreement, express or implied. **See civil affairs/military government; military government.**

CIVIL AFFAIRS AGREEMENT: An agreement which governs the relationship between United States armed forces located in a friendly country and the civil authorities and people of that country. **See civil affairs.**

CIVIL AFFAIRS/MILITARY GOVERNMENT: A grouping of terms employed for convenience to refer to either civil affairs or military government, depending upon the context. **See civil affairs; military government.**

CIVIL AFFAIRS/MILITARY GOVERNMENT UNIT: A military unit organized to perform military government functions in occupied areas and civil affairs functions in friendly territory.

CIVIL CONTEMPT: An offense against a party in whose favor a mandate is issued.

CIVIL DISTURBANCE: Acts of violence and disorder on the part of the civil population prejudicial to law and order. **See domestic disturbance.**

CIVILIAN: A person who is not a member of an armed service by virtue of enlistment, commission, or warrant; a person neither obliged nor permitted to wear military dress.

CIVILIAN COMPONENT: (NATO Agreement) the civilian personnel accompanying a force of Contracting Party who are in the employ of an armed service of that Contracting Party, and who are not stateless persons, nor nationals of any State which is not a Party to the North Atlantic Treaty, nor nationals of, nor ordinarily resident in, the State in which the force is located.

CIVILIAN COUNSEL: Counsel provided by the accused to represent him.

CIVILIAN INTERNEE: A civilian who is interned during armed conflict or occupation for security reasons or for protection or because he has committed on offense against the detaining power.

CIVIL LAW: The law of the Romans under Emperor Justinian was condensed and digested into a code known as Corpus Juris Civilis. The laws of Justinian were lost in the Western Empire during the early Dark Ages, but a complete copy was found about 1137. The laws were then revised and became the basis of jurisprudence for most of continental Europe. The present law on the continent is therefore referred to as the Roman or civil law.

CIVIL REMEDY: A remedy by suit or action brought by an individual for a private right.

CIVIL RIGHTS: Rights appertaining to a person by virtue of citizenship.

CLAIM: Means any claim filed under oath by the commissioned, appointed, enrolled and enlisted personnel of the armed forces, and by civilian employees of the Defense Department, for damage destruction, capture or abandonment of their personal property incident to their service.

CLAIMANT AGENCY: An agency of the Federal Government responsible for the computation of, consolidation, and planning for the production of materiel requirements (including the presentation of claims against national resources of that portion of the economy it represents) to support the national economy and the Armed Forces in time of war.

CLANDESTINELY: In disguise, secretly, stealthily, under concealment, or by misrepresentation.

CLASSIFIED CONTRACT: Any contract that requires access to classified information or material by the contractor or his employee in the performance of a contract. This is not limited to the contract document.

CLASSIFIED DEFENSE INFORMATION: Official information the safeguarding of which is necessary in the interests of national defense, and which is classified for such purpose by appropriate classifying authority.

CLASSIFIED MATTER: Information or matter in any form or of any nature which in the public interest must be safeguarded in the manner and to the extent required by its importance.

CLAUSTROPHOBIA: A morbid fear of being confined in an enclosed place.

CLEMENCY: Term used to describe the fusion of mercy with justice; the reduction, suspension or remission of part or all of the legal punishment, because of the meritorious conduct of the accused or mitigating or extenuating circumstances.

CLERICAL ERRORS IN CHARGES AND SPECIFICATIONS: Those of spelling, punctuation, etc., correction of which does not alter fact.

CLOSE ABOARD: Means passing within six hundred yards for ships and four hundred yards for boats.

CLOSE CONFINEMENT: The confinement of prisoners under conditions of close custodial supervision, separate from the main prisoner group and in quarters specially designated by the commanding officer for that purpose. Normally this includes only those prisoners undergoing disciplinary segregation and those undergoing administrative segregation.

CODE: A body of law covering one general subject established by the legislative authority of the state.

CODICIL: A supplement to a will.

CODIFICATION: The process of collecting and arranging the laws of a country or a state into a code, i.e., into a complete system of positive law.

COERCION: Coercion is the application to another of such force, either physical or moral, as to induce or constrain him to do against his will something he would not otherwise have done. A person coerced by another to perform an act is not legally liable for the act performed.

COHABIT: To live together under the representation or appearance of being married.

COITUS: Sexual intercourse.

COLLATERAL FACTS: Facts not directly connected with the matter in dispute.

COLLATERAL ISSUE: A side issue that has no direct bearing on the main issue in controversy.

COLLUSION: An agreement between two or more persons to defraud a person of his rights by the forms of law, or to obtain an object forbidden by law.

COLONEL: A commissioned rank or person in the AF, Army, or Marine Corps, immediately above lieutenant colonel.

COLORS: A term applied collectively to the United States ceremonial flag and to one or more of the ceremonial departmental flags.

COMBATANT: 1. Combatants in the full sense are the regularly authorized military and naval forces of the states. They are liable to the risks and entitled to the immunities of warfare, and if captured become prisoners of war. 2. Person taking part in active fighting.

COMITY: 1. A term designating the practice by which one court follows the decision of another court on a like question, though not bound by the law of precedent to do so. 2. Courtesy, respect, willingness to grant a privilege, not as a matter of right, but out of deference and good will.

COMITY OF NATIONS: The obligation granted by courtesy to the laws of one nation within the territories of another, when they do not conflict with the laws of the latter.

COMMAND: 1. The authority vested in an individual of the armed forces for the direction, coordination and control of military forces. 2. An order given by a commander; that is, the will of the commander expressed for the purpose of bringing about a particular action. 3. A unit, or units, an organization, or an area under the command of one individual.

COMMANDANT OF THE COAST GUARD: The highest ranking officer of the United States Coast Guard, with the rank of admiral.

COMMANDANT OF THE MARINE CORPS: The highest ranking officer of the United States Marine Corps, a four-star general, appointed by the President for a four-year term.

COMMANDER: A senior naval officer below the rank of captain and above that of lieutenant commander.

COMMANDER IN CHIEF: The officer or official having supreme command of the armed forces of a country; In the United States this is the president; The commander of a theater of war; The commander of a force directly under the Joint Chiefs of Staff.

COMMANDER OF THE GUARD: The officer or sergeant of the guard responsible for the instruction and discipline of, and the performance of duty by, the guard.

COMMANDING GENERAL: A general officer commanding an installation or organization.

COMMANDING OFFICER: A commissioned officer, esp. other than a general officer, commanding an organization or installation.

COMMAND JURISDICTION: The sphere in which a commander exercises his command; The jurisdictional control exercised in this sphere, esp. as it relates to the control or responsibility reserved by a commander over a person or unit of his command even when such person or unit is attached to another command for operational and administrative control and for logistic support.

COMMERCIA BELLI: Agreements entered into by belligerents, either in time of peace to take effect in event of war, or during the war itself, by which arrangement is made for non-hostile intercourse.

COMMISSION: 1. To put in, or make ready for, service or use, as to commission an aircraft or a ship. 2. A written order giving a person rank and authority as an officer in the armed forces. 3. The rank and the authority given by such an order.

COMMISSIONED OFFICER: The individual who derives his authority from a commission signed by the President and confirmed by the Congress.

COMMITMENT: 1. Assignment of units and/or resources to given courses of action or uses. 2. Promise or pledge of such assignment. 3. The act of sending a person to prison by means of a warrant or order; the warrant or order itself.

COMMITTEE: A body of persons, either military or civilian, or both, appointed by appropriate authority as a permanent (standing committee) or temporary (ad hoc committee) advisory body to the appointing authority. It makes recommendations to the appointing authority on such matters as are placed before it. Membership is in addition to the primary duty assigned the individuals concerned, except that an individual may be assigned the primary duty of secretary or recorder, or as a member of an ad hoc committee during a specified period of time.

COMMODORE: A wartime commissioned rank in the Navy, immediately above captain, and corresponding to brigadier general; a person of such rank; A rank in the Coast Guard equivalent to a brigadier general in the Army.

COMMON BARRATRY: Is the offense of frequently exciting and stirring up suits and quarrels either at law or otherwise. A single act is not sufficient to constitute the crime, but there must be a series of acts, the essence of the offense being that the offender shall be a "common" barrator.

COMMON LAW: A system of law, or body of legal rules, derived from decisions of judges based upon accepted customs and traditions. It was developed in England. It is known as the common law because it is believed that these rules were generally recognized and were in full force throughout England. Common law is now the basis of the laws in every state of the Union, except Louisiana, which bases its laws upon the early laws of France.

COMMON LAW LARCENY: Included in larceny (wrongful taking with intent to permanently deprive).

COMMON-LAW-MARRIAGE: An agreement by a man and woman

to enter into the marriage relationship without ecclesiastical or civil ceremony.

COMMON TRIAL: If two or more persons are charged with the commission of an offense or offenses which, although not jointly committed, were committed at the same time and place and are provable by the same evidence, the convening authority may in his discretion direct a common trial for such offenses only.

COMMONWEALTH: A republican frame of government in which the welfare and rights of the entire mass of people are the main consideration, rather than the privileges of a class or the will of a monarch.

COMMUNITY: in the military service "community" includes an organization, post, camp, base, ship, or station.

COMMUNITY PROPERTY: In some states a system exists whereby all earnings of either husband or wife constitute a common fund of the husband and wife. The property is known as community property.

COMMUTATION: To change a punishment to one of a different nature.

COMMUTATION OF SENTENCE: Is a reduction of the penalty and is granted by governors or the president by executive order. Such reductions are granted in view of extenuating circumstances warranting leniency. The guilt of the prisoners is not thereby denied. A sentence is frequently commuted so that it expires at once. A commutation of sentence does not restore civil rights as does a pardon.

COMMUTE: Is to change a punishment to one of a different nature, may be exercised by the President and by the Secretary of a Department (or such Under Secretary or Assistant Secretary as may be designated by him). However, when a convening authority or a board of review finds the evidence insufficient to sustain a finding of guilty of an offense for which the death sentence was adjudged, and affirms only a finding of a lesser included offense for which the death sentence is not authorized, the convening authority and the board of review have the power to commute the death sentence to such a period of confinement as may be legal for the offense affirmed.

COMPANY: A military unit ordinarily consisting of a headquarters and at least two or more platoons (60 to 250 or more men) which is usually commanded by a captain. It is the lowest administrative unit of most branches of the Army.

COMPANY-GRADE OFFICER: A commissioned officer below the grade of major.

COMPARATIVE NEGLIGENCE: The degree of negligence in which each of the parties may be shown to have been responsible for the injury complained of.

COMPETENCY: The legal fitness or capacity of a witness to testify on the trial of a case; also, the quality of evidence offered which makes it proper to be received.

COMPETENT EVIDENCE: To be competent, evidence must primarily be material, and relevant.

COMPLAINT: The formal accusation of crime made under oath to some competent officer as the commencement of a criminal prosecution.

COMPLAINTS OF WRONGS: Any member of the armed forces who believes himself wronged by his commanding officer, and upon application is refused redress, may complain to any superior officer who shall forward the complaint to the officer having general court martial jurisdiction over the officer against whom it is made. That officer shall examine into the matter and take proper measures for redressing the wrong complained of, and, as soon as possible, transmit to the Department concerned a true statement of the matter with proceedings had thereon.

COMPLEX: A group of ideas, largely unconsciousness, with a strong emotional coloring. Behavior may appear unreasonable because its motivation is essentially unconscious, hence such behavior could be ascribed to a specific complex; or the behavior might seem reasonable, but its apparent cause could be sheer rationalization. Its real cause might then be a complex.

COMPOS MENTIS: Of sound mind.

COMPOUND: Enclosed place or yard, such as a place for confining prisoners.

COMPOUND LARCENY: Larceny committed under certain aggraavating circumstances, by reason of which it is punished more severely than simple larceny. Thus— 1. At common law, robbery is a compound larceny—a felonious taking and carrying away of the property of another from his person or in his presence, by violence or by putting him in fear. 2. By statute in most jurisdictions larceny under certain circumstances is made a compound larceny. The principal statutory compound larcenies are: a. Larceny from the person of another, not by violence or putting in fear. b. Larceny from particular places, as a dwelling house, house, shop, vessel, etc., not accompanied by a breaking and entry with intent to steal, as in burglary.

COMPOUNDING A FELONY: The gravamen of this offense consists in the stiffling of a public prosecution or in some way perverting public justice.

COMPOUNDING CRIME: The offense of compounding a crime is committed where one who knows that it has been committed agrees, for a consideration, not to prosecute it.

COMPOUNDING OFFENSES: Taking goods or other amends on an agreement not to prosecute. Compounding a felony is, at common law, equally criminal with the felony, and is also a misdemeanor against public justice. The material facts are knowledge of the actual commission of the crime, the taking of the money or property of another, and the intent to conceal or to compound the felony.

COMPROMISE: An arrangement arrived at, either in court or out of court, for settling a dispute upon what appears to the parties to be equitable terms, considering uncertainty regarding the facts or the law and the facts together. Proof of an offer to compromise the controversy involved in litigation, or the fact that an offer to compromise was made, is generally held to be inadmissible in evidence.

COMPULSION: A repeated urge to do something which the patient himself knows is foolish. Kleptomania, for example, is a compulsion. In kleptomania the patient has an urge to steal, knows it is wrong, tries to resist the impulse, but develops mounting tension which can be released only by yielding to the urge. Not all compulsion, of course, are "criminal." Most compulsions take the form of performing minor acts, touching certain objects in a ritualistic way, etc. The essence of a compulsion is that it is contrary to the patient's conscious "will." If the patient wants to do what he is doing, then his action is not, strictly speaking, a compulsion.

COMPULSIVE NEUROSIS: A psychoneurosis marked by obsessive ideas and an urge to perform complicated and senseless acts.

COMPULSORY SELF-INCRIMINATION: Compelling a person to be a witness against himself.

CONATION: Will or drive. The word is usually used in contrast with "cognition," which means knowledge. Thus, the McNaghten rule uses a purely "cognitive" test; that is, it seeks to determine whether the defendant knew that the act was wrong. In states where irresistible impulse is a defense, a "conative" element is added; it then is a matter of finding out whether the defendant wanted to do the act and whether the drive was irresistible.

CONCEALED WEAPON: A weapon carried by a person but intentionally covered or kept from sight.

CONCLUSIVE PRESUMPTIONS: Presumption which forbids inquiry into the real facts and the party against whom it operates is not permitted to offer any evidence pertaining thereto, for the facts in question, explained or unexplained, contradicted or uncontradicted, are, by law, made conclusive. Many authorities prefer to describe these conclusive presumptions as substantive rules of law.

CONCURRENT JURISDICTION: Applied in those instances wherein, in granting to the United States over an area authority which would otherwise amount to exclusive jurisdiction, the State concerned reserves to itself the right to exercise, concurrently with the United States, all of the same authority.

CONCUSSION: A shaking up of the brain with no substantial structural damage to that organ.

CONDEMNATION: Property of private owner is taken for public use, without consent but with payment of just compensation; a forced sale.

CONDITIONAL PARDON: The offender's guilt is wiped away on condition that he conform to certain specified requirements. These requirements may involve performing certain acts or refraining from certain acts such as abstaining from intoxicating liquors or leaving the state. The conditional pardon becomes void if its beneficiary fails to perform the required acts. He may then be returned to prison for the remainder of his original term.

CONDITIONED REFLEX: A response that results from learning or training, whereby the subject associates a primary stimulus with a secondary stimulus until the point is reached where he reacts to the secondary (previously neutral) stimulus alone.

CONDONATION: A public wrong cannot be forgiven, nor consented to, by a private person. By statute certain crimes have been allowed to be condoned. Usually these are misdemeanors where the injured party has a civil action. But in the absence of statute, it is obvious that no person can condone nor consent to that which the state says shall not be done. The State may grant immunity through its proper officers. By statute the majority of the states require that the district attorney obtain the court's consent before entering nolle prosequi. This must usually be done before the jury has been impaneled. In the absence of statute the power is generally vested in the prosecuting officer alone.

CONDUCT: An action or omission and its accompanying state of mind, or where relevant, a series of acts and omissions.

CONDUCT UNBECOMING AN OFFICER AND GENTLEMAN: Action or behavior in an official capacity which, in dishonoring or disgracing the individual as an officer, seriously compromises his character as a gentleman; or action or behavior in an unofficial or private capacity, which, in dishonoring or disgracing the individual personally seriously compromises his standing as an officer.

CONFABULATION: The type of story-telling which occurs when a patient has a genuine loss of memory and fills in the gaps with fantasies. While in plain English this word means telling lies, in psychiatry it has a more restricted meaning. In true confabulation (as the word is used in psychiatry) the patient usually believes what he is saying. The lies told by the psychopath, on the other hand, are not technically "confabulations" because the psychopath knows that they are lies.

CONFESSION: A voluntary declaration of guilt by a person accused of a crime. If it is made out of court, it is technically called an extra-judicial confession.

CONFESSIONS AND ADMISSIONS: A confession is an acknowledgment of guilt whereas an admission is a self-incriminatory statement falling short of an acknowledgment of guilt. A confession or admission of the accused must be voluntary to be admissible in evidence.

CONFIDENTIAL: Information and material (MATTER), the unauthorized disclosure of which would be prejudicial to the interests or prestige of the nation, or would cause unwarranted injury to an individual, or be of advantage to a foreign nation.

CONFIDENTIAL COMMUNICATION: A statement made to a lawyer, physician, or clergyman in confidence and impliedly understood that it shall remain a secret.

CONFINEMENT: The authorized restraint of an individual within fixed limits by a physical force.

CONFINEMENT ON BREAD AND WATER: Involves confinement in a place where the prisoner can communicate with no unauthorized person, the daily rations to consist solely of bread and water except that, while serving such sentence, no accused shall be deprived of a full ration for a period longer than three consecutive days.

CONFIRMING AUTHORITY: The commanding officer or commander in chief who is required by military law to approve the action of a board of review or reviewing authority in certain kinds of court-martial actions before the sentence can become effective, or operative.

CONFISCATION: The appropriation of property taken from an enemy, or seized for a violation of law, to the use of the state.

CONFLICT OF LAWS: The variance between the laws of two countries or states relating to the subject-matter of a suit brought in one of them, when the parties to the suit, or some of them, or the subject-matter, belong to the other.

CONFRONTATION: In matrimonial and other actions, the bringing of witnesses face with the parties or the accused in a criminal action.

CONGENITAL INSANITY: Insanity existing from birth. There is no difference between congenital and hereditary insanity.

CONNIVANCE: An agreement or consent, indirectly given that something unlawful shall be done by another.

CONQUEST: The status of a territory which has come permanently under the jurisdiction of an enemy as distinct from military occupation, which is a simple act supported by force.

CONSANGUINITY: The relation subsisting among all the different persons descending from the same stock or common ancestor.

CONSCIOUS MIND: The end-organ of the brain, ever on guard during our waking state to transmit impressions from the outside world by means of the senses. Its function is the state of awareness or consciousness.

CONSIDERATION: The waiving of, or a promise to waive, a legal right at the request of another. It is, in reality, the price which the offeror demands for agreeing to carry out his part of the contract.

CONSPIRACY: A combination or confederacy between two or more persons formed for the purpose of committing, by their joint efforts, some unlawful act or for the purpose of using unlawful means for the commission of an act lawful in itself.

CONSTRUCTION OF STATUTE: The reading of a statute according to its spirit and intent.

CONSTRUCTIVE: The term "constructive" generally applies to that which amounts in the eyes of the law to an act, although the act itself is not necessarily performed. The law presumes an act to have been performed, and applies the term to many situations to prevent a miscarriage of justice.

CONSTRUCTIVE BREAKING: When the entry is gained by a trick.

CONSTRUCTIVE CONDONATION OF DESERTION: If an officer exercising general court-martial jurisdiction unconditionally restores a deserter to duty without trial with knowledge of the alleged desertion, this action amounts to a constructive condonation of the desertion and may be interposed in bar of trial subsequently ordered.

CONSTRUCTIVE INTENT: Where a person, engaged in an unlawful act, commits another unlawful act, unintended by him, the intent to commit the first act is carried over to the act actually committed, and is called "constructive intent." Generally, constructive intent is limited in its use to situations in which the first act is malum in se. It is sufficient in cases which require only general intent, but has no application in cases which require specific intent.

CONSTRUCTIVE KNOWLEDGE: Knowledge is constructive when it is shown that the order was so published that the accused would in the ordinary course of events, or by the exercise of ordinary care, have secured knowledge of the order.

CONSTRUCTIVE NOTICE: Notice imputed to a person not having actual notice.

CONSTRUE: To show the meaning of; to explain or interpret.

CONSUL: An officer of a commercial character, appointed by a sovereign state to watch over the commercial interests of the appointing state and of its subjects in foreign countries.

CONSULAR CONVENTION: An agreement or treaty between two countries establishing the rights and duties of their respective consuls.

CONSULAR COURTS: Courts held by the consuls of one country, within the territory of another under authority given by treaty for the settlement of civil, or in some instances, criminal cases.

CONTEMPT OF COURT: Contempt of court is the willful disobedience to, or open disrespect of, the valid rules, orders, or process, or the dignity and authority of a court of justice, whether by disorderly, contemptuous, or insolent language or behavior, or other disturbing conduct, in presence of a court, or by mere failure to obey its orders. Contempt may also be an offense against a legislative body. The power of punishing for contempt is incident to all superior courts. Inferior courts are usually restricted to the punishment of contempts done in the presence of the court.

CONTEMPT TOWARD OFFICIALS: The use by any officer in the armed forces of words which are contemptuous in themselves and words which are contemptuous because of the connection in which they are used against the President, Vice-President, Congress, Secretary of the Defense, or a Secretary of a Department, a Governor or a legislature of any State, Territory or other possession of the United States in which such officer is on duty or present.

CONTIGUOUS: Adjoining.

CONTINENTAL SHELF: The extension of the land mass of a littoral country into and under the sea up to a certain depth.

CONTINUANCE: If for reasonable cause the defense counsel will will not be ready to try the case on the date set for trial or is unable to proceed during the course of the trial, he should request a continuance. If the court is in session, the request for continuance should be made to the court. If the court is not in session and the defense counsel desires a substantial delay in the trial of the case, he should present a written request, signed by the accused and himself, through counsel.

CONTRA: Opposite, otherwise decided.

CONTRABAND: Certain classes of goods, such as arms and amunition, which, by the rules of International Law, cannot lawfully be furnished or carried by a neutral nation to belligerent nations.

CONTRA BONOS MORES: Against good morals.

CONTRACEPTION: The prevention of conception (fertilization of the ovum by the sperm). Usually applies to any method used for this purpose.

CONTRACT: An agreement between two or more competent persons, having for its purpose a legal object, wherein both persons agree to act or to refrain from acting in a certain manner.

CONTRACTING OFFICER: Any officer or civilian employee authorized to enter into and administer contracts and to make determinations and findings with respect thereto.

CONTRALATERAL: On the opposite side.

CONTRAVENE: To come in conflict with; prevent or obstruct the operation of.

CONTRECOUP: Injury of a part opposite to that struck.

CONTRIBUTORY NEGLIGENCE: Negligence on the part of the plaintiff which results in injury to his person or property.

CONTROVERT: To dispute, deny or oppose by reasoning.

CONVENING AUTHORITY: The officer who convened the court, an officer commanding for the time being, a successor in command or any officer exercising general court-martial jurisdiction. The convening authority cannot delegate his functions as such to anyone. The power of an officer to take initial action as convening authority on a record of trial vests in the office, not in the person, of the authority so acting. Normally the convening authority who takes initial action on the record of trial of the case is the officer who convened the court-martial. In a case in which a command has been inactivated or has been alerted for immediate overseas movement, action upon a sentence adjudged by a court-martial appointed by the commander prior to such inactivation or movement may be taken by any officer exercising general court-martial jurisdiction.

CONVENTION: A pact or agreement between states or nations in the nature of a treaty.

CONVERSION: A wrongful exercise of dominion over the personal property of another.

CONVERSION HYSTERIA: A psychoneurosis in which there is gross loss or impairment of some function, and in which the disorder so protects the patient that there is little or no obvious anxiety.

CONVEYANCE: A transfer of legal title to land.

CONVICT: 1. A person who has been finally condemned by a court. 2. To find a person guilty of a crime.

CONVICTION: The act of proving, finding, or determining an individual or number of individuals to be guilty of an offense. Specifically, it is the act of finding or the state of being found guilty of a crime before any legal tribunal, such as a jury or court-martial.

CONVULSION: An involuntary, massive, muscle-contraction.

COORDINATION CONTROL: That necessary direction of separate units to insure adequately integrated relationships between all of these units.

COPROLALIA: A compulsion to use obscene words.

COPROPHAGY: The eating of ordure.

COPY: A true transcript of an original writing.

CORONER: A public officer, whose principal duty it is to hold an inquisition, with the assistance of a jury, over the body of any person who has died an accidental or violent death, for the purposes of determining the cause or causes of death.

CORONER CONVENES AN INQUEST: When the coroner is informed of the death of a person in his county where the circumstances surrounding it are suspicious, obscure or mysterious. A jury of six residents is summoned; they are sworn over the body of the deceased and directed to inquire into the cause of death.

CORPORAL: 1. In the US Army, an enlisted rank or person immediately above private first class, corresponding to airman 1st class in the AF; In the Marine Corps, an enlisted rank or person immediately above private first class, corresponding to airman 2nd class in AF; Formerly in the AF, an enlisted rank or person immediately above private first class, but now designated 'airman 2nd class'. 2. Relating to the body; as corporal punishment.

CORPS: Any large identifiable group, as a cadet corps or AF officer corps; One of several groups of officers identified by the professional training of its members, such as the Medical Corps: etc.; A major branch of an army or service, as the US ARMY Signal Corps; An Army tactical unit usually made up of two or more divisions.

CORPUS DELICTI: "The body of the crime." It has to do with the rules of evidence which govern proof of the commission of crimes, particularly as concerns the act element thereof and the commission of the act by human agency.

CORRECTIONAL INSTITUTION: 1. Type of institution that has the rehabilitation of inmates as its aim. 2. In the Federal prison system a minimum or medium security institution, generally for prisoners whose sentences do not exceed five years.

COUNSEL: The appointed trial counsel and defense-counsel or special court-martial and their assistants, if any, and any individual counsel (civilian or military).

COUNT: A declaration; an allegation of an offense in an indictment.

COUNTENANCE: Means to encourage by a favoring aspect and means more than to witness.

COUNTERCLAIM: A cause of action existing in favor of the defendant against the plaintiff.

COUNTERSIGN: A word given from the principal headquarters of a command to aid guards and sentinels in ther scrutiny of persons who apply to pass the lines. It consists of a secret challenge and a password. A parole is a word used as a check on the countersign; it is imparted only to those who are entitled to inspect guards and to commanders of guards.

COURT-MARTIAL: A military tribunal composed of one or more eligible members of the armed forces (the number depending upon the kind of court), the functions of which are to decide whether a person subject to military law has committed a violation of the Uniform Code and, if it finds him guilty, to adjudge punishment for the offense.

COURT-MARTIAL JURISDICTION: The authority of a commander to convene courts-martial for the trial of persons assigned to his own command or of persons attached to his command for administrative support or control; the sphere of authority within such authority is exercised.

COURT-MARTIAL ORDER: Order that is published promulgating the result of trial by a general or special court martial.

COURT-MARTIAL REPORTS: Extracts from the records of the proceedings of courts-martial and the action of the convening and reviewing authorities, opinions of the Judge Advocate General, and other legal matters for the information and guidance of the armed forces.

COURT OF ADMIRALTY: A court having jurisdiction of causes arising under the rules of admiralty law.

COURT OF INQUIRY: Board of three or more officers and a recorder appointed by the President, or other competent authority, to examine into the nature of any transaction of, or accusation on imputation against, military personnel.

COURT OF MILITARY APPEALS: This court is composed of three civilian judges, appointed by the President and confirmed by the Senate, to act as a supreme court of appeals on decisions of the Board of Review.

COWARDICE: Pusillanimity; fear; misbehavior through fear in relation to some duty to be performed before an enemy.

COWARDLY CONDUCT: The refusal or abandonment of a performance of duty before in the presence of the enemy as a result of fear.

CREDIBILITY: The weight given the testimony of a witness. This is a question for determination by the fact-finding body.

CRETINISM: A congenital disease due to lack of the secretion of the thyroid gland, characterized by a thickness of the neck, shortness of the extremities, a large protruding tongue, arrested mental development.

CREW: Covers all persons engaged to serve in any capacity aboard ship, other than master.

CRIME: The commission or omission of an act which the law forbids or commands under pain of a punishment to be imposed by the state by a proceeding in its own name. In most cases the law requires that the commission or omission of the act must be accomplished by an unlawful intent.

CRIMEN FALSI: A term borrowed from the civil law and is used to describe that class of crimes which involves falsification, that is to say, "1, by forgery; 2, by false declarations or false oaths, perjury; 3, by acts, as by dealing with false weights and measures, by altering the current coin, by making false keys, and the like."

CRIMINAL CONTEMPT PROCEEDINGS: Those prosecuted to preserve the power and vindicate the dignity of the courts, and to punish for disobedience of their orders.

CRIMINAL JURISDICTION: In general, the power which exists for the trial and punishment of criminal offenses (crimes).

CRIMINAL LAW: A body of specific rules regarding human conduct which have been promulgated by political authority, which apply uniformly to all members of the classes to which the rules refer, and which are enforced by punishment administered by the state. The characteristics of these rules regarding human conduct are therefore, politicality, specificity, uniformity, and panel sanction. These rules are found in the constitutions, treaties, common law, enactments by the legislatures of the state and of its subdivisions, and in judicial and administrative regulations.

CRIMINAL LIBELS: Libels on private persons. The crime of libelling a private person consists in the malicious publication of any writing, sign, picture, effigy, or other representation, tending to expose any person to hatred, contempt, or ridicule. The gist of the offense is its tendency to provoke a breach of the peace.

CRIMINAL PROCEDURE: The method pointed out by law for the apprehension, trial, and prosecution, and fixing the punishment, of those persons who have committed crimes.

CRIMINALLY RECEIVING: A person who buys, receives, withholds or conceals any stolen property is guilty of a felony. The purchaser or receiver must assume the burden of making reasonable inquiry to ascertain the right of the seller to dispose of such property. When stolen property is found in the posession of a person, such person must be able to prove that he made a reasonable inquiry. If such inquiry was not made, then he is subject to arrest.

CRUEL AND UNUSUAL PUNISHMENT PROHIBITED: Punishment by flogging, or by branding, marking, or tattooing on the body, or any other cruel or unusual punishment, shall not be adjudged by any court-martial or inflicted upon any person subject to this UCMJ. The use of irons, single or double, except for the purpose of safe custody, is prohibited.

CRYPTOCLEARANCE: A security clearance given a qualified person to handle cryptographic materials. A cryptoclearance is distinguished from other security clearances, i.e. possession of a Secret or Top Secret clearance does not of itself entitle one to handle cryptomaterials.

CULPABLE INEFFICIENCY: Inefficiency for which there is no reasonable or just excuse.

CULPABLE NEGLIGENCE: A degree of carelessness greater than simple negligence; it is a negligent act or omission accompanied by a culpable disregard for the foreseeable consequences to others of such act or omission.

CUMULATIVE EVIDENCE: Additional evidence tending to prove facts of the same general character as those supported by other evidence previously produced. Such evidence merely repeats in substance and effect what has already been put in proof by other evidence of the same character.

CUMULATIVE SENTENCING: The attempt at one trial to multiply a single offense into several offenses, for each of which a separate punishment can be imposed.

CUNNILINGUS OR CONNILINCTION: Placing the mouth against the female genitalia, particularly if the tongue is inserted into the vulvar orifice. If it represents simple kissing of the vulva as a prelude to normal coitus, it is not generally considered a perversion. However, if this is the participant's primary sexual aim and if this represents the acme of his sexual satisfaction, then cunnilingus is classed as a perversion.

CURTESY: The legal right or interest which the husband acquires by marriage in land owned by his wife.

CUSTODIAN OF AN OFFICIAL RECORD: A person who has custody thereof by authority of law, regulation, or custom, that is, a person in whose office the record is officially on file.

CUSTODY: Means to have them in charge, safe-keeping, and implies temporary physical control merely and does not connote dominion or supremacy of authority as does possession in its full significance.

CUSTOM: The principal conditions to be fulfilled in order to constitute a valid custom are (a) It must be long continued; (b) It must be certain and uniform; (c) It must be compulsory; (d) It must be consistent; (e) It must be general; (f) It must be known; (g) it must not be in opposition to the terms and provisions of a statute or lawful regulation or order.

CUSTOMS OF THE SERVICE: Military customs, practices, and procedures not prescribed by law or regulation but which by tradition and practice have become of binding force.

CYLOID: The type of temperament lying between cyclothmic and the abnormal or manic depressive psychosis.

CY PRES DOCTRINE: "As nearly as may be"; a rule permitting a court to carry out as nearly as may be, the intention of the donor of a charitable trust.

D

DAMAGE: Consists of any physical injury to property.

DAMAGES: The sum allowed by law as compensation for an injury or loss caused by another. The amount of damages to be recovered is usually a matter for the jury to determine.

DAMAGE STATEMENT: Is a document containing a breakdown of the claim arising out of collision and includes as exhibits copies of documentary data indicating the ability to establish as legally recoverable each item of the claim.

DAMNIFY: To cause damage or injurious loss to a person or put him in a position where he must sustain it.

DANGER AREA: A specified area within, below, or over which there may exist activities constituting potential danger to aircraft flying over it, or to persons, property, and traffic on land or sea.

DANGEROUS WEAPON: A weapon is dangerous when used in such a manner that it is likely to produce death or grievous bodily harm.

DAY OF ABSENCE: Day during which an officer or enlisted man is on off duty status and away from his organization. It is used as a unit in figuring leave time, or as a unit in figuring the time an officer or enlisted man is absent without leave.

DEATH GRATUITY: Payment of a lump sum to beneficiaries of military personnel on active duty, who die from wounds or disease not a result of misconduct, of an amount equal to 6 months' pay, excluding allowances.

DEBAUCH: To corrupt one's manners, to make lewd, to mar or spoil; to seduce and vitiate a woman; enticing and corrupting.

DECLARANT: One who makes a declaration or unsworn allegation of fact.

DECLARATIONS AGAINST INTEREST: Declarations, oral or written, of deceased persons, made while the declarants were in a position to know of the matters stated, and which are against pecuniary or proprietary interest, are admissible as an exception to the hearsay rule.

DECREE: The court's decision in Equity. A decree usually directs the defendant to do or not to do some specific thing, as opposed to a judgment for damages in a court of law.

DEED: A conveyance of realty in writing signed by grantor, whereby title to realty is transferred from one to another.

DE FACTO: Actually; in fact; in reality; in contrast to de jure.

DEFAULT JUDGMENT: A judgment entered after the defendant has failed to appear when properly served with process.

DEFENDANT: A person whose conduct is the actual subject of investigation.

DEFENSE: 1. In the law of procedure, an affirmative setting up of facts in answer to a complaint or counterclaim. 2. The conduct of a trial either criminal or civil on the part of the defendant, or of the plaintiff in a counterclaim. 3. Any act of a person in resisting an act of aggression against his person or property or against any person he is legally or morally justified in seeking to protect.

DEFENSE DEPARTMENT: The Department of Defense.

DEFENSE COUNSEL: Includes, unless otherwise indicated by the context, the appointed defense counsel, appointed assistant defense counsel, if any, and any individual counsel.

DEFENSIVE AREAS: During all wars certain areas have been especially dangerous because in the neighborhood of hostile operations, and into areas in which hostilities were actualy going on neutrals came at their own risk. Neutrals have in recent years been excluded from areas which were regarded by the belligerent as of particular military importance. These were termed by Japan in 1904 "defensive sea areas" and have at other times been named "strategical areas." The United States established such areas by executive orders April 5, 1917, and other states had already issued similar orders.

DEFRAUD: The depriving of a person or property or something of value by trick, deceit, chicanery, or overreaching.

DE JURE: Of right; by lawful title.

DELIBERATELY: By the use of the word "deliberately" in describing a crime the idea is conveyed that the perpetrator weighs the motives for the act and its consequences, the nature of the crime, or the things connected with the intention, with a view to a decision thereon; that he carefully considers all these, and that the act is not suddenly committed.

DELIBERATION: Reflection, however brief, upon the act before committing it; fixed and determined purpose, as distinguished from sudden impulse.

DELIRIUM: A combination of excitement, confusion, disorientation, and some sensory disturbance, such as hallucinosis.

DELIRIUM TREMENS: The result of alcoholic poisoning, manifested by great mental excitement, insomnia, incoherent speech, tremors, disordered intellect, and terrifying hallucinations of sight and hearing.

DELIVER UP: Synonymous with surrender.

DELUSION: An idea which is (a) contrary to fact, (b) inappropriate to the person's education, intelligence or culture, and (c) adhered to in spite of plain evidence that it is false. Many normal persons have delusions. A man may think he is smarter than he is, a woman may think she is charming and beautiful when she is neither. These are delusions. However, in psychiatric practice, the word is generally reserved for false ideas which are more bizarre than those. The three commonest delusions are (1) delusions of persecution, (2) delusions of grandeur, and (3) delusions of personal unworthiness.

DEMENTIA: A gross impairment of mental faculties, such as enfeeblement of intelligence or serious disorientation, or major loss of contact with reality. In general, dementia occurs more often in organic diseases of the brain than in psychoses without known organic basis. In many psychoses there is no dementia at all. Delusions often exist without dementia.

DEMENTIA PRAECOX: A term embracing a large group of psychoses characterized by disorientation, loss of contact with reality, and splitting of the personality.

DEMONSTRATIVE EVIDENCE: Physical objects such as maps, diagrams, photographs, models used at a trial not for the purpose of proving a point in itself, but rather to illustrate and clarify a witness' testimony on a point.

DEMURRAGE: The charge made when a ship is delayed while loading or unloading cargo.

DEMURRER: An objection made by one party to his opponent's pleading, alleging that he ought not to answer it for some defect of law in the pleading.

DE NOVO: Anew; afresh.

DEPARTMENT: A designation for any of the main subdivisions of the executive branch of the government, as in 'Department of Defense'; A designation for any of the three main subdivisions of the Department of Defense, as in the 'Department of the Army..

DEPARTMENT OF THE AIR FORCE: One of the three departments of the Department of Defense. It includes the Department of the Air Force at the seat of government and all field headquarters, forces, reserve components, installations, activities, and functions under the control or supervision of the Department of the Air Force.

DEPARTMENT OF THE ARMY: The executive part of the department and all field headquarters, forces, reserve components, installations, activities, and functions under the control or supervision of the secretary of the department.

DEPARTMENT OF THE NAVY: One of the three departments of the Department of Defense that includes the Department of the Navy at the seat of government; the headquarters, United States Marine Corps; the entire operating forces of the United States Navy, including naval aviation, and of the United States Marine Corps, including the reserve components of such forces; all field activities, headquarters, forces, bases, installations, activities, and functions under the control or supervision of the Department of the Navy; and the United States Coast Guard when operating as a part of the Navy pursuant to law.

DEPENDENCY: A territory distinct from the country in which the supreme sovereign power resides, but subject to the laws and regulations which the sovereign may think proper to prescribe.

DEPENDENT: Includes at all times and in all places the lawful wife and unmarried legitimate children, over 21 years of age, who are incapabe of self-support because of being mentally defective or physically incapacitated, and who are in fact dependent on such member for over half of his or her support, and also includes stepchildren or adopted children when such stepchild or adopted child is in fact dependent; in case of female members of the uniformed services the term "dependent" also includes a husband provided such husband is in fact dependent upon said female member for over half of his support.

DEPONENT: He who makes a deposition.

DEPOSITION: A written declaration, under oath, made upon notice to the adverse party, for the purpose of enabling him to attend and cross-examine. It must be taken in the presence of a competent official, usually a court officer or a notary public.

DEPRECIATION: Loss in value from any cause.

DEPREDATION: A plundering; a laying waste.

DEPRESSION: A syndrome manifested by sense of inadequacy, "blue feeling," self-depreciation, melancholy, and guilt feelings.

DERILICTION IN THE PERFORMANCE OF DUTIES: A person

is derilict in the performance of his duties when he willfully or negligently fails to perform them, or when he performs them in a culpably inefficient manner.

DERMATOLOGIST: A physician who specializes in the treatment, care and diagnosis of diseases of the skin.

DESERTION: Any member of the armed forces of the United States who (1) without proper authority goes or remains absent from his place of service, organization, or place of duty with intent to remain away therefrom permanently; or (2) quits his unit or organization or place of duty with intent to avoid hazardous duty or to shirk important service; or (3) without being regularly separated from one of the armed forces enters any foreign armed service except when authorized by the United States is guilty of desertion; any officer of the armed forces who, having tendered his resignation and prior to due notice of the acceptance of the same, quits his post or proper duties without leave and with intent to remain away therefrom permanently is guilty of desertion.

DESIGN: Wrongful act is designed when it is intended or when it results from conduct so shockingly and grossly devoid of care as to leave room for no reasonable inference.

DESTROYED: To be destroyed, property need not be completely demolished or annihilated, but need be only sufficiently injured to be useless for the purpose for which it was intended.

DETAINED PAY: Ultimately returned to the accused when he is separated from the service and therefore amounts to enforced saving.

DETAINERS: A warrant filed against a person already in custody with the purpose of insuring that, after the prisoner has completed his present term, he will be available to the authority which has placed the detainer. Wardens of institutions holding men who have detainers on them invariably recognize these warrants and notify the authorities placing them of the impending release of the prisoner.

DETENTION OF PAY: It is of the same nature as a "forfeiture" with the following exceptions: (a) The detained pay is returned to the accused when he is separated from the service. (b) All pay may never be detained. The maximum amount that can be detained is ⅔ pay per month for a period of 3 months. (c) It may never apply to "allowances." Reason—it is limited to ⅔ pay per month.

DETENTION ROOM: The room where arrested persons are temporarily confined by the military police.

DETENTION WARD: The ward in a military hospital for prisoners undergoing medical treatment or care.

DETERMINE: To ascertain the exact truth about.

DEVISE: A gift of real property by the last will and testament of the donor.

DIANA COMPLEX: A psychological reaction found amongst young females, sometimes referred to as "the virility complex."

DICTA: An opinion of the court upon some question of law not necessary to the decision of the case being considered.

DICTUM: An opinion expressed by a court, but which, not being necessarily involved in the case, lacks the force of an adjudication.

DIMINISHED RATIONS DEFINED: It is food consisting of 2100 or more calories daily and including balanced portions of the regular ration excluding—meat, eggs, butter, sweets, condiments, and desserts.

DIPLOMACY: The art and science of international negotiation.

DIPLOMATE: A physician who has attained a high degree of professional skill in a specialized field, and whose proficiency has been recognized and accredited by a diploma of the college of his specialty.

DIPSOMANIA: Periodic and compulsive drinking.

DIRECT CONTEMPT: An act committed in the presence of the court which tends to interrupt its proceedings and subvert justice.

DIRECTED VERDICT: A verdict which a jury returns as directed by the court.

DIRECT EVIDENCE: That which tends to prove the fact at issue without the intervention of proof of any other fact.

DIRECT EXAMINATION: The initial examination of a witness by the party calling him is known as the direct examination. The direct examination must cover all of the facts which the party expects to elicit from the witness.

DIRECTIVE: 1. A military communication in which policy is established or a specific action is ordered. 2. A plan issued with a view to placing it in effect when so directed, or in the event that a stated contingency arises. 3. Broadly speaking, any communication which initiates or governs action, conduct or procedure.

DISABILITY: 1. The want of legal capacity to perform an act. 2. An illness or injury which makes an individual unfit for and incapable of active service.

DISAFFECTION: Imports disgust or discontent with, or ill will, disloyalty, or hostility toward, an authority to whom respect, obedience, or allegiance is due.

DISAPPROVAL OF A SENTENCE: Nullifies it as a basis for punishment.

DISBURSEMENT: The amount of expenditure checks issued less refunds received and travel advances returned.

DISBURSING OFFICER: Officer who receives, is responsible for, and pays out public funds. He may also command the finance detachment and advise his commanding officer on financial matters.

DISCHARGE: The separation of a person from the service by means other than retirement or death; also short for discharge certificate.

DISCHARGE WITHOUT HONOR: Form of discharge formerly given when service was not honest and faithful, when a character rating was "fair" or "poor," or when a dishonorable discharge could not be given. **See undesirable discharge.**

DISCIPLINARY ACTION: All authorized measures, including courts-martial, nonjudicial punishment, and reprimand (as distinguished from administrative reprimand), taken to punish acts of misconduct by military personnel.

DISCIPLINARY AND ADJUSTMENT BOARD: A board of at least three officers at a correctional installation appointed by the commandant to consider infractions of rules and regulations, to recommend appropriate disciplinary action therefor, and to consider and assist in the solution of adjustment problems of inmates referred to it by the commandant or other members of the staff.

DISCIPLINARY BARRACKS: Military correctional installation for confinement, retreating, and restoration of prisoners to honorable duty status or return to civil life.

DISCIPLINARY GUARD: Enforces military orders and regulations governing conduct, employment security, discipline, and management of prisoners at military confinement facilities.

DISCIPLINARY LAWS OF THE COAST GUARD: The regulations and laws of the oCast Guard; superseded by the Uniform Code of Military Justice on May 31, 1951.

DISCIPLINARY SEGREGATION: The close confinement of prisoners as a disciplinary measure imposed in accordance with regulations. See **administrative segregation.**

DISCIPLINARY TRAINING CENTER: Army correctional institution in overseas territories used in periods of national emergency as a vehicle for rehabilitating or restoring prisoners to duty.

DISCIPLINE: Active and cooperative obedience to the orders and commands of one's superior officers; Procedures and rules established for and to be followed in specific operations or situations.

DISCOVERY: The right of a party to an action to require an opponent to disclose, prior to trial, certain relevant and material facts within his opponent's knowledge. This may include the contents of documents, the name of an expected witness, or the tenor of his testimony. Originally, discovery was confined to suits in equity and was not permitted in actions at law. Even in this country discovery as a method of securing information is limited.

DISCREDIT: To injure the reputation of. Examples of this conduct may include acts in violation of local law, or one's attitude toward his private indebtedness or his creditors such as to thereafter reflect discredit upon the service to which he belongs.

DISHONORABLE DISCHARGE: Reserved for those who should be separated under conditions of dishonor, after having been convicted of offenses usually recognized by the civil law as felonies, or of offenses of a military nature requiring severe punishment.

DISHONORABLY: Imports that the failure of the accused to pay a just debt was characterized by fraud, deceit, willful evasion, bad faith, gross indifference, or false promise. A mere negligent failure to pay a just debt is not an offense punishable under the Uniform Code of Military Justice.

DISLOYALTY: Imports not being true to or being unfaithful toward an authority to whom respect, obedience, or allegiance is due.

DISMISSAL: Dismissal from the service, the separation from the service of an officer as a result of court-martial.

DISOBEYING SUPERIOR OFFICER: The willful disobedience contemplated is such as shows an intentional defiance of authority, as when an enlisted person is given a lawful command by an officer to do or cease doing a particular thing at once and refuses or deliberately omits to do what is ordered.

DISORDERLY: Any disturbance of a contentious or turbulent character.

DISORDERLY CONDUCT: Means not merely noisy and boisterious behavior, but includes within its legal signification whatever strikes openly at the organization or interferes with the orderly relations of civil or military society.

DISORIENTATION: Failure to identify the time, place, or persons around. Disorientation may be partial. A patient might know the year and season, but not the month or day of the week; then he would be "partly disoriented for time."

DISPLACED PERSON: A civilian who is involuntarily outside the national boundaries of his country.

DISPLACEMENT: Transfer of emotion to an inappropriate idea or object.

DISPOSAL: The act of getting rid of records, documents, excess, obsolete, or surplus property under proper authority. Disposal may be accomplished by, but is limited to, transfer, donation, sale, abandonment, or destruction, but does not include redistribution.

DISPROPORTIONATE PUNISHMENT: A punishment is disproportionate to the offense when it is excessive for the offense committed, considering all matters in mitigation and extenuation.

DISRESPECT TOWARD A SUPERIOR OFFICER: The disrespectful behavior that detracts from the respect due to the authority and person of a superior officer.

DISSENTING OPINION: A minority opinion the decision of a case.

DISTRESS: The taking of a personal chattel out of the possession of a wrong-doer into the custody of the party injured, to procure a satisfaction for a wrong committed. Seizure for unpaid rent.

DIVISION OFFICER: A division officer within the meaning of the Navy Regulations, is one regularly assigned by the commanding officer to command a division of the ship's organization

DIVORCE: A judicial severance of the tie of matrimony.

DOCTRINE: Principles, policies, and concepts, applicable to a subject, which are derived from experience or theory, compiled, and taught for guidance. It represents the best available thought that can be defended by reason.

DOCTRINE OF ENTRAPMENT: One who is instigated, induced or lured by an officer of the law for the purpose of prosecution, into the commission of a crime which he had otherwise no intention of committing, may avail himself of the defense of "entrapment."

DOCTRINE OF SUPERIOR ORDERS: Refers to the defense of immunity claimed by a person of inferior rank who owes a duty of obedience to his superior giving the order.

DOCUMENT: Any form of recorded information. It includes printed, mimeographed, typed, photostated, and written matter of all kinds to include electrically transmitted messages; maps, relief maps, photomaps, and air photographs and mosaics; drawings, sketches, notes, and blueprints, or photostatic copies; photographs, and photographic negatives; recorded engineering data; correspondence and plans relating to research and development projects; and all other similar matter.

DOCUMENTARY EVIDENCE: "Any substance having any matter expressed or described upon it by marks capable of being read," and when "produced for the inspection of the court or judge, such documents are called documentary evidence."

DOMESTIC DISTURBANCE: Civil unrest or tension which takes the form of demonstration or rioting; a situation which arises within the continental United States, its Territories and possessions, from acts of violence or disorder, and which is prejudicial to the maintenance of law and order. See civil disturbance.

DOMICILE: Residence at a particular place, accompanied by an intention, either positive or presumtive, to remain there permanently or for an indefinite or unlimited length of time.

DOUBLE CRIMINALITY: A principle applied in extradition proceedings under which a crime must be punishable in the country in which the crime was committed as well as in the country from which surrender of the fugitive from justice demanded.

DOUBLE JEOPARDY: The defense in a criminal action that the accused has already been tried for the same offense as that with which he is now charged either by indictment or information. The term is derived from the Fifth Amendment to the Constitution of the United States and to similar provisions in the Constitutions of the several states. The "due process" clause of the Fourteenth Amendment to the U.S. Constitution would in any case extend it to all the states. The plea is liberally construed to cover all criminal prosecutions, even those not strictly involving "life and limb." **See Former Jeopardy.**

DOWER: The legal right or interest which the wife acquires by marriage in the estate of her husband.

DRAFT: A written order drawn upon one person by another, requesting him to pay money to a designated third person.

DRAWS OR LIFTS UP ANY WEAPON AGAINST: Covers any simple assault committed in the manner stated.

DRUMHEAD COURT-MARTIAL: A summary court-martial to try offenses on the battlefield or line of march.

DRUNK: One who has lost the normal control of his bodily and mental facilities.

DRUNKENNESS: Any intoxication from alcoholic liquor which is sufficient sensibly to impair the rational and full exercise of the mental and physical faculties to a degree that will incapacitate for the proper performance of any duty which a person of the rank or rate of the accused could properly be called upon to perform.

DRUNK ON DUTY: The term "duty" as used means military duty.

Every duty which an officer or enlisted person may legally be required by superior authority to execute is necessarily a military duty. Whether the drunkenness was caused by liquor or drugs is immaterial and any intoxication which is sufficient sensibly to impair the rational and full exercise of the mental and physical faculties is drunkenness.

DUBITANCY: Uncertainty; hesitancy; doubt.

DUCES TECUM: You bring with you.

DUEL: A combat between two persons for private reasons fought with deadly weapons by prior agreement.

DUELING: Any fighting of two persons, one against the other, by agreement, is a duel, but the term, as commonly used, implies such a fighting with deadly weapons. In some countries it is not unlawful, but it is a misdemeanor at common law in England and in this country.

DUE PROCESS OF LAW: In each particular case means such an exertion of the powers of government as the settled maxims of the law permit and sanction, and under such safeguards for the protection of individual rights as those maxims prescribe for the class of cases to which the one in question belong.

DULY PLACED IN MEDICAL QUARANTINE: Imports that the accused, for medical reasons, was ordered by a person in authority to remain within certain specified limits for a definite or indefinite period of time and that the accused was aware of this order and of his duty to obey the same. The term "broke" imports that the accused transgressed or went beyond the limits of the alleged medical quarantine while the same was still in effect.

DUM-DUM BULLET: A kind of expanding bullet, inhumane because of the type of injuries it inflicts.

DURESS: Personal restraint, or fear of personal injury or imprisonment.

DUTY: A moral obligation imposed upon, or felt by, a person by virtue of some circumstance or set of circumstances; also the sense of this obligation; That which a person is required to do in the performance of his assignment; Military service under assignment by competent authority; the work connected with this service.

DUTY ASSIGNMENT: The duty to which an individual is officially assigned.

DUTY HOUR: Any one of the hours during which a person is actually at work as required by assignment.

DUTY MOS: The military occupation speciality in which a person actually performs duty.

DUTY OFFICER: An officer on duty, or ready for duty, during periods when other personnel are normally off duty; An officer charged with being personally present and on the job to take care of certain matters requiring instant and continuous attention as they arise.

DUTY ROSTER: A roster showing the time or times at which various persons are scheduled for particular duties.

DUTY STATION: The station or base at which a person is assigned for a regular duty; also a place at which a person performs an assigned duty.

DUTY STATUS: The status of an individual with respect to his duty.

DUTY TIME: Any time considered time spent on duty; In a restricted sense, the time actually spent at work, as opposed to off-duty time.

DUTY TO HOSPITAL: The designation for a duty status report, indicating that the person or persons concerned have been transferred from a present duty status to a sick in the hospital status.

DUTY TO SICK IN QUARTERS: The designation for a report in change of duty status, indicating that the person or persons concerned have been transferred from a present for duty status to a sick in quarters status.

DWELLING HOUSE: Includes outhouses within the common inclosure, farmyard, or cluster of buildings used as a residence.

DYING DECLARATIONS: In trials for homicide (murder, manslaughter and negligent homicide) the dying declaration of the alleged victim concerning the circumstances of the act which induced the dying condition, including the identity of the person or persons who caused the injury, is admissible in evidence to prove such circumstances. The reason for the rule is that the dying statement of the victim would be unavailable otherwise and was based presumably on a moral obligation to tell the truth. The declaration must have been made while the victim was in extremity and under a sense of impending death, although it is not necessary to show that the victim asserted that he was under this impression if that fact is otherwise established.

DYSPLASTIC: Refers to certain body types which show a marked digression from the average in that they are morphologically closely associated to endocrine pathology.

DYSTONIC ALGOLAGNIA: A condition resulting from a basically psychopathic character make-up.

E

EARNEST MONEY: Money paid to bind a bargain.

EASEMENTS: A right, granted by the grantor to the grantee, to use real property. For example, the grantor may convey to the grantee a right of way over his land, the right to erect a building which may shut off light or air, the right to lay drain tile under the land, or the right to extend wires over the land. If these rights of easement are reserved in the deed conveying the property, they pass along with the property to the next grantee and are burdens upon the land.

ECSTASY INTOXICATION: That moment when the sadist has reached the zenith of affectivity, the sensation of pain is suppressed by the stronger urge and sensation of desire.

EFFICIENCY REPORT: Report prepared by the immediate superior, on the manner in which officers, enlisted personnel, and civilians perform their assigned duties. Efficiency reports are prepared at stated intervals, usually annually and upon temporary duty of 60 days or more and upon permanent change of station.

EGO: The perception, control of purposeful activity of testing reality, judgment, etc.

EJECTMENT: An action for the recovery of real property.

EJUSDEM GENERIS: While unqualified general terms are usually to be given their natural and full signification, yet when general words follow in a statue words of particular and special meaning, if there be not a clear manifestation of different legislative intent, they are construed as applicable to persons and things, or cases of like kind, as are designated by the particular words.

ELECTRA COMPLEX: Sexual desire of the daughter towards her father; with hostility towards her mother.

ELEMENTS: The acts or omissions of action, which form the bases of any particular offense.

ELIGIBLE FOR COMMAND AT SEA: Construed to apply to all officers of the line of the Navy, except those designated for the performance of engineering, aeronautical engineering, or special duties, and except those officers of the Naval Reserve and those limited duty officers not authorized to perform all deck duties afloat.

EMANCIPATED MINOR: Freed from the custody, control and service of the parents during infancy:

EMBARGO: A proclamation or order of a state usually issued in time of war or threatened hostilities, prohibiting the departure of ships or goods from the ports of such state.

EMBASSY: The residence or office of an ambassador; sometimes the functions, business, or position of an ambassador.

EMBEZZLE: To fraudulently appropriate another's property intrusted to one's care, or which has come lawfully into one's hands.

EMBEZZLEMENT: The fraudulent appropriation of property by a person to whom such property has been entrusted, or into whose hands it has lawfully come.

EMBRACERY: To attempt, by any means whatever, except by the production of evidence and argument in open court, to influence and instruct any juryman, or to incline him to be more favorable to the one side than to the other, in any judicial proceeding, whether any verdict is given or not, and whether a verdict, if given, is true or false.

EMINENT DOMAIN: The power of government to take private property for public use.

EMPLOYEE OF THE GOVERNMENT: Includes officers or employees of any Federal agency, members of the military or naval forces of the United States, and persons acting on behalf of a Federal agency in an official capacity, temporarily or permanently in the service of the United States, whether with or without compensation.

ENDOCRINOLOGIST: A physician who specializes in the study, diagnosis and treatment of disorders of the ductless (and endocrine) gland system.

ENDOGENOUS: Originating in oneself.

ENEMY: Includes not merely the organized forces of the enemy in time of war, but also imports any hostile body that our forces may be opposing, such as a rebellious mob or a band of renegades.

ENGLISH COMMON LAW: That portion of the law of England which is based not upon legislative enactment but upon immemorial usage and the general custom of the people.

ENGRAM: Memory picture from a psychic experience.

ENJOIN: To forbid or command by injuction.

ENLISTED MAN: Any male member of the Army who is below the grade of a commissioned officer, warrant officer, or cadet. The term is sometimes used to include the female enlisted persons in the Army; however, the terms enlisted person and enlisted personnel are preferred when referring to both the male and female members of the Army:

ENLISTED PERSON: Construed to refer to any person who is serving in an enlisted grade in any armed force.

ENLISTED WOMAN: An enlisted member of the WAC or of the WAF, WAVES, SPARS, and Women Marines.

ENLISTEE: A person who has voluntary enlisted for service in the AF or other service.

ENLISTMENT: A voluntary entrance into military service under enlisted status, as distinguished from induction through Selective Service; A period of time, contractual or prescribed by law, which an enlisted person serves between enrollment and discharge; The act of enrollment in military service.

ENLISTMENT ALLOWANCE: Allowance paid to an enlisted member for past service who reenlists within 3 months after being given an honorable discharge. The amount of payment is based on the number of years served in the enlistment period from which last discharged.

ENSIGN: In the U.S. Navy, the lowest commissioned rank, corresponding to second lieutenant in the other services; a person holding this rank; the title of a person.

ENTRAPMENT: An agent of the Government conceives an offense against the law and then incites a person to commit that offense for purposes of prosecution.

ENURITICS: Psychopaths who are interested in urine.

ENVOY: A public minister of the second class, ranking next after the ambassador.

EPILEPSY: A chronic nervous affection characterized by periodic seizures in which there is loss of consciousness together with a series of tonic or clonic convulsions. It is not a form of insanity, but it is recognized as a cause of insanity. The violent form of disease is called grand mal; the milder form, petit mal.

EQUITABLE LIEN: A lien which is not conditioned upon the possession of the thing sought to be charged.

EQUITABLE MERGER: Any situation where the reviewing authority, confronted with the conviction of two or more offenses, as to all of which the accused may legally stand convicted, sets aside the findings on one or more of the offenses because the plural offenses arose out of the same act or the same course of action extending over a comparatively short period of time; no aggravating circumstances existed precluding equitable action; and evidence as to one offense tended in some degree to support the other.

EQUITY: That portion of remedial justice which is exclusively administered by a court of equity.

ERRORS IN SUBSTANCE IN CHARGES AND SPECIFICATIONS: Those of such a nature as to vitiate the entire proceedings and render them liable to review by civil tribunals; such, for example, as failure to show jurisdiction on the part of the court.

ESCAPE: Where a person who is in lawful custody for any criminal offense whether it be treason, felony, or misdemeanor, regains his liberty before he is delivered in due course of law; It is an offense on the part of the person in custody, and of the officer in whose custody he is.

ESCAPE FROM CONFINEMENT: Any completed casting off of the restraint of confinement, before being set at liberty by proper authority, and lack of effectiveness of the physical restraint imposed is immaterial to the issue of guilt.

ESCAPE OF A PRISONER: His deliberate absence from his place of confinement or custody, or from the supervision of his guard.

ESCHEAT: Reversion of property to the state in consequence of want of any individual competent to inherit.

ESTATE: The interest which one has in lands, or in any other subject of property.

ESTOPPEL: A bar which precludes a person from denying the truth of a fact which has in contemplation of law become settled by the acts and proceedings of judicial or legislative officers, or by the act of the party himself, either by conventional writing or by representations, express or implied, in pais.

ET AL: "And another" or "and others."

ET CETERA: And others; and other things.

ET SEQUENTIA: And the following.

EVENT: May be considered to include the words "act," "transaction," and "occurrence," and to be included within the meaning of the word "fact."

EVICTION: Dispossession with or without process of law; by judgment of law.

EVIDENCE: Limited in its scope to only those matters that may be legally presented at a trial by the act of the parties, through the aid of such concrete facts as witnesses, admissions in court, confessions, photographs, charts, records or other documents;

applies to factors, introduced by the prosecution or defense, that generate proof.

EVIDENCE, PRIMARY: That evidence which suffices for the proof of a particular fact until contradicted or overcome by other evidence.

EVIDENCE, SECONDARY: Oral testimony or a copy admitted to prove the contents of a lost original document, or one which the other party can produce but will not.

EXCLUSIVE JURISDICTION: That which gives to one tribunal sole power to try the case.

EXECUTIVE ACTION: An action carried out by an executive under powers inherent in his position, and done to forward or modify policy, to expedite accomplishment of a task or mission, or to commence or modify a program.

EXECUTIVE AGENCY: An agency of the executive branch of the government, or of one of its executive departments.

EXECUTIVE DEPARTMENTS: One of the departments of the executive branch of the government headed by a cabinet member.

EXECUTIVE OFFICER: An assistant to a commanding officer responsible for seeing that the policies of the command as applied to the details of day-to-day operations are carried out.

EXECUTIVE ORDER: A rule or regulation having the force of law, issued by the President with congressional authorization.

EXCEPTION: An objection; a reservation; a contradiction.

EXCHANGE: The exchange of prisoners of war is a purely voluntary act on the part of the states at war. This takes place under an agreement called a "cartel." The exchange is usually rank for rank, number for number, value for value, though it is sometimes necessary to agree upon certain conventional values when those of the same rank are not among the captives, as in 1862, when the United States exchanged a captain in the army for six privates, etc.

EXCLUSIVE JURISDICTION: In domestic law plenary authority of Federal Government over certain real property under Federal control, arising from the acceptance thereof by the Federal Government (pursuant to Federal Statute since 1940) and consent thereto by statute of the State Government or Territorial Government whose authority is excluded except where the right to serve civil and criminal process is served. In international law, that situation in which either the civil authorities of a receiving State or military authorities of a sending State, but not the authorities of both, have the right to exercise civil or criminal jurisdiction over certain of the members of, or persons accompanying, the visiting armed force in all or in specified categories of cases.

EX CONTRACTU: From a contract.

EXCUSABLE HOMICIDE IN GENERAL: Is homicide committed under circumstances that constitute, not a justification, but merely an excuse. It is of two sorts: 1. Homicide per infortunium, or by misadventure—where a person unfortunately kills another in doing a lawful act, without any intent to hurt, and without criminal negligence. 2. Homicide se defendendo, or in self-defense, upon a sudden affray—where a person necessarily kills another, after becoming engaged in a sudden affray, in order to save himself from reasonably apparent danger of death or great bodily harm.

EX DELICTO: Actions which arise in consequence of a crime, misdemeanor or tort.

EXECUTED AND EXECUTORY CONTRACTS: An executed contract is one which has been fully carried out by the contracting parties. An executory contract is one which is yet to be performed. An agreement may be executed on the part of one party and executory on the part of the other. Thus, a contract for the purchase of a suit of clothes on credit, followed by the delivery of the suit, is executed on the part of the dealer and executory on the part of the purchaser.

EXECUTION OF JUDGMENT OR DECREE: Embraces all appropriate means of putting into effect a final judgment of court.

EXECUTIVE AGREEMENT: Agreement of the United States and a foreign country negotiated by direction of the President which usually takes effect upon signature and is not submitted to the Senate for ratification.

EXECUTIVE OFFICER: The chief assistant to a commanding officer.

EXECUTIVE ORDER: Order issued by the President by virtue of the authority vested in him by the Constitution or by an act of Congress. It has the force of law.

EXECUTOR: Person appointed by testator to carry out directions in his will according to its provisions.

EXECUTORY CONTRACTS: **See Executed.**

EXEMPLARY DAMAGES: Additional damages awarded because of the malicious character of the acts complained of.

EXEMPT: The condition of not being legally required to perform an act.

EXEQUATUR: (Latin: let it be executed) A certificate issued by the foreign department of a state to a consul of another state, recognizing his official character, and authorizing him to fulfill his duties.

EX GRATIA: Of favor; of grace.

EXHIBITIONISM OR INDECENT EXPOSURE: The exposure of the genitalia to one of the opposite sex constitutes, in general parlance, the perversion of exhibitionism. Usually this offense is committed by the male in the presence of one or more females.

EXISTED PRIOR TO SERVICE: Term added to a medical diagnosis to signify that there is clear and unmistakable evidence that the disease or injury, or the underlying condition producing the disease or injury, existed prior to the individuals' entry into military service.

EX MERO MOTU: Of mere motion; a court-martial under certain conditions may, ex mero motu, exclude certain evidence.

EX NESSITATE REI: From the necessity of the case.

EX PARTE: An ex parte proceeding is one by and for one purpose only, without notice to or opposition by another. It necessarily presupposes a right to petitioner to which there is no party.

EXPATRIATION: The voluntary act of abandoning one's country and becoming the citizen or subject of another.

EXPANDABLE PROPERTY: Property that may be consumed in use or loses its identity in use and may be dropped from stock record accounts when it is issued or used.

EXPENDABLE SUPPLIES: 1. Articles which are consumed in use, such as oil, ammunition, paint, fuel, forage, surgical dressings, drugs, medicines, cleaning and preserving materials, etc. 2. Articles such as repair parts and components which when issued for immediate installation, are used to repair or complete other articles and thereby lose their identity. 3. Expendable items as applied to repairs and uitilities operations applies to items which, when issued, are consumed in maintenance operations, or construction activities, and are, therefore, dropped from accountability.

EXPENDITURE: A payment entered as a final charge against an appropriation.

EXPERT OPINION: The testimony of an expert stating his opinion on a question of science, skill, or trade.

EXPERT TESTIMONY: Special knowledge or experience as distinguished from common, and judicial knowledge, and is in the nature of conclusions or judgments that are based on an assumed state of facts and rendered by any witness shown to be qualified beyond that of persons in general. Such testimony somewhat tends to invade the province of the jury, or to supplant its work in proportion to the amount of reasoning in such testimony.

EXPERT WITNESS: One who is skilled in some art, trade, profession or science or who has knowledge and experience in relation to matters which are not generally within the knowledge of men of common education and experience.

EX POST FACTO: Subsequently; from what is done afterwards.

EX POST FACTO LAWS: One which, in its operation, makes that criminal which was not so at the time the action was performed, or which increases the punishment, or, in short, which in relation to the offense or its consequences, alters the situation of a party, to his disadvantage.

EXPRESS CONTRACT: An actual agreement of the parties, the terms of which are openly uttered or declared at the time of making it—stated in distinct and explicit language either orally or in writing.

EXPRESSIO UNIS EST EXCLUSIO ALTERIUS: Expression of One Thing an Exclusion of Others. Applies in the construction of penal statutes. Thus, where a statute provided that certain games of chance might be kept on being licensed, and declared that certain others should be unlawful, it was held that all games not mentioned in the statute were legalized.

EX PROPRIO VIGORE: By its own force.

EX RELATIONE: At the information of; by the relation.

EXTENUATION: Those matters which explain the circumstances surrounding the commission of the offense, including the motives or reasons therefor, but which do not amount to a legal justification.

EXTERRITORIALITY: The privilege of those persons (such as foreign ministers) who, though temporarily resident within a state, are not subject to the opertion of its laws.

EXTORTION: The communication of threats to another with the intention thereby to obtain anything of value, or any acquittance, advantage or immunity of any description.

EXTRADITION: The surrender of a criminal by a foreign state in which he has taken refuge, to the state in which the crime was committed.

EXTRAJUDICIAL: That which does not belong to the judge or his jurisdiction, notwithstanding which he takes cognizance of it.

EXTRATERRITORIALITY: The operation of laws upon persons, beyond the limits of the enacting state. The term is often used in the same sense as exterritoriality.

EXTREMIS: When a person is sick beyond the hope or recovery and near death he is said to be in extremis.

EX VI TERMINI: From, or by the force of the term.

EYEWITNESS: One who saw the act or fact to which he testifies.

F

FACT: "The fundamental conception of a fact is that of a thing as existing or being true." "It is not limited to what is tangible, or visible, or in any way the object of sense; things invisible, mere thoughts, intentions, fancies of the mind, when conceived of as existing or being true, are conceived of as facts."

FAIL: In naval procedure, means substantially the same as "neglect."

FALSE: Deliberately deceitful; As regards the false making or altering of a writing, "false" refers not to the contents of the writing or to the facts stated therein but to the making or altering of it.

FALSE AND FRAUDULENT CLAIMS: Include not only those containing some material false statement, but also claims which the claimant knows to have been paid or for some other reason knows he is not authorized to present or upon which he knows he has no right to collect.

FALSE IMPRISONMENT: Any unlawful restraint of a person's liberty, and is committed whenever a person detains the body of another, by force actual or constructive, without his consent and without legal cause. False imprisonment is a misdemeanor at common law and generally under the statutes.

FALSE SWEARING: The making under lawful oath of any statement, oral, or written, not believing the statement to be true.

FALSUS IN UNO, FALSUS IN OMNIBUS: (false in one part, false in all) is a maxim occasionally mentioned. This does not mean that the whole of the witness' testimony is to be rejected. It refers only to wilful false statements and not to unintentional mistakes.

FAMILY ALLOWANCE: Regular monthly payment through the Army Finance Center, to a member of the family of an enlisted person, and financed in part by a contribution from the Government and in part by a charge against the enlisted person's pay as provided for in the Servicemen's Dependents Allowance Act of 1942. Now authorized only for a limited number of personnel comming within the "savings provision" of the Career Compensation Act of 1949.

FAUCES TERRAE: Jaws of the land; projecting headlands or promontories, including arms of the sea.

FEAR: A natural feeling of apprehension when going into battle.

FEDERAL AGENCY: Any agency of the federal government; specif. any executive agency, or any establishment under the legislative or judicial branch of the government.

FEDERAL REGISTER: A publication of the National Archives, used chiefly for the publication of regulations issued by various administrative agencies of the government.

FEDERAL SERVICE STRIPE: A diagonal stripe worn by enlisted persons on the left sleeve of the uniform, each stripe representing three years of active duty in the US armed forces. Usually called a 'service stripe.'

FEE: Estate in land, an absolute inheritance clear of any condition, or restricted to particular heirs, but descendible to heirs generally.

FELLATIO: Oral copulation; use of the mouth on the male sex organs.

FELLOW-SERVANT RULE: The common law doctrine that if the employer has provided safe and suitable tools, machinery and appliances, in accordance with the duty imposed upon him by law, he is not liable for an injury to an employee resulting from the misuse or nonuse of the instrumentalities by another employee.

FELONIOUS HOMICIDE: The killing of a human being without legal justification or excuse, and is either murder or manslaughter.

FELONIOUS INTENT IN LARCENY: To constitute larceny at common law there must be what is technically called a "felonious" intent, or "animus furandi," and this intent must exist both in the taking and in the carrying away. By this it is meant that there must be: 1. A fraudulent intent, and not a mistake or bona fide claim of right. 2. And an intent to deprive the owner permanently of his property in the goods, or of their value or a part of their value. 3. Some of the authorities require that the taking shall be lucri causa—that is, for the sake of gain; but by the weight of authority this is not necessary.

FELONIOUSLY: Generally, with criminal intent, malignantly, maliciously, with deliberate evil intent; and, second, specifically, as meaning with intent to commit the particular crime with which the defendant is charged .

FELONY: Designates a crime of a graver or more atrocious nature than those designated as misdemeanors. In many states felony is defined as any public offense on conviction of which the offender is liable to sentence of death or imprisonment in a penitentiary or state prison; in contrast, misdemeanor is a general name for criminal offenses of every sort which do not amount to the grade of felony.

FEME SOLE: A single woman.

FEMME COVERT: A married woman.

FEMUR: The thigh bone; the thigh.

FETISH: A symbol arousing sexual excitation; the substituting of a part of an article for the sexual object.

FETISHISM: A compulsive perversion of the substitutive type in which an object possessed by the loved person replaces the love for that person herself. Thus, the fetishist employs the art of magic in investing an intimate object with the attractive evaluation of the individual himself. The object which serves as a fetish is a symbol. It embodies mysterious qualities which are considered by the victim to emanate from the loved one. By overevaluating an object, such as a shoe or a stocking, the hair or any other portion of the loved one's body, the fetishist relinquishes the aim of accomplishing the normal heterosexual act and accepts a mystical substitute which to him offers even more miraculous qualities. A perverted sense of smell frequently accompanies the perversion of fetishism. The odor is often that of a portion of the body of the love object.

FIBROSIS: The development of fibrous tissue.

FIDUCIARY: One holding a position of trust or confidence with respect to the money or property of another.

FIELD DUTY: Service or duty performed in operation against actual or potential enemy, or performed in maneuvers, war games, field exercises, or similar operations, as distinguished from training duty, rear-area duty, or the like; In a restricted sense, duty performed in combat operations against an enemy.

FIELD EXERCISE: A training exercise conducted under simulated war conditions in the field, and in which the troops and equipment of one side are present wholly or in part while the opposing side is either imaginary or represented by only a few troops and pieces of equipment.

FIELD GRADE: An officer's grade covering major, lieutenant colonel, and colonel.

FIGHTING: To constitute this offense at common law and under the statutes as well, there must be fighting between two or more persons. And there must be actual fighting. Mere quarrelsome and threatening words are not enough.

FILIATION ORDER: The fixing of the paternity of a child and the obligation to support it.

FINAL INDORSEMENT: Indorsement on the service record that is filled out only when a soldier is separated from the service by discharge, death, etc.

FINALLY APPROVED: A sentence is "finally approved" within the sense of NS MCM section 0122 when it is approved by the supervisory authority in the case of a special court-martial where the approved sentence does not involve a bad-conduct discharge, or promulgated by the Navy Department after final appellate action in all other general and special court-martial cases.

FINANCE AND ACCOUNTING OFFICER: The staff officer assigned to perform the duties set forth in prescribed regulations and charged with maintaining the system of accounts and financial procedures through which his commander's responsibilities are stated and discharged in monetary terms. He may also be a disbursing officer if he disburses public funds in connection with his duties.

FINDING OF FACTS: Will include only those things which the court believes the evidence establishes, and nothing further.

FINE: Has no relation to the pay of the accused and can best be compared to the fine known in civilian court where a person is fined a certain amount. In order to enforce collection, the sentence may include an alternate of confinement.

FINGER PRINTS: Embraces any impression, print or stain, made by the tips of the fingers or thumbs, or by the palmer surfaces of the hands. The papillary ridges, or friction skin, regardless of the portion of the body from which it is taken, is permanent and unchanging in its character. In the commission of crime, any portion of the inner or palmer surfaces of the hands may leave its imprint, and wherever any of these may be found, identity may be established by comparison with the prints of an individual.

FIRE: To discharge a gun; to shoot a projectile from, or discharge a cartridge in, a gun; to ignite and launch a rocket; To cause a gun or rocket to discharge.

FIREARM: A small arm, as a pistol or rifle, designated to be carried and used by an individual; Also used in a general sense, a gun.

FIRE-WATER COMPLEX: This condition is often found as a part of the symptom complex occurring in sexually psychopathic incendiarists. After lighting a fire there is a period of exhibitionism followed by a desire to urinate.

FIRST SERGEANT: The chief administrative position for a noncommissioned officer.

FIXTURE: A chattel attached to realty, becoming part and parcel of it.

FIXTURES: Personal property which has been attached to realty—may become a part of the real property or be of such a character that they continue to be treated as personalty. In reaching their decisions as to whether fixtures are real property or personal property, the courts have considered four distinct factors: 1. the mode of annexation; 2. the intention of the person who attaches the fixture; 3. the relationship between the fixture and the use to be made of the real property; and 4. the relationship existing between the parties engaged in the controversy.

FLAGELLATION: A psycho-sexual perversion characterized by a passion for whipping; encountered among sado-masochists; may be either active or passsive.

FLAG OFFICER: As used in Navy Regulations, shall mean an officer of the Navy above the grade of captain.

FLAG RANK: A Naval rank of commodore or higher.

FLEET: An organization of ships, aircraft, Marine forces and shore-based fleet activities, all under the command of a commander or commander-in-chief who may exercise operational as well as administrative control.

FLEET ADMIRAL: The highest commissioned rank in the US Navy, corresponding to general in the Army; a person holding this rank.

FLIGHT SERVICE: An activity or organization within the Military Air Transport Service established to promote the safe and efficient extended flight operation of military aircraft within the US.

FORCE: (NATO Agreement) the personnel belonging to the land, sea or air armed services of one Contracting Party when in the territory of another Contracting Party in the North Atlantic Treaty area in connection with their official duties, provided that the two Contracting Parties concerned may agree that certain individuals, units or formations shall not be regarded as constituting or included in a "force" for the purposes of the present Agreement.

FORCE A SAFEGUARD: Any trespass on the protection established by a detachment, guard, detail, or order posted by a commander for the purpose of protecting some person, place, or property.

FORECLOSURE: A termination of the rights of the mortgagor or his grantee in the property covered by the mortgage.

FORCE MAJEURE: Superior or irresistible force.

FORCIBLE ENTRY AND DETAINER: Forcible entry occurs where a person violently enters upon real property occupied by another, with menaces, force, and arms, and without the authority of law. Forcible detainer is detention of the possession of the property by the use of force and violence, and may occur where the original entry was forcible or where it was peaceable.

FOREIGN DUTY: Duty outside the continental limits of the US, except that duty performed in a territory or possession of the US by a resident of such territory or possession is not considered foreign duty.

FOREIGN SERVICE: For a resident of the US, service outside the continental US; For a resident of a US territory or possession, service in an area other than the continental US and other than the area of his residence.

FORENSIC: Relating to the courts.

FORFEITURE: Deprives the accused of all or part of his pay.

FORFEITURE OF ALL PAY AND ALLOWANCES: Construed to mean the forfeiture of all pay and allowances becoming due on and after the date a lawfully adjudged sentence is approved by the convening authority.

FORFEITURE OF PAY: It is the deprivation of a specified amount of the accused's pay for a stated number of months (or days). The amount of pay to be forfeited is determined by the court.

FORGERY: The false making or altering with intent to defraud of any signature to, or any part of, any writing which would, if genuine, apparently impose a legal liability on another or change his legal right or liability to his prejudice; or the uttering, offering, issuing, or transferring, with intent to defraud, of such writing known by the offender to be so made or altered.

FORGING OR COUNTERFEITING: Any fraudulent making of the signature of another, whether or not an attempt is made to imitate the handwriting.

FORMER JEOPARDY: Is where: 1. No person shall, without his consent, be tried a second time for the same offense; 2. No proceeding in which an accused has been found guilty by a court-martial upon any charge or specification shall be held to be a trial until the finding of guilty has become final after review of the case has been fully completed. 3. A proceeding which, subsequent to the introduction of evidence but prior to a finding, is dismissed or terminated by the convening authority or on motion of the prosecution for failure of available evidence or witnesses without any fault of the accused shall be a trial.

FORNICATION: Unlawful sexual intercourse between two unmarried persons. Further, if one of the persons be married and the other not, it is fornication on the part of the latter, though adultery for the former. In some jurisdictions, however, by statute, it is adultery on the part of both persons if the woman is married, whether the man is married or not.

FORUM: A court of justice or judicial tribunal.

FRAUD: A generic term which embraces all the multifarious means which human ingenuity can devise and are resorted to by an individual to gain an advantage over another by false suggestion, or by suppression of the truth.

FRAUDULENT: Deliberately deceitful.

FRAUDULENT ENLISTMENT: An enlistment procured by means of a willful misrepresentation in regard to a qualification or disqualification, which has had the effect of causing the enlistment of a man not qualified to be enlisted, and who, but for such false representation or concealment, would have been rejected.

FRONTALIER: Civilian living in the immediate vicinity of frontier whose business, health, or welfare requires frequent frontier crossings to locations in the immediate vicinity of the frontier.

FROTTEURS: Addicts of a form of masturbation, closely associated with buttock fetishism; the male subject usually rubs or presses against the buttocks of a female, and sometimes a male, while in a crowd. In this condition there is usually a homosexual element.

FUGITIVE FROM JUSTICE: One who, having committed a crime, flees from the jurisdiction within which it was committed, to escape justice.

FUGITIVE WARRANT: Is a warrant which recites that the individual is a fugitive from another State or jurisdiction and is being arrested for return to that other State for trial. Delivery will be refused in this instance or if, for any other detectable reason, the warrant is deemed improper.

FUNCTIONS: The appropriate or assigned duties of an individual, office or organization. As defined in the National Security Act of 1947, amended, the term "function" includes functions, powers and duties. As defined in Functions of the Armed Forces and Joint Chiefs of Staff, approved by the Secretary of Defense 1 October 1953, the term "function" includes responsibility, missions, and tasks.

G

GANGRENE: Death of a part of a body for failure of nutrition.

GARNISHMENT: The right of a judgment creditor to compel a third party owing money to, or holding money for, a judgment debtor to pay the money to the creditor instead of to the debtor.

GASTRO ENTEROLOGIST: A physician who specializes in the diagnosis and treatment of diseases and disorders of the digestive tract.

GENERAL ALLOTMENT: Allotment which limits the amount that may be obligated under available appropriations without limiting a portion of the total to any specific appropriation or project account; allotment under which obligations may be charged against more than one appropriation.

GENERAL ARTICLE: This Article covers all offenses not specifically mentioned in the UCMJ. It includes 1. all disorders and neglects to the prejudice of good order and discipline; 2. all conduct of a nature to bring discredit upon the armed forces, and 3. all crimes and offenses not capital. Offenses in violation of this Article are triable by a general, special or summary court, according to the nature and degree of the offense, and punishable at the discretion of such court.

GENERAL COURT-MARTIAL: Highest type of court-martial, consisting of not fewer than five members not including the law officer, having power to try any offense punishable by the Uniform Code of Military Justice.

GENERAL COURT-MARTIAL ORDER: An order issued by AF, Army, Navy organization to convene a general court-martial, in which is announced the results of trial by a general court-martial, and the mitigation, remission, suspension, or vacation of a sentence of a general court-martial.

GENERAL DISCHARGE: Form of discharge, under honorable conditions, service satisfactory, given to a soldier not qualifying for an honorable discharge.

GENERAL DUTY: The duty status of a person who is physically qualified to serve in any given military duty. Distinguished from limited duty; A term sometimes applied to an aircraft or other piece of equipment, signifying that it has been designed or designated for use in any of numerous duties, as in fighting, bombing, or reconnaissance.

GENERAL EDUCATIONAL DEVELOPMENT TESTS: Comprehensive test to measure an individual's acquired knowledge relative to that acquired at high school and college levels.

GENERAL HEADQUARTERS: A commander's headquarters, esp. for all field forces.

GENERAL ISSUE: A plea which denies or traverses at once the whole indictment or declaration, without offering any special matter to evade it.

GENERAL MOBILIZATION: A mobilization of the entire military forces of a nation, either to engage in hostilities already begun, or in preparation for an all-out war.

GENERAL OFFICER: Any officer of the AF, Army, or Marine Corps above the rank of colonel, i.e. a brigadier general, major general, lieutenant general, general of the Air Force, or general of the Army.

GENERAL ORDER: An official order given in writing by a headquarters, affecting or relating to the entire command.

GENERAL ORDERS: 1. Permanent instructions, issued in order form, that apply to all members of a command, as compared with special orders, which affect only individuals or small groups. General orders are usually concerned with matters of policy or administration. 2. A series of permanent guard orders that govern the duties of a sentry on post.

GENERAL OWNER OF PROPERTY: A person who has title to it, whether or not he has possession of it.

GENERAL PARTICIPATION CLAUSE: Clause contained in some treaties providing that the treaty shall only be effective in a war in which all belligerents are parties to this treaty.

GENERAL PROCUREMENT BOARD: Agency set up to supervise, co-ordinate, and control all procurement by United States forces in a theater of operations.

GENERAL PURCHASING AGENTS: Agents who have been appointed in the principal oversea areas of operations to supervise, control, coordinate, negotiate, and develop the local procurement of supplies, services, and facilities by United States Armed Forces, in order that the most effective utilization may be made of local resources and production.

GENERAL REPUTATION: Implies "common opinion" or "consensus", although, naturally, there may be a few dissenters to this general opinion.

GENERAL VERDICT: Embodies and declares the result of an inquiry into a question of law as well as of fact.

GENERALIA SPECIALIBUS NON DEROGANT: Things general do not derogate things special.

GENEVA CONVENTION: An international agreement made in Geneva in 1864 concerning the treatment, by belligerents, of prisoners of war, the sick, and the wounded; this agreement, with its later amendments, has been accepted and is obeyed by all of the civilized nations.

GERONTOPHILIA: The choice of older persons of the opposite sex as sexual objects or partners.

GIST: The essential ground or object of the action in point of law, without which there would be no cause of action.

GOOD CONDUCT MEDAL: A service award granted to enlisted

men in recognition of exemplary behavior; the medal worn in recognition of this award.

GOOD OFFICES: The offer of one nation to act as intermediary in a dispute between two other nations.

GOVERNMENT AGENCY: Executive department, board, bureau, commission, or other agency in the executive branch of the Federal Government, or any corporation wholly owned, either directly or through one or more corporations, by the United States.

GOVERNMENT FURNISHED PROPERTY: All tangible property of the Government furnished to the contractor, including both property acquired by the Government and delivered to the contractor and property acquired by the contractor for the account of the Government.

GRADE: Graduation in authority and pay among enlisted man and officers.

GRAND JURY: A jury of inquiry who are summoned and returned by the sheriff to each session of the criminal courts and whose duty is to receive complaints and accusations in criminal cases, hear the evidence adduced on the part of the state, and find bills of indictment in cases where they are satisfied a trial ought to be had. At common law, a grand jury consisted of not less than 12 nor more than 23. In some states, the number is otherwise fixed by statute: Oregon and Utah 7; Texas 12; Idaho 16; California 19; New Mexico 21.

GRAND MAL: A form of epilepsy characterized by periods of coma and convulsions.

GRAVAMEN: The grievance complained of; the substantial cause of the action.

GREENSTICK FRACTURE: A fracture in which one side of the bone is broken, the other being bent.

GRIEVOUS BODILY HARM: Does not include minor injuries, such as a black eye or a bloody nose, but does include fractured or dislocated bones, deep cuts, torn members of the body, serious damage to internal organs and other serious bodily injuries.

GROSSLY NEGLIGENT ACTS: Acts which evidence a reckless disregard for the consequences, either to one's self or to others exposed to its dangerous effects.

GROSS NEGLIGENCE: An utter indifference to the consequences of one's actions, a total abandonment of the standard of reasonable care coupled with a wanton disregard for the safety of others.

GROUP: An AF unit immediately subordinate to a wing.

GUARD: A person charged with the constant watch and protection of a person, building, gate, piece of equipment; A person charged with restraining another person or persons; The action or duty of serving as a guard.

GUARDHOUSE: A building that accommodates the members of a military guard and provides space for the detention or confinement of military prisoners.

GUARDHOUSE LAWYER OR SEA LAWYER: A sailor or soldier

who is in the habit of twisting the regulations in his favor and advises his fellow sailors and soldiers in doing so.

GUARDIAN AD LITEM: One appointed by the court to look after the interests of an infant in litigation.

GUARD REPORT: Report submitted to the proper authority by the commander of a guard at the close of each period of duty.

GUERILLA: A member of an independent body of armed men, not regularly or organically connected with the armies of either belligerent, which carries on irregular war.

GUIDANCE: Policy, direction, decision, or instruction, having the effect of an order when promulgated by a higher echelon.

GUN: A mechanism consisting essentially of a barrel, receiver, and breech mechanism, using controlled explosives to shoot projectiles or signal flares; A cannon, as distinguished from a small arms.

GYNANDRY: The extreme grade of degenerative homosexuality in females.

GYNECOLOGIST: A physician specializing in the diagnosis and treatment of diseases and disorders peculiar to the female (especially the sexual organs).

H

HABEAS CORPUS: The appropriate remedy to ascertain whether any person is rightfully in confinement or not, and the cause of his confinement, and if no sufficient ground of detention appears, the party is entitled to his immediate discharge.

HABENDUM: Portion of the deed defining the extent of ownership in the thing granted to be held and enjoyed by the grantee.

HABIT FORMING NARCOTIC DRUG: See narcotic.

HALLUCINATION: A sensation without any external object to account for it. To hear voices in a quiet room is to have an auditory hallucination. To see something that isn't there is to have a visual hallucination, and so with the other senses.

HARBOR: To hide or help the escape of someone wanted by lawful authority.

HARBORING OR PROTECTING THE ENEMY: Shielding, either physically or by use of any artifice, aid, or representation, from any injury or misfortune which in the chance of war may befall him.

HARD LABOR WITHOUT CONFINEMENT: Imposition of work in addition to the accused's normal duties, which duties must be performed outside of the accused's normal working hours.

HARMLESS ERROR: Any error which does not present a fair risk of harm to the accused. An error is therefore "harmless" when: the right of the accused involved is not a "substantial" right, or the record of trial indicates the error did not influence the court to any material extent.

HAZARD: To put in danger of loss or injury.

HAZARDOUS DUTY: Or "important service" may include such service as duty in a combat or other dangerous area; embarkation for foreign duty or for sea duty; movement to a port of embarkation, etc. Drill, target practice, maneuvers, and practice marches will not ordinarily be regarded as included.

HAZARDING OF VESSEL: Willful and wrongful putting a vessel of the armed forces in danger of loss is punishable by death or such other punishment as a court-martial may direct. If such hazarding is merely negligent, the death penalty is not authorized.

HEADQUARTERS: Construed either as a singular or plural. The command echelon of a unit or other organization, consisting of a commander and his staff.

HEARSAY: A statement which is offered in evidence to prove the truth of the matters therein stated, but which is not made by the author when a witness before the court at the particular trial at which it is so offered is heresay.

HEARSAY EVIDENCE: Evidence not proceeding from the personal knowledge of the witness but from the mere repetition of what he has heard others say.

HEARSAY RULE: Prohibits the use of a person's assertion as equivalent to testimony to the facts asserted, unless the asserter is brought to testify in court on the stand, where he may be probed and cross-examined as to the grounds of his assertion and his qualifications to make it.

HEIR: The person appointed by law to succeed to the estate in case of intestacy.

HEMATOLOGIST: A physician who specializes in the diagnosis and treatment of diseases and disorders of the blood and blood forming organs.

HEMATOMA: A swelling containing blood.

HEMO: A prefix referring to blood.

HEREDITAMENTS: Property that can be inherited.

HETEROSEXUAL: Pertaining to the opposite sex.

HETEROSEXUALITY: Sexual attraction to persons of the opposite sex.

HIGH SEAS: All parts of the sea which are outside the boundary of any country.

HIGH SEAS, FREEDOM OF: A status which requires freedom of navigation and free use for all.

HIGHWAY TRAFFIC CONTROL: The enforcement of the rules of the road, traffic regulations, and road discipline, including spot direction. It is a function of the provost marshal and military police.

HIGHWAY TRAFFIC CONTROL POST: Point on the highway at which the military police enforce highway traffic control and furnish information and directions.

HIRE: Has application to the more menial, manual, or mechanical employments, and commonly implies employment for short periods, as a day or a week; and is distinguished from the word "salary" in that the latter has reference to the more mental forms of employment and implies greater permanence of employment and payment at long intervals.

HIS SUPERIOR OFFICER: With respect to a person who is a member of one armed force, an officer of another armed force who is duly placed in the chain of command over such person is, "his superior officer".

HOLDER IN DUE COURSE: The holder of a negotiable instrument who takes it in good faith and for value, with no notice of any defect in the title of the person from whom he took it.

HOLD-OVER: To retain possession as tenant of property leased, after the end of the term.

HOLOGRAPHIC (OLOGRAPHIC) WILL: One that is entirely written, dated, and signed by the hand of the testator himself.

HOME: A dwelling place of a person, distinguished from other dwelling places of that person by the intimacy of the relation between the person and the place.

HOMICIDE IN GENERAL: Homicide is the killing of a human being by a human being and is either justifiable, excusable, or felonious.

HOMOSEXUAL: A person whose major or primary source of sexual satisfaction is from contact with others of the same sex. Among females, homosexuality is generally known as Lesbianism.

HOMOSEXUALITY: A condition in which there is a sexual fixation or erotic sexual attachment to persons of the same sex.

HONORABLE DISCHARGE: Form of discharge given to a soldier whose service has been honest and faithful, and who has been given conduct ratings of at least Good; has been given efficiency ratings of at least Fair; has not been convicted by a general court-martial; and has not been convicted more than once by a special court-martial.

HONOR GUARD: A specially chosen guard detailed to escort a distinguished person, or one detailed to escort a deceased person at a military funeral.

HOSTAGE: A person who is given into the possession of the enemy in time of war, his freedom or life to stand as security for the performance of a promise made by the other belligerent power.

HOSTILITY: A state of open war, actual fighting.

HOUSEBREAKING: The unlawful entering of the building or structure of another with intent to commit a criminal offense therein.

HOVERING VESSEL: Any vessel which is found or kept off the coast of the United States within or without the custom waters, if, from the history, conduct, character, or location of the vessel, it is reasonable to believe that such vessel is being used or may be used to introduce or promote or facilitate the introduction or attempted introduction of merchandise into the United States in violation of the laws respecting the revenue.

HUMERUS: The bone of the upper arm.

HYPERACTIVE: Overactive, restless, constantly moving.

HYPERTHYMIC: Pertains to temperament, showing increase in excitability and vivacious tempo; at times irritability and explosiveness.

HYPERTROPHY: The morbid enlargement or overgrowth of an organ or part due to an increase in size of its constituent cells.

HYPNOSIS: Putting a subject to sleep by inducing a trance or an amnesia by means of psychological suggestion.

HYPOCHONDRIASIS: A morbid overconcern about disease. It is a psychoneurosis. The person who has this neurosis is a hypochondriac. The diseases which worry the patient are, in a sense, imaginary; but the psychoneurosis is certainly real. The patient really is sick; not sick with the tuberculosis which he dreads, but sick with the emotional conflict which produced the hypochondriasis.

HYPOPLASIA: Imperfect development.

HYPOSPADIA: Opening, usually congenital, occurring on the underside of the penis; an opening of the urethra into the vagina.

HYPOTHECATION: The act of pledging personal property as collateral security.

HYPOTHETICAL QUESTION: A form of question which is put to an expert witness, in which things counsel claims to have proved are stated as a supposition and the witness is asked to state and explain the conclusion which in his opinion results.

HYSTERECTOMY: An operation for the removal of the uterus.

HYSTERIA: A psychoneurosis in which there is gross loss of, or impairment of, the function of one or more organs; as, for example, hysterical blindness or hysterical convulsions; also used for conversion hysteria. The term is also used, somewhat amateurishly, as a synonym for temper tantrums.

I

IBIDEM: The same; the same book or place; the same subject.

ID: The unconscious reservoir of instincts, urges, and drives.

IDEAL SADISM: Fancied, imaginary sadism; in this condition sadistic acts exist solely in the imagination of the subject. It may precede actual sadistic acts.

IDEM: The same.

IDEM SONANS: Doctrine of absolute accuracy in spelling name is not required. If name as misspelled conveys to the ear a sound practically identical with the correct name it is sufficient.

ID EST: That is.

IDIOPATHIC INSANITY: This is a form of insanity resulting from disease of the brain, injury to the cortex, anemia of the brain, etc.

IGNORANTIA JURIS NON EXCUSAT: Ignorance of the law is no excuse.

ILLUSION: A perception which is misinterpreted.

IMAGINATION: Psycho-imagery arranged in logical categories according to rhythmical and stylistic principles; the ability to build up abstract thoughts into concrete.

IMBECILITY: Feebleness of mind. In idiocy there is practically an absence of mind; in imbecility the mental defectiveness is less, there is a glimmering of intelligence.

IMMIGRANT ALIEN: Any person lawfully admitted into the United States under an immigration visa for permanent residence.

IMMUNIZATION: The act of rendering safe from the attack of a disease.

IMPEACHING A WITNESS: Introducing evidence which tends to prove that a witness who has testified is unworthy of belief.

IMPEACHMENT: To call in question the veracity of a witness, by means of evidence adduced for that purpose, or the adducing of proof that a witness is unworthy of belief.

IMPERSONATE: The term "impersonate" means to assume or act the person or character of another.

IMPLEADED: Included in a case with another person.

IMPLIED CONTRACT: One not created or evidenced by the explicit agreement of the parties, but inferred by law, as a matter of reason and justice from their acts of conduct, the circumstances surrounding the transaction making it reasonable, or even a necessary assumption that a contract existed between them by tacit understanding.

IMPORTANT SERVICE: **See hazardous duty.**

IMPOSSIBLE CONDITIONS: Those which can not be performed in the course of nature.

IMPOTENCE: Lack of strength; lack of sexual virility.

IMPROPER USE OF COUNTERSIGN: Any person who in time of war discloses the parole or countersign to any person not entitled to receive it or who gives to another who is entitled to receive and use the parole or countersign a different parole or countersign from that which, to his knowledge, he was authorized and required to give.

IMPULSE: An animal vital urge towards satisfaction of a biological need.

IMPULSIVE: Actuated by an impulse or impulses.

IMPULSORY: Actuated by an impulse or impulses but deviated prior to fulfillment of its original goal.

INCARCERATION: Imprisonment or confinement.

INCENDIARY: A person guilty of the crime of arson or the burning of a building.

INCENTIVE PAY: Additional pay given a person as an incentive to perform a special kind of duty, as flying, demolition, etc.

INCEST: A person who marries or cohabits or has sexual intercourse with an ancestor or descendant, a brother or sister of the whole or half blood, or an uncle, aunt, nephew or niece of the whole blood. Cohabit means to live together under the representation or appearance of being married. The relationships referred to herein are blood relationships without regard to legitimacy.

INCEST COMPLEX: Desire for sexual relations with a near relative, usually a parent.

INCITERS OR ACCESSORIES BEFORE THE FACT: Those who aid, counsel, command, or encourage the commission of a crime without being present actually or constructively at its perpetration.

INCLOSURE: Thing inclosed; document that is not part of a communication but is included with it. An inclosure may explain, or may give evidence in support of information in the communication.

INCRIMINATING QUESTIONS: No person, under the federal constitution and the state constitutions, can be required to incriminate himself. This provision is declaratory of the common law and applies not only to parties accused, but to witnesses as well. It guarantees a person against being compelled to give evidence in any proceeding either civil or criminal, which might be used against him in any subsequent criminal prosecution. No witness can be required or compelled to answer a question, if, in the opinion of the court, it seems evident that to answer it truthfully would tend to incriminate him or even subject him to the danger of a criminal prosecution.

IN CUSTODIA LEGIS: In the custody of the law.

INDECENCY: Acts which are indecorous as well as those which offend the moral senses or which are morally unfit to be seen or heard.

INDECENT: Offensive to common propriety, offending against modesty or delicacy, grossly vulgar, or obscene.

INDECENT ACTS WITH A CHILD UNDER THE AGE OF 16 YEARS: The taking of any immoral, improper, or indecent liberties with, or the commission of any lewd or lascivious act upon or with the body of, any child of either sex under the age of 16 years with the intent of arousing, appealing to, or gratifying the lust or passions or sexual desires, either of the person committing the act, or of the child, or of both.

INDECENT ASSAULT: The act of a male person taking indecent liberties with the person of a female; or fondling her in a lewd and lascivious manner without her consent and against her will, but with no intent to commit rape.

INDECENT EXPOSURE: **See Exhibitionism.**

INDECORUM: Impropriety in behavior or manners which violates the conventions of civility, custom or etiquette.

INDEMNITY: A collateral contract by which one person engages to secure another against an anticipated loss or to prevent him from being damnified by the legal consequences of an act or forbearance on the part of one of the parties or of some third person.

INDEPENDENT CONTRACTOR: A person who contracts with another to do something for him, but who is not controlled by the other nor subject to the other's right to control with respect to his physical conduct in the performance of the undertaking.

INDETERMINATE SENTENCE: When the time of release of a prisoner is determined by an administrative board and the court merely imposes minimum and maximum limits of the penalty, the sentence is known as an indeterminate sentence. Technically, the sentence is not indeterminate if the limits are fixed by the court or by the legislature, and it should be called indefinite rather than indeterminate. However, no state has sentences that are completely indeterminate and the general practice is to call these indefinite sentences indeterminate. The "indeterminate sentence" refers to the fact that the exact period of custody is not fixed before the custody begins. A person on an indeterminate sentence may be released either conditionally on parole or unconditionally and completely without parole.

INDICTMENT: An accusation founded on legal testimony of a direct and positive character, and the concurring judgment of at least 12 of the grand jurors that upon the evidence presented to them the defendant is guilty.

INDIRECT CONTEMPT: An act committed, not in the court's presence, but at a distance from it, which tends to degrade the court or to obstruct or defeat the administration of justice.

INDIVIDUAL COUNSEL: Refers to military counsel selected by the accused or to civilian counsel provided by him.

INDORSEMENT: 1. Reply or forwarding note added to a basic communication by an office or commander in the chain of communication. The indorsement becomes a part of the communication. 2. Form giving data on the Service Record as to change of status or station of a soldier, his financial credits, and his character and efficiency ratings. It is completed when the soldier is transferred, dropped as a deserter, or separated from the service.

INDUCE: To lead on, to influence, to move by persuasion or influence.

INDUCTION: Where an individual successfully passes the physical examination and is accepted by the service for training and duty, and all the steps prescribed by staute and regulations having the force of law have been taken, whether he takes the oath administered to him or not.

INDUSTRIAL SECURITY: That portion of internal security which is concerned with the protection of classified information in the hands of United States industry.

INDUSTRIAL SECURITY OFFICE: Any command, office, unit, agency, or person within a military department, designated by that department as being responsible for exercising control over industrial security matters at a facility for which they are cognizant.

IN ESSE: In being; in existence; alive.

IN EXTENSO: Fully; at length.

IN EXTREMIS: In his last moments; at point of death.

INFAMOUS CRIMES: At common law an infamous crime was one, the commission of which was inconsistent with the common principles of honesty and humanity. Infamous crimes were treason, felony, all offenses founded in fraud and which came within the general notion of the crimen falsi of the civil law, piracy, swindling, cheating, barratry, and the bribing of a witness to absent himself from a trial in order to get rid of his evidence. Within the meaning of the phrase as used in the United States Constitution, a crime is infamous if it be punishable by imprisonment in a penitentiary or by any imprisonment accompanied by hard labor. In some states the rule is that infamy may be determined either by the nature of the crime, as at common law, or by the nature of the punishment which may be inflicted, as in the federal cases.

INFANTICIDE: The murder of an infant.

INFANTRY: A branch of the Army in which soldiers are organized, trained, and equipped to fight on foot.

INFECTION: The communication of disease from one body to another.

INFERENCE: A deduction which the reason of the jury makes from the facts proved without an express direction of law to that effect.

INFERIORITY COMPLEX: The feeling of inadequacy regarding one's role in life.

IN FLAGRANTI DELICTO: In the act of doing the wrong or crime.

INFORMATION: An accusation in the nature of an indictment, from which it differs only in being presented by a competent public officer on his oath of office instead of by a grand jury on their oath.

INFORMATION COPY: A copy of any document, letter, report or the like, sent for information and not for action.

INFRA: Below, under, beneath.

IN FUTURO: At a future time.

INHABITED DWELLING: Includes the outbuildings that form part of the cluster of buildings used as a residence.

INHIBIT: To prevent or retard.

INJUNCTION: A prohibitive writ issued by a court of equity, at the suit of a party complainant, directed to a party defendant in the action or to a party made a defendant for that purpose, forbidding the latter to do some act or to permit his servants or agents to do some act which he is threatening or attempting to commit, or restraining him in the continuance thereof because such act is unjust and inequitable, injurious to the plaintiff, and not such as can be adequately redressed by an action at law.

INJURY: A term comprising such conditions as fractures, wounds, sprains, strains, dislocations, concussions, and compressions. In addition, it includes conditions resulting from extremes of temperature or prolonged exposure. Acute poisonings, except those due to contaminated food, resulting from exposure to a toxic or poisonous substance are also classed as injuries.

IN LOCO PARENTIS: In the place of a parent.

INNOCENT PASSAGE: The right of the vessels of one nation to navigate peacefully through the territorial waters of another nation.

IN PAIS: In the country as distinguished from in court; out of court or without judicial process; by deed or not of record.

IN PARI DELICTO: Equally at fault.

IN PARI METERIA: Upon the same matter or subject.

IN RE: In the matter of.

IN REM: Against a thing and not against a person.

INSANITY: A form of mental incapacity which may be urged, as existing at the time of arraignment or trial, to prevent going to trial; which may be urged, as existing at the time the alleged crime was committed, in order to prevent a finding of criminal liability therefor; which may be urged, as existing at the time of sentencing, in order to prevent the imposition of sentence.

INSANITY (MORAL): State of those persons who, while knowing the difference between right and wrong, are deficient in moral judgment.

INSIGHT: Correct orientation; logical interpretation of reality situations.

INSPECTOR GENERAL: An officer detailed as an inspector general who examines and reports on every phase of activity that affects the discipline, efficiency, and economy of a command, installation, or activity.

INSPECTOR GENERAL INSPECTION REPORT: A report prepared in a prescribed format by inspectors general to advise commanders of the performance of mission and state of discipline, efficiency, and economy of a command.

INSPECTOR GENERAL INVESTIGATION: An examination by an inspector general into an allegation, report of conditions, or a situation, including the systematic procurement, examination, and evaluation of sworn testimony and documentary and physical evidence, for the purpose of providing the directing authority with a sound basis for just and intelligent action with respect to the allegation. condition, or situation. A report is rendered in a prescribed format.

INSPECTOR GENERAL SURVEY: The development of factual data on a specific subject or field of activity based upon a careful examination and evaluation of information obtained by means of inquiries or inspections.

INSTALLATION: Real estate and improvements thereon under the control of the Department of the Army at which functions of the Department of the Army are carried on and which has been established by order of the Department of the Army. Where installations are located contiguously or on the same reservation, the combined property is designated as one installation and the separate functions as activities of that installation.

INSTINCT: Fore-knowing through innate or inherent components of the total affectivity, which adhere firmly and systematically to certain vital aims (endogenous urge).

INSTRUCTION BY THE COURT: An exposition of the rules or principles of law applicable to the case of some branch or phase of it, which the jury are bound to accept and apply.

INSTRUCTIONS: The court members are informed of the necessary elements of the offense charged and are thus enabled to determine intelligently whether the facts found by them constitute such an offense. Without these and appropriiate additional instructions the court members would be left unguided and unconfined. It is therefore necessary and desirable that the president explain to the court members the law and the issues involved and bring into focus the relationship of the evidence to those issues.

INSULIN: The active principle secreted by the pancreas, controlling sugar metabolism. Injected subcutaneously, it creates mental disturbances, and it is therefore used in shock therapy.

INSURANCE: A contract by which, for a consideration, one party assumes particular risks of the other party and promises to pay him or his nominee a certain or ascertainable sum of money on a specified contingency.

INSURGENTS: Are organized bodies of men who, for public political purposes, are in a state of armed hostility to an established government.

INSURRECTION: A rebellion, or rising of citizens or subjects in resistance to their government.

INTELLECT: The thinking function of the mind (understanding); the capacity to acquire and utilize concepts; the innate faculty of the mind to think subjectively and objectively.

INTELLIGENCE: Imports that the information conveyed is true or implies the truth, at least in part.

INTENT: The particular state of mind, differing in different crimes, which is required to exist in concurrence with the criminal act.

INTENT TO STEAL: An intent permanently to deprive and defraud another of the use and benefit of property or permanently to appropriate the property to his own use or the use of any person other than the true owner.

INTENTIONALLY: The act was done deliberately and on purpose, through design, or according to plan, and not merely through carelessness, by accident, or under a good-faith error of law made before, during, or after a trial.

INTER ALIA: Among other things or matters.

INTERIM: In the meantime; meanwhile.

INTERN: To confine the activities of a person to a specified place, or within specified boundaries.

INTERNAL SECURITY: 1. Measures taken to prevent enemy and enemy inspired action, other than military attack, against United States resources, industries, and institutions. Internal security is a multiple responsibility of governmental agencies at all levels concerned with maintenance of law and order, of citizens; of ownership and management; and of the Department of Defense. The Department of Defense responsibilities include provision of internal security of facilities within its own jurisdiction; support to civil authorities when an emergency renders their resources inadequate; emergency protection of Government installations; and advice and assistance as to the protection of vital industries and installations. 2. Condition resulting from the measures taken within a command to safeguard defense information coming under its cognizance, including physical security of documents and materials.

INTERNATIONAL LAW: A body of rules and principles governing the relations of nations between each other. Since these rules could not be enforce by any definite supernational agency, their validity has long depended on the extent to which any particular nation chose to recognize them.

INTERNATIONAL RULES: That part of the Rules of the Road established by agreement between maritime nations concerning the governing of the navigation of the high seas.

INTERNED: Definitely known to have been taken into custody of a nonbelligerent foreign power as the result of and for reasons arising out of any conflict in which the Armed Forces of the United States are engaged.

INTERNEE: A person who, during war, is kept within a particular country or is forced to stay in a certain place. Protected persons as defined in the Geneva Conventions of 1949 may only be made internees in accordance with the requirements therein stated.

INTERESTED PARTY: A person who has only some "interest" in the subject matter of the investigation.

INTERNMENT CAMP: An activity or installation established for the internment and complete administration of civilian internees only. **See civilian internee.**

INTERLOCUTORY: Something which is done between the commencement and the end of action which decides some point or matter, which, however, is not a final decision of the matter in issue.

INTERPRETATION OF STATUTE: The reading of a statute to discover its meaning either in part or as a whole.

INTERROGATORY: A question; sets of questions in writing intended to be proposed to a witness.

INTER SE: Among themselves.

INTERVENTION: The attempt of one or more states, even by use of force, to coerce another state in its purely state action. When a state directly interferes with the exercise of the lawful state authority in or by another state, it constitutes intervention. There is no right of intervention, as has been sometimes argued, though an act of intervention may be sometimes justifiable in itself.

INTER VIVOS: Between the living; where property passes by conveyance from one living person to another.

INTESTACY: The state of dying without having made a valid will.

INTESTATE: A person is said to die intestate when he dies without making a will. The word is also often used to signify the person himself.

IN THE EXECUTION OF HIS OFFICE: An officer is in the execution of his office when engaged in any act or service required or authorized to be done by him by statute, regulation, the order of a superior, or military usage.

IN THE FIELD: Construed to refer not only to land, but to any place, whether on land or water, apart from permanent cantonments or fortifications where military operations are being conducted.

IN TOTO: Wholly; completely.

INTRA: A prefix meaning within.

INTRA VIRES: An act is said to be intra vires (within the power) of a person or corporation when it is within the scope of his or its powers of authority; opposite of ultra vires.

INVASION: Occurs when the military forces of a belligerent state penetrate enemy territory by force of arms.

INVASION OF PRIVACY: Invading one's right to be "left alone" to live in seclusion without being subjected to unwarranted or undesired publicity.

INVERT: An individual with erotic inclinations towards his own sex. (Homosexual.)

INVESTIGATING OFFICER: As applied to a particular offense shall be understood to include a person, who, has investigated that offense or a closely related offense alleged to have been committed by an accused; the term also includes any other person who, as counsel for, or member of, a court of inquiry, or as an investigating officer or otherwise, has conducted a personal investigation of a general matter involving the particular offense.

INVOLUNTARY MANSLAUGHTER: Is homicide unintentionally caused and without malice, resulting from the commission of an unlawful act not amounting to a felony, or from negligence, or lack of caution, or absence of skill in the commission of a lawful act, or from failure to perform a legal duty.

IPSO FACTO: By the fact itself, by the mere fact.

IPSO JURE: By the operation of law.

IRREGULAR PLEADING: Includes such contradictory pleas as guilty without criminality or guilty to a charge after pleading not guilty to all specifications thereunder.

ISSUE: 1. Descendants; all persons who have descended from a common ancestor. 2. A single certain and material point arising out of the allegations of the parties—generally made up of an affirmative and a negative.

ITA LEX SCRIPTA EST: The law is so written.

J

JETTISON: Voluntary throwing of goods overboard in case of extreme peril to lighten the ship.

JOINTLY AND SEVERALLY: Together and separately.

JOINT OFFENSE: One committed by two or more persons acting together in pursuance of a common intent.

JUDGE ADVOCATE: Officer on the staff of a commander, usually referred to as a staff judge advocate. The Judge Advoate of a command is the legal adviser of the commanding officer thereof, and as to that command he performs duties corresponding in general nature and scope to those discharged by The Judge Advocate General with relation to the Department of the Army. With regard to military justice, his duties include, among others, the duties devolved upon The Staff Judge Advocate by the Uniform Code of Military Justice.

JUDGE ADVOCATE GENERAL, THE: This term refers, severally, to The Judge Advocates General of the Army, Navy, and Air Force, and, in Coast Guard matters when not attached to the Navy, to the General Counsel of the Treasury Department. The Judge Advocates General have supervision of the administration of military justice in their respective Departments. They shall prescribe uniform rules of procedure for boards of review and shall meet periodically to formulate policies and procedure for the review of court-martial cases in their offices and by boards of review.

JUDGMENT: The decision or sentence of the law given by a court or other tribunal as the result of proceedings instituted therein.

JUDGMENT BY DEFAULT: One taken against a defendant when, having been summoned or cited in an action, he fails to enter an appearance at the proper time.

JUDGMENT NOTE: The maker may sign a contract as additional security, which permits a judgment to be taken against him without a trial in case he fails to pay on the due date. This form of note is called a judgment note.

JUDGMENT NOTWITHSTANDING THE VERDICT: In cases where a motion for a directed verdict should have been granted but was denied, the court may on its own motion or on the motion of the aggrieved party render judgment notwithstanding the verdict of the jury.

JUDICIAL CONFESSION: Where the accused confesses his guilt in open court.

JUDICIAL COUNCIL: A board of three general officers in the Judge Advocate General's Corps which examines certain cases requiring confirming action under the appellate procedure of the former Articles of War.

JUDICIAL DETERMINATION: Determination by decision of a court of justice.

JUDICIAL NOTICE: Simply means that the court will take cognizance of the existence of certain facts necessary to establish a party's claim or defense without requiring the party to produce evidence of those facts. Although no definite criterion has been established as to what facts will be judicially noticed, it may be stated, in general, that facts of common knowledge require no evidence. Thus, at a glance, it appears that notoriety serves as the keynote for judicial notice. It is not necessarily required that the judge actually know or remember the fact; it is sufficient if the fact can readily be ascertained by reference. Since notoriety serves as the basis for the principle of judicial notice, it is held that the private knowledge of the judge of a fact not commonly known, cannot be judicially noticed.

JUDICIAL OPINION: The reason or reasons given by the court for its judgment.

JUDICIAL PROCEEDING: Includes a trial by court-martial.

JURISDICTION: 1. The authority of the commander over the lands, persons, and property in areas of projected, actual, or completed military operations as defined by the international rules of war or delimited by consent of agreement. 2. Jurisdiction means a court's power to try and determine a case.

JURISDICTION, CIVIL: The right and authority to hear and determine a cause in a civil action such as contracts, torts.

JURISDICTION, CONCURRENT: Jurisdiction of several different tribunals, each authorized to deal with the same subject matter.

JURISDICTION, CRIMINAL: The right and authority to hear and determine a cause in criminal actions.

JURISDICTIONAL IMMUNITIES: Freedom from jurisdiction of a court.

JURISDICTION OF THE UNITED STATES: Includes any lands reserved or acquired for the use of the United States, and under the exclusive or concurrent jurisdiction thereof, or any place purchased or otherwise acquired by the United States by consent of the legislature of the State in which the same shall be, for the erection of a fort, magazine, arsenal, dockyard, or other needful building.

JURISDICTION OVER PERSONS NATIONALITY: Varies according to their relations to a state. The question of nationality is one of the most important. Nationality involves the reciprocal relations of allegiance on the part of the person and protection on the part of the state. The term is often used as corresponding to citizenship in the broad sense of the term.

JURISDICTIONAL WATERS: A zone on the high seas, twelve miles from the beaches at low tide, within which the vessels of the United States Coast Guard are allowed to cruise, make custom searches, and otherwise enforce the various custom laws of the United States.

JURISPRUDENCE: The philosophy of law, or the science which treats of the principles of positive legal and law relations.

JURY: A certain number of persons, selected according to law, who are sworn to inquire of certain matters of fact and declare the truth upon evidence to be laid before them.

JUS SANGUINIS: The child born in the foreign country is a subject of the state of which his parents are citizens. That the child inherits the nationality of his father is a common maxim known as jus sanguinis.

JUS SOLI: Certain states follow the rule of jus soli, maintaining that the place of birth determines the nationality.

JUSTICE: The constant and perpetual disposition to render every man his due.

JUSTICIABLE: Proper to be examined in courts of justice.

JUSTIFIABLE AND EXCUSABLE HOMICIDE: The necessary killing of another in the performance of a legal duty, or the exercise of a legal right, the slayer not being at all in fault. A homicide is justifiable, so that no blame whatever attaches, in the following case: When a person convicted of a capital offense, and sentenced to death by a court of competent jurisdiction, is executed by the proper officer in accordance with the sentence.

K

KIDNAPPING: A false imprisonment aggravated by conveying the person imprisoned to another place. In some states a false imprisonment accompanied by a mere intent so to convey is sufficient to constitute the crime. It is a misdemeanor at common law, but has been made a felony, generally, by the state statutes.

KITING: The unethical and sometimes illegal practice of issuing checks against a bank account in which there are not sufficient collected funds to cover the check, with the expectation that before the check drawn is presented for payment funds will be deposited to make good the withdrawal.

KLEPTOMANIA: The desire to steal or appropriate articles. In many cases psychopathic personalities manifesting the impulsory desire to steal come under the heading of fetish-thieves and during the act of stealing receive sexual gratification, sometimes to the point of orgasm.

KNOWINGLY: That state of mind which exists when the accused person is in possession of facts under which he is aware he cannot lawfully do a particular act, but nevertheless proceeds to do it. It is also intended to exclude mistakes of fact or accidents.

KOPROLAGNIA: A condition usually found in masochism, wherein the subject is sexually excited through the senses of taste and smell by articles of filth, such as excrement (urine and feces).

L

LACHES: Inexcusable delay.

LACTATIONAL INSANITY: Insanity occurring after confinement, during the period of suckling, or after weaning.

LANDLORD: Owner of an estate in land, who has leased it for a term of years, on a rent reserved, to another person, called the tenant.

LARCENY AND WRONGFUL APPROPRIATION: Any person who wrongfully takes, obtains, or withholds, by any means whatever, from the possession of the true owner or of any other person any money, personal property, or article of value of any kind— 1. with intent permanently to deprive or defraud another person of the use and benefit of property or to appropriate the same to his own use or the use of any person other than the true owner, steals such property and is guilty of larceny; or 2. with intent temporarily to deprive or defraud another person of the use and benefit of property or to appropriate the same to his own use or the use of any person other than the true owner is guilty of wrongful appropriation.

LASCIVIOUS: Tending to excite lust, obscene, relating to sexual impurity, or tending to deprave the morals in respect to sexual relations.

LATENT: Hidden, concealed, dormant; doesn't appear on the face.

LATENT AMBIGUITY: Ambiguity that does not appear upon the surface of the document, but is only brought out where inquiry is made as to its application.

LAW: The most general term for all rules to which people in any society conform, whether by custom or by enforcible governmental regulation.

LAW, CODIFIED: The laws embodied in a complete system of positive law, in a code.

LAW, COMMON: A system of law, developed in England, which comprises the body of those principles and rules which derived their authority solely from usages and customs, or from the judgment and decrees of the courts enforcing such usages and customs.

LAW, CUSTOMARY: Law developed by long custom and usage in contrast to law based on legislative enactment.

LAW, DOMESTIC: The law in effect within one country.

LAWFUL ORDER: An order requiring the performance of a military duty or act is presumed to be lawful and is disobeyed at the peril of the subordinate.

LAWFUL SEARCH: Search with warrant; search pursuant to arrest; search required to prevent removal of criminal goods; search with consent; search authorized or directed by Commanding Officers; search made in accordance with military custom.

LAW, INTERNATIONAL: A system of rules governing the relations between sovereign nations.

LAW, MUNICIPAL: Same as domestic law; it is the law of an individual state or nation.

LAW MEMBER: **See law officer.**

LAW OFFICER: This term, refers to the official of a general court-martial. A law officer must be appointed by the convening authority for each general court-martial. He must be a member of the bar of a Federal court or the highest court of a State, and be certified as qualified for such duty by The Judge Advocate General of the armed force to which he belongs. No person is eligible for the office in a case where he is the accuser or a witness for the prosecution or has acted as investigating officer in the same case.

LAW OF PRIOR DECISION: A rule of law based on decisions of courts in contrasts to rules of law based on legislative enactment.

LAW SPECIALIST: This term as used in the UCMJ refers to an officer of the Navy or Coast Guard on special duty (law). It corresponds to "judge advocate" in the Army and Air Force.

LAW, SUBSTANTIVE: That part of the law which the courts are established to administer, as opposed to the rules according to which the substantive law itself is administered.

LAW, TREATY: The system of rules of International Law embodied in treaties in the broad sense.

LAW, UNWRITTEN: Same as customary law.

LAW, WRITTEN: Same as codified law.

LEADING QUESTION: Is one which suggests the desired answer to the witness, and is, therefore, generally objectionable on direct examination. Leading questions may be divided into three general classes: 1. Those questions which call for no other answer but a simple affirmative or negative in which the witness merely assents to the language of the interrogator; 2. Those questions framed in such a manner as to suggest the desired answer; 3. Those questions which assume a fact in controversy so that the answer admits the fact in dispute. An example: "What was the plaintiff doing when the defendant struck him?"

LEASE: Any agreement which gives rise to relationship of landlord and tenant; contract for exclusive possession of lands or tenements for determinate periods usually.

LEAVE: The authorized absence of an individual from a place of duty, chargeable against such individual.

LEAVE OF ABSENCE: Authorized absence from assigned duty. Military personnel accrue leave credit at the rate of 2½ calendar days for each month of active service. See delay en route; pass.

LEAVING POST BEFORE BEING RELIEVED: A sentinel or lookout who, in time of war leaves his post before being regularly relieved is punishable by death or such other punishment as a court-martial may direct; if not in time of war, the penalty is such as a court-martial may direct, other than death.

LEGACY: A disposition of personalty by will.

LEGAL ASSISTANCE PLAN: Plan sponsored by the Department of the Army and the American Bar Association to make adequate legal advice and assistance available to military personnel and their dependents.

LEGAL DUTY: An obligation arising from contract of the parties or the operation of the law.

LEGAL ETHICS: That branch of moral science which treats of the duties which a member of the legal profession owes to the public, to the court, to his professional brethren and to his client.

LEGAL MERGER: Any situation where the reviewing authority, confronted with a conviction of two or more offenses arising out of the same act or the same transaction, sets aside the findings on one as a matter of legal necessity because: 1. Courts provides that it is a lesser included offense of another of which the accused is also convicted, the same evidence proving both offenses; or 2. it appears that the elements of each offense are the same and are proved by the same evidence; or 3. it appears that all the elements of one offense are included in, but less than the elements of the greater offense, the same evidence proving the elements of the lesser offense and the corresponding elements of the greater offense.

LEGAL OFFICER: This term as used in the code refers to an officer of the Navy or Coast Guard designated to perform legal duties for a command. It corresponds to "staff judge advocate" in the Army and Air Force.

LEGAL RELEVANCY: Requires that the proposed evidence must be of sufficient probative value. Evidence which is too remote and merely collateral does not tend to establish the fact in issue and is excluded because it is not sufficiently probative. Introduction of such evidence would not serve as a legal basis for an inference on the issue. Such evidence would tend only to cloud the case, confuse the minds of the jury, and waste the time of all parties.

LEGAL REPRESENTATIVE: One who stands in place of and represents the interests of another such as executors or administrators.

LESBIAN: A female whose major source of sexual gratification is by contact with other females. Lesbianism is homosexuality in the female.

LESSER INCLUDED OFFENSE: If all the elements of a different offense are present with others in an offense charged in an indictment, such different offense is a lesser included offense.

LESSER OFFENSE: When the crime charged necessarily embraces a lesser offense as part and parcel of it and the latter is included in the description in the indictment, the accused may be found guilty of the lesser offense. Thus, on an indictment for murder the defendant may be convicted of manslaughter.

LESSEE: The tenant.

LESSOR: He who grants a lease; the landlord.

LETTER OF CENSURE: Any letter of censure to a subordinate from any officer in command is a nonjudicial punishment, except when issued pursuant to the sentence of a court-martial, if a copy thereof is forwarded to any headquarters; any other criticism, reproof, or instructions, written or oral shall not in itself constitute a punishment in that sense.

LETTER ROGATORY: A formal request addressed to a court in another state asking the latter to interrogate the witness. The court to which the letter rogatory, or request, is addressed, is under no compulsion to respect it. It is within its discretion to refuse to honor it. It is a matter resting upon the principle of comity. But if it be a court of appropriate jurisdiction, there is no question as to its power to honor it and by its process execute it.

LEVY: To assess; raise; execute; exact; collect; gather; take up; seize.

LEWD: Lustful or lecherous and signifies that form of immorality which has relation to sexual impurity or incontinence carried on in a wanton manner.

LEX DE FUGA: The law of flight.

LEX FORI: Law of the forum, the jurisdiction where the cause is heard.

LEX LOCI CONTRACTUS: Law of the place where the contract was made.

LEX NIL FACIT FRUSTRA, NIL FUBET FRUSTA: The law does nothing and commands nothing in vain.

LEX NON SCRIPTA: The unwritten or common law, which includes general and particular customs, and particular local laws.

LEX SCRIPTA: Statute law.

LIABILITY: The state of being bound or obliged in law or justice to do, pay, or make good something. A legal liability is one which courts of justice recognize and enforce as between parties litigant.

LIBEL: That which is written or printed, and published, calculated to injure the character of another by bringing him into ridicule, hatred or contempt. **See Slander.**

LIBERTY: Authorized absence of an individual from a place of duty, not chargeable as leave.

LIBIDINOUS: Excessively lustful.

LIBIDO: The energy of the sexual instincts, which is normally directed to an outside object.

LICENSEE: A person whose presence on the premises of the proprietor thereof is not invited, but is tolerated.

LIEBER'S CODE: General Orders No. 100 of the Army of the United States of 1863, the basis of many subsequent codes.

LIE DETECTING MACHINE: Any device which records involuntary bodily responses associated with conscious lying.

LIEN: A charge upon property for the payment of a debt or duty; a right by law to have a debt satisfied out of a particular thing.

LIEUTENANT: A commissioned person in the AF, Army, or Marine Corps, in either of two grades, that of first lieutenant or of second lieutenant; In the US Navy, a commissioned rank or person immediately above lieutenant junior grade, corresponding to captain in the other services.

LIEUTENANT COLONEL: A commissioned rank or person in the AF, Army, or Marine Corps, immediately above major; the title of this person.

LIEUTENANT COMMANDER: In the US Navy, an officer ranking immediately above lieutenant, corresponding to major in the other services; the title of this officer.

LIEUTENANT GENERAL: A commissioned rank or person in the Army, AF, or Marine Corps, ranking immediately above major general; the title of this person.

LIEUTENANT JUNIOR GRADE: In the US Navy, an officer ranking immediately above ensign, corresponding to first lieutenant in the other services.

LIMITED DUTY: The duty status of a person who is physically disqualified for performing military duty in certain categories.

LIMITED JURISDICTION: That which extends only to certain specified causes.

LINE-OF-DUTY INVESTIGATION: An investigation to determine whether or not a sickness, injury, or death was incurred in line of duty.

LINE OFFICER: An officer engaged in operational duties, especially combat duties.

LIQUID: Anything readily convertible into cash.

LIS PENDENS: Litigation pending.

LITIGATION: A contest in a court of justice to enforce a right; a lawsuit.

LITTORAL STATE: A state adjacent to a shore.

LOBOTOMY: Cutting into the brain for the purpose of relieving pain, grief, or excitement; a form of psychosurgery.

LOCAL PAROLE: Status of trustworthy prisoners in confinement who have freedom of movement outside the enclosure but within a defined area.

LOCOMOTOR ATAXIA: (Tabes dorsalis)—A disease of the spinal cord caused by a previous syphilitic infection.

LOCUS CRIMINUS: The locality or place of a crime.

LOCUS DELICTI: The place of the commission of the crime or tort.

LOCUS SIGILLI: The place of the seal.

LOITER: To stand around, to move about slowly, to spend time idly, to saunter, to linger, or to lag behind when such conduct is in violation of known instructions or accompanied by a failure to give complete attention to duty.

LOOTING AND PILLAGING: Unlawfully seizing or appropriating property located in enemy or occupied territory, which has been left behind or was owned by, or in the custody of, the enemy or occupied state or a person who is or was under the protection of the enemy or occupied state. The unauthorized removal or appropriation of any part of the equipment of a seized or captured vessel, or the unlawful seizure or appropriation of property owned by or in the custody of the officers, crew, or passengers on board a seized or captured vessel, constitutes the offenses of looting and pillaging wherever the vessel may be located at the time of the offense.

LOSS OF NUMBERS: The dropping of the accused officer in grade on the appropriate lineal list, the stated amount of numbers thereby making the intervening officers senior to him and retarding the date of his next promotion to the extent of the numbers lost.

LUCID INTERVAL: A temporary recovery from insanity.

LUCRI CAUSA: Expectation of gain or benefit to the thief; and that it is not enough that he fraudulently intends to deprive the owner of his property.

LUST MURDER: Murder committed in sadistic brutal fashion; the victim's body usually shows evidence of being mutilated particularly the genitalia.

LOCUS PENITENTIAE: A place of repentence; the opportunity of withdrawing from a projected contract before the parties are finally bound; or of abandoning the intention of committing a crime before it has been completed.

M

MAIMING: Any person who, with intent to injure, disfigure, or disable, inflicts upon the person of another an injury which— 1. seriously disfigures his person by any mutilation thereof; or 2. destroys or disables any member or organ of his body; or 3. seriously diminishes his physical vigor by the injury of any member or organ is guilty of maiming.

MAINTENANCE: The officious intermeddling in a suit that in no way belongs to one, by maintaining or assisting either party with money or otherwise to prosecute or defend it. Thus one who is in no way concerned in a suit is as a rule guilty of maintenance if he bears the expense thereof or retains counsel for a party, but this is not true if he has an interest, as that of reversioner, or where he is related to the party he assists. A landlord may assist his tenant, or a master his servant, and one may assist a poor man to carry on his suit.

MAJOR: A commissioned rank or person in the AF, Army, or Marine Corps, immediately above the rank of captain; the title of this person.

MAJOR GENERAL: A commissioned rank or person in the AF, Army, or Marine Corps, immediately above brigadier general; the title of this person.

MAJORITY: The rank or position held by a major.

MALA FIDES: Bad faith (opposite of bona fides).

MALA IN SE: Acts wrongful in themselves.

MALA PROHIBITA: Acts wrongful because the law prohibits them.

MALFEASANCE: The wrongful or unjust doing of some act which the doer has no right to perform or which he has stipulated by contract not to do.

MALICE: A wrongful act done intentionally without just cause or excuse or which the doer knows will injure another; a disposition to injure another; a willful disregard of the rights or safety of others; a spiteful or malevolent design; deliberate cruelty; the expression of a wicked and depraved heart and mind.

MALICE AFORETHOUGHT: Malice aforethought does not necessarily mean an actual intention to kill the deceased, nor does it necessarily imply deliberation, but denotes purpose and design as contrasted with accident and mischance. It is present when there is an intention to cause death or grievous bodily harm, or knowledge that one's acts will probably so result, when committed in the commission of a felony or in obstructing an officer who is making an arrest or preventing a riot.

MALICE PREPENSE: Malice aforethought.

MALICIOUS MISCHIEF: All acts of unnecessary and malicious injury to the property of others, which impair the utility or diminish the value of such property to a material extent. It was generally indictable at common law, and proof of the destruction of the property was necessary: now, statutes are found in most states defining the crime, regulating its punishment and sometimes expressly enumerating what acts must be proved to constitute it. These statutes are made to protect the owner of property rather the property itself.

MALICIOUS PROSECUTION: A judicial proceeding instituted against an individual out of the prosecutor's malice and ill will, with the intention of injuring him, without probable cause to sustain it.

MALICIOUSLY: An act is, in contemplation of law, done maliciously where it is wrongful and is done intentionally.

MALINGER: To pretend to be sick so that one may escape from work or duty.

MALINGERING: The feigning of illness, mental or physical disablement, or intentional self-injury, for the purpose of avoiding work, duty, or service.

MALPRACTICE: The treatment of a case by a physician or surgeon in a manner contrary to accepted rules, and with injurious results.

MALTREATMENT: To strike, to subject to improper punishment, or to deprive of benefits, if done without justifiable cause.

MALUM IN SE: An act inherently wrong in itself.

MALUM PROHIBITUM: An act declared wrong by statute or local order.

MANAGEMENT CONTROL: The direction exercised, in other than military matters, by an authority of the Naval Establishment over a unit of the naval shore establishment in the administration of its local operating functions.

MANDAMUS: A writ which issues from a court of superior jurisdiction and is directed to a private or municipal corporation or any of its officers or to an executive, administrative or judicial officer or to an inferior court, commanding the performance of a particular act therein specified and belonging to his or their public, official or ministerial duty, or directing the restoration of the complainant to rights or privileges of which he has been illegally deprived.

MANDATE: An authoritative command; order.

MANDATES UNDER THE LEAGUE OF NATIONS: Former colonies and territories of countries defeated in World War I and "mandated" to other countries for administration under the League of Nations.

MANIA: A disorder of the mind marked by great mental and emotional excitement, hallucinations, delusions, and a tendency to violence.

MANIC: That phase of a manic-depressive psychosis in which the patient is overactive and expansive. In its milder form, it is called "hypomania." A patient afflicted with this form of the psychosis is also called "a manic."

MANIC-DEPRESSIVE PSYCHOSIS: A mental disease characterized by either 1. a more or less prolonged period of depression; 2. a period of overactivity and euphoria; or 3. swings between these two phases.

MANIFEST: A document specifying in detail the passengers or items carried for a specific destination.

MANSLAUGHTER: The unlawful killing of a human being without malice express or implied.

MANUAL FOR COURT-MARTIAL: Regulation issued by the President, prescribing the detailed procedure to be followed before military tribunals, including the manner of proof and rules of evidence.

MARINE CORPS: Within the Navy Department, includes land combat and service forces and such aviation as may be organic therein.

MARITIME CONTROL AREA: Area generally similar to a defensive sea area in purpose except that it may be established any place on the high seas. Maritime control areas are normally established only in time of war.

MARITIME LAW: The system of law which relates to commerce and navigation, to business transacted at sea or relating to navigation, to ships and shipping, to seamen, to the transportation of persons and property by sea, and generally to marine affairs. The law relating to harbors, property of ships, duties and rights of masters and seamen, contracts of affreightment, salvage etc.

MARKETABLE TITLE: A title, not merely defensible, but which is free from plausible or reasonable objections.

MARTIAL LAW: The exercise of the power which resides in the executive branch of the government to preserve order and to insure the public safety in time of emergency when other branches of the government are unable to function, or their functioning would itself threaten the public safety.

MARTINET: An unreasonably harsh officer.

MASOCHISM: The correlative complex of sadism, which like its correlative, may be heterosexual or homosexual; the desire to experience pain and suffering.

MAST: Procedure used in imposing non-judicial punishment or in otherwise disposing of charges against an accused, i.e., the hearing and determination.

MASTER: The person having actual command of the vessel.

MAST PUNISHMENTS: Commanding officers' nonjudicial punishments.

MASTURBATION (onanism, ipsation): Causation of sexual excitement through manual manipulation of the genitalia; auto-eroticism through friction or rubbing.

MATERIAL EVIDENCE: Evidence is material when the fact it tends to prove is part of an issue of the case.

MATERIALITY: The proposed evidence goes to prove a fact not properly in issue. The fact in issue, that is, the controversy, depends upon the substantive law and the rules of pleading. Stipulating that the controversy is explicit, and of course it is, immaterial evidence is evidence which would be of probative force upon another issue, but not upon this one. It is totally immaterial and foreign to the question to be decided. It does not go to prove the case at all. It may be of great probative force upon another issue but it has no bearing upon the particular case in court. For instance, in the tort of conversion, the minority of a defendant would be immaterial, but in an action on a contract, made by the same defendant, his infancy would be material.

MATERIA MEDICA: The science of drugs or agents used in medicine.

MATRICIDE: The killing or murder of a mother.

MATTER IN AGGRAVATION: When the judge advocate has knowledge that the offense as actually committed was of a more grave nature than appears merely on the face of the specification it is his duty to offer such testimony as tends to show the aggravating nature of the offense, but this should not relate to a separate and distinct offense.

MATTER IN EXTENUATION: The accused will be given an opportunity to explain the commission of the offense, including the reasons that actuated the accused, but which do not extend to legal justification or excuse.

MATTER IN MITIGATION: Has for its purpose the lessening of the punishment to be assigned by the court or the furnishing of grounds for a recommendation for clemency.

MAXIMUM SECURITY INSTITUTION: The designation given to disciplinary barracks in which the more serious offenders are usually confined and so constructed as to reduce the possibility of escape of prisoners to a minimum. Such an institution may be inclosed by walls, and the prisoners are normally quartered in cells, with most activities conducted within the inclosure.

MAYHEM: The act of unlawfully and violently depriving another of the use of such of his members as may render him less able in fighting, either to defend himself or annoy his adversary. (The definition has been broadened by statute in some jurisdictions.)

MEDIATION: A form of intervention of a third state in the dispute of two states with a view towards persuading them to settle their disputes.

MEDICAL BOARDS: Consist, whenever practicable, of three medical officers of the Navy or Naval Reserve serving on active duty; constituted to evaluate and report upon the present state of health of members of the Navy or Marine Corps, including the Reserve compenents thereof.

MEDIUM SECURITY INSTITUTION: The designation given to disciplinary barracks or rehabilitation centers in which less serious offenders may be committed for confinement, and usually inclosed with a fence rather than a wall. Prisoners are normally housed in barracks or dormitories.

MELANCHOLIA: The depressed phase of manic-depressive psychosis. The term may also be applied to involution melancholia and is sometimes loosely used to indicate any depression.

MEMORANDUM: 1. Routine directive by which subordinate headquarters gives instructions, advice or information; used when a general order, letter, circular, or regulation is inappropriate. 2. Written communication between individuals dealing with official matters.

MEMORANDUM RECEIPT: Document formally acknowledging receipt of articles issued for temporary use, the accountability for which remains with the issuing supply officer. A credit memorandum receipt is a similar formal document signed by the accountable officer acknowledging return of the property.

MENINGITIS: An inflammation of the membranes of the brain or spinal cord.

MENS REA: A guilty mind, a guilty or wrongful purpose; a criminal intent.

MENTAL DEFECT, DISEASE OR DERANGEMENT: Comprehends those irrational states of mind which are the result of deterioration, destruction, or malfunction of the mental, as distinguished from the moral, faculties.

MENTAL IMPAIRMENT: Not amounting to legal insanity may nevertheless affect a person's capacity to entertain a specific intent, to premeditate, or to possess the requisite knowledge which may be an element of the offense.

MERGER OF OFFENSES: As a rule, at common law, where a person by the same act commits two crimes, one a felony and the other a misdemeanor, the misdemeanor merges in the felony; but, if the crimes are of the same degree, both felonies or both misdemeanors, there is no merger.

METATROPHISM: The conversion of certain sexual and erotic attitudes which takes effect as masculine inclusion of the impulse life of the female, and a female inclusion of the impulse life of the male, without leading to homosexuality.

METES AND BOUNDS: Measures and boundaries.

MIDSHIPMAN: A student naval officer.

MILEAGE FEE: An allowance of a certain sum per mile to a witness to attend a distant court.

MILITARY: Construed to refer to any or all of the armed forces.

MILITARY COMMAND: The authoritative direction exercised over activities of the military establishments in military matters together with the power to exercise authoritative direction in all matters when circumstances dictate.

MILITARY COMMISSION: A court convened by military authority for the trial of persons not usually subject to military law who are charged with violations of the laws of war; and in places subject to military government or martial law, for the trial of such persons when charged with violations of proclamations, ordinances, and valid domestic civil and criminal law of the territory concerned.

MILITARY COURT: Any tribunal convened by military authority. Military commissions, courts-martial, and provost courts are examples.

MILITARY COURTESY: Rules of conduct that are required, either by regulation or by tradition, for military personnel.

MILITARY CRIMINAL JURISDICTION: In general, the power which exists in properly convened courts-martial for the trial and punishment of criminal offenses under the code committed by individuals subject to the code.

MILITARY DEPARTMENT: The Department of the Air Force, the Department of the Army, the Department of the Navy, as distinguished from an executive department.

MILITARY DISCIPLINE: State of individual and group training that creates a mental attitude resulting in correct conduct and automatic obedience to military law under all conditions. It is founded in respect for, and loyalty to, military law and authority.

MILITARY GOVERNMENT: A condition wherein the U. S. military has assumed authority over or the exercise of governmental functions in a country in which national sovereignty has been lost or suspended as a result of war.

MILITARY GOVERNMENT COURT: Court established by commander having military government responsibility, with jurisdiction over cases arising under enactments of military government, or indigenous law over all persons in the occupied territory, except members of the occupying and allied forces who are subject to military law.

MILITARY GOVERNMENT OFFICER: A military officer who, as a member of a military government staff or unit, is charged with the discharge of the commander's relationship with or control over a civil population, its government, and economy.

MILITARY GOVERNMENT ORDINANCE: An enactment, on the authority of a military governor, promulgating laws or rules regulating the occupied territory under his control.

MILITARY GOVERNOR: The military commander or other designated person who in an occupied territory exercises supreme authority over the civil population subject to the laws and usages of war and to any directive received from his government or from his superior.

MILITARY JURISDICTION: The power and authority to impose military law. The administration of military law, usually exercised by military courts.

MILITARY JUSTICE: The application of military law to persons subject thereto and accused of the commission of offenses under the Uniform Code of Military Justice.

MILITARY LAW: Those laws relating to the government of the Armed Forces. That body or system of rules for the conduct of military personnel; in a limited sense the Uniform Code of Military Justice.

MILITARY NECESSITY: The principle of military necessity permits a belligerent to apply only that degree and kind of regulated force, not otherwise prohibited by the law of war, required for the partial or complete submission of the enemy with the least possible expenditure of time, life, and physical resources.

MILITARY OCCUPATION: A condition in which territory is under the effective control of a foreign armed force. Only "occupied territory" may be under "military occupation".

MILITARY PAYMENT CERTIFICATE: A special monetary certificate printed as scrip, used as currency at certain overseas bases and stations. Often called 'scrip'.

MILITARY PERSONNEL OR CIVILIAN EMPLOYEES: Include all military personnel of the Dept. of Defense, prisoners of war and interned enemy aliens engaged by the DOD in labor for pay, and volunteer workers, and others serving as employees of DOD with or without compensation.

MILITARY POLICE: The police force of the Army.

MILITARY POLICE CRIMINAL INVESTIGATION DETACHMENT: A unit of the Military Police Corps composed of qualified and accredited criminal investigators, generally assigned to a command or attached to a military police organization.

MILITARY POLICE CRIMINAL INVESTIGATOR: A military policeman accredited by The Provost Marshal General to investigate the commission, or probable commission, of criminal offenses by personnel subject to military law or by civilians against military personnel, property, or installations.

MILITARY PRISONER: Person in custody or in confinement within military jurisdiction.

MILITARY PROPERTY: All movable property acquired or issued for use in the military service and all immovable property devoted to military use.

MILITARY RESERVATION: Land set apart or acquired for military use; land area within the boundaries of a military installation.

MILITARY SERVICE: 1. Duty in any branch of the Armed Forces. 2. Training for duty with the Armed Forces. 3. A branch of the Armed Forces of the United States, established by act of Congress, in which persons are appointed, enlisted, or inducted for military service and which operates and is administered within a military or executive department. The military services are: the U. S. Army, the U. S. Navy, the U. S. Air Force, the U. S. Marine Corps, and the U. S. Coast Guard.

MINISTER: The general term for diplomatic representatives sent by one state to another.

MINISTERIAL ACT: An act which a person performs in a given state of facts, in a prescribed manner, in obedience to the mandate of legal authority, without regard to, or the exercise of, his own judgment upon the propriety of the act done.

MINOR OFFENSE: Whether an offense may be considered "minor" depends upon its nature, the time and place of its commission, and the person committing it; generally speaking the term includes misconduct not involving moral turpitude or any greater degree of criminality than is involved in the average offense tried by summary court-martial.

MINUTES OF UNDERSTANDING: The official records made of proceedings at a meeting; in international law, these minutes provide agreed interpretation of certain provisions of a treaty or agreement discussed at the meeting.

MISBEHAVIOR BEFORE THE ENEMY: Any member of the armed forces who, before the enemy 1. runs away; or 2. shamefully abandons or surrenders any command, place or military property which it is his duty to defend; or 3. by disobedience, neglect, or intentional misconduct endangers the safety of any such command, place or property; or 4. casts away his arms or ammunition; or 5. is guilty of cowardly misconduct; or 6. quits his place of duty to plunder of pillage; or 7. causes false alarms; or 8. willfully fails to do his utmost to engage, defeat, capture or destroy the enemy and his equipment; or 9. fails to afford all practical relief and assistance to the armed forces of the United States and their allies when engaged in battle.

MISBEHAVIOR OF SENTINEL: Any sentinel or lookout who, in time of war, is found drunk or sleeping upon his post, or leaves it before he is regularly relieved, shall be punished by death or such other punishment as a court-martial may direct; or if at any other time than war, by such punishment, other than death, as a court-martial may direct.

MISCARRIAGE: Sometimes used interchangeably with abortion, i.e. The late expulsion of the foetus, between the fourth and sixth months of pregnancy.

MISCEGENATION: A mixing of races; intermarriage between white and colored or other prohibited races.

MISCONDUCT: Wrongful conduct; mere negligence or carelessness is not misconduct; the fact that an act violates a law, regulation or order does not, of itself, constitute a basis for a finding of misconduct; in order to support a holding of misconduct it must be found that the death, injury or disease was incurred intentionally, or was the result of wrongful conduct, either willful or grossly negligent, demonstrating a reckless disregard for the consequences.

MISCONDUCT BEFORE THE ENEMY: Any act of insubordination, treason, cowardice and the like, committed by a member of the armed forces in battle or in the face of the enemy; This offense is punishable by death.

MISCONDUCT OF A PRISONER: Unauthorized conduct by a prisoner of war in the hands of the enemy which tends to ameliorate his condition to the detriment of other prisoners.

MISDEMEANORS: Crimes of lesser importance than felonies were originally called trespasses, but later came to be known as misdemeanors. It has been said frquently in the cases that misdemeanors include all indictable offenses inferior to felonies. Misdemeanors have also been defined as those crimes to which the law has not given particular names. Neither of these definitions is sufficiently inclusive, however, because many minor or petty offenses may be prosecuted without indictment, either upon informations or summarily, before magistrates; and some misdemeanors have particular names while some felonies, newly created by statutes, have not.

MISFEASANCE: The improper performance of some act which a person may lawfully do.

MISNOMER: A misdescription of the party. The court usually has the right to amend the indictment by inserting the correct name.

MISPRISION OF FELONY: One who sees another commit a felony, or knows of its commission, and uses no means to apprehend him, or bring him to justice, or to prevent the felony, is guilty of a misdemeanor known as "misprision of felony."

MISSING MOVEMENT: The act whereby any person subject to the Uniform Code of Military Justice through neglect or design misses the movement of a ship, aircraft, or unit with which he is required in the course of duty to move.

MISTRIAL: The law officer (president of a special court-martial) may declare a mistrial whenever in his judgment, taking all circumstances into consideration, such action is manifestly necessary in the interests of justice. The declaration of a mistrial is not a bar to further prosecution and is an interlocutory question.

MITIGATION: General or specific good character of the accused, including specific acts. Examples: 1. Previous honorable discharges. 2. Awards, citations. 3. Desires as concerns the service. 4. Financial problems. 5. Youth and good work of the accused.

MITIGATION OF SENTENCE: To reduce a punishment imposed by courts-martial or other military tribunal in quantity or quality, the general nature of the punishment remaining the same.

MODERATE SPEED IN A FOG: Any speed which will enable a vessel to come to a dead stop within half the distance of visibility.

MODICUM: A little; a small quantity or portion; a limited amount or supply.

MODUS OPERANDI: A mode of operating.

MOIETY: One of two equal parts; an indefinite part.

MOOT COURT: A practice court where law students conduct fictitious suits.

MORAL TURPITUDE: An act of baseness, vileness, or depravity in the private and social duties, which a man owes to his fellow men, or to society in general, contrary to the accepted and customary rule of right and duty between man and man. Conduct contrary to justice, honesty, modesty, or good morals.

MORNING REPORT: The daily record or log of any one of certain military units or unit sections required to keep records on the daily strength and official status of personnel assigned or attached to a command.

MORTALITY TABLE: A table based on the experiences of life insurance companies, showing the probable number of years any man or woman of a given age and race may be expected to live.

MORTGAGE: A transfer of property passing conditionally as security for debt.

MORTGAGOR: He who gives a mortgage.

MORTGAGEE: He who holds a mortgage.

MOST FAVORED NATION'S: This clause has been common in treaties of commercial nature. This clause in its unconditional form ordinarily binds the state to grant to its co-signer all the privileges similarly granted to all other states, and such as shall be granted under subsequent treaties. In its conditional form when priviliges specifically are granted by one state in exchange for privileges granted by another, as in a reciprocal reduction in tariff duties, a third state can lay claim to like reduction only upon fulfillment of like conditions.

MOTION: An application made to the court to obtain a rule or order directing some act to be done in favor of the applicant.

MOTION FOR ACQUITTAL: Motion for judgment of acquittal of one or more offenses charged in the indictment or information after the evidence on either side is closed.

MOTION TO DISMISS: Properly relates to any defense or objection raised in bar to trial.

MOTION TO ELECT: A motion that the prosecution be required to elect upon which of two or more specifications it will proceed.

MOTION TO GRANT APPROPRIATE RELIEF: One made to cure a defect of form or substance which impedes the accused in properly preparing for trial or conducting his defense.

MOTION TO QUASH: Directed to the sufficiency of the information or indictment to charge an offense against the accused. The motion may be directed to such defects as affect the substance of the indictment or information to an extent that it will render the indictment or information insufficient to support a judgment or to such defects which do not affect the substance of the charge but go to the form of the indictment or information.

MOTION TO SEVER: A motion by one of two or more co-accused to be tried separately from the other or others. Occasion for the motion may arise in either a joint or a common trial. The more common grounds for this motion are that the mover desires to use at his trial the testimony of one or more of the co-accused, or the testimony of the wife of one, or that a defense of the other accused is antagonistic to his own, or that evidence as to the other accused will in some manner prejudice his defense.

MOTION TO VACATE: An attack on a judgment. Any ground which questions the trial court's power or shows a defective judgment will support a motion to vacate. If the motion is based upon a matter not appearing of record, it should be supported by affidavits. In practice the motion to vacate may serve another useful purpose. It can be used to raise federal and state constitutional questions which arise during trial or which may result from the verdict or finding.

MOTIVE: That which incites one to form the intention. It is a clear principle of law that motive does not enter into any crime as an essential ingredient. And while defendant's motive is always inquirable into for the purpose of establishing an antecedent probability of his committing the offense, neither failure to prove any motive nor proof of a good motive will prevent a conviction.

MOVEMENT: Does not include practice marches which are to be short duration with a return to the point of departure contemplated, nor does it include minor changes in the location of ships, aircraft, or units, as when a ship is shifted from one berth to another in the same shipyard or harbor or when a unit is moved from one barracks to another on the same post.

MURDER: The unlawful killing of a human being without justification or excuse. If the killing is done with premeditated design, or when the killer is engaged in the perpetration or attempted perpetration of burglary sodomy, rape, robbery, or aggravated arson the penalty is death, or imprisonment for life, as a court-martial may direct; if committed with intent to kill or inflict great bodily harm, or while the killer is engaged in an act inherently dangerous to others with a wanton disregard of human life, the penalty shall be such as a court-martial may direct.

MURDER IN THE FIRST DEGREE: The deliberate, premeditated killing of a human being, unless it is excusable or justfiable,

MURDER IN THE SECOND DEGREE: The killing of a human being, committed with a design to effect death, but without deliberation and premeditation.

MUTINY: A rebellion or revolt against military authority.

MUTINY ON THE HIGH SEAS: This is a crime of the high seas, committed by any member of a ship's crew who usurps the command of the ship from the captain or deprives the captain of authority and command on board, or resists or impedes or prevents the captain in the lawful and free exercise of his command or authority, or transfers such command and authority to some one not lawfully entitled to it.

MUTISM: Failure to speak or refusal to answer questions because of mental illness.

MYOCARDIUM: The heart muscle.

N

NARCISM: Admiration and love of self; gratification from self-admiration. (Also narcissism.)

NARCOSYNTHESIS: Putting a patient to sleep, or into a semi-somnolent state by chemical injections, then getting him to talk about his problems, or to relive previous painful experiences in the hope of freeing him from the effects of such experiences; and then suggesting to him, while he is still party somnolent that he will be free of symptoms.

NARCOTIC: Opium and coca leaves and the innumerable alkaloids derived therefrom, the best known of these alkaloids being morphia, heroin, and codeine, obtained from opium, and cocaine derived from the coca plant; all compounds, salts, preparations, or other derivatives obtained either from the raw material or from the various alkaloids; Indian hemp and its various derivatives, compounds, and preparations, and peyote in its various forms.

NATIONAL AGENCY CHECK: A security check which consists of the investigation of the records kept on a particular person by such agencies as the Federal Bureau of Investigation and the Office of Naval Intelligence.

NATIONAL DEFENSE BUILDING: The Pentagon.

NATIONALITY: The political status of an individual with reference to his allegiance to a certain country.

NATIONAL OF THE UNITED STATES: 1. A citizen of the United States. 2. A person who, though not a citizen of the United States, owes permanent allegiance to the United States.

NATIONAL SECURITY AGENCY: An agency that functions under the Department of Defense, but serves other agencies of the government concerned with communications security and other technical matters.

NATIONAL SECURITY COUNCIL: A council serving as an advisory body to the President on the integration of domestic, foreign, and military policies relating to the national security in order that the armed forces and other departments and agencies of the government may cooperate effectively.

NATIONAL WAR COLLEGE: An educational institution established in 1946 at Washington, D. C. to prepare students for high-level policy, command, and staff functions and for the performance of strategic planning duties.

NATURALIZATION: An act by which a foreigner is admitted to citizenship in a state. The method of naturalization is in accord with local law and varies greatly in different states.

NAVAL ACTIVITY: Construed to mean a unit of the Naval Establishment, of distinct identity, and established under an officer in command or in charge.

NAVAL BARRACKS: An activity established to house, mess, clothe, pay, and maintain records for naval personnel who, in general, are in a nontransitory status.

NAVAL CLEMENCY BOARD: Composed of five members, meets regularly in Washington, D. C., and makes recommendation to the Secretary of the Navy relative to remission, reduction or suspension of any or all of the sentence; shall consider for clemency such cases as may be referred to it relative to Naval or Marine Corps personnel awaiting punitive discharges or Naval or Marine Corps personnel serving a period of confinement in a corrective institution or prison.

NAVAL CONTROL OF SHIPPING OFFICER: When assigned, a naval officer who, in a port or base designated by the Commander-in-Chief, Atlantic or Pacific Fleets, controls and coordinates the routing and movements of merchant convoys and independently sailed merchant ships in or out of that port or base, subject to the directives of the Operational Control Authority.

NAVAL CONTROL OF SHIPPING ORGANIZATION: The organization within the Navy which carries out the specific responsibilities of the Chief of Naval Operations to provide for the control and protection of movements of merchant vessels in time of war.

NAVAL COURIER: Construed to apply to a person who has been so designated and accredited by competent authority to receive, transport, and deliver specific grades of classified matter.

NAVAL COURTS AND BOARDS: The Navy regulations of court-martial procedures, boards of inquiry, deck courts, etc. now superceded by the Uniform Code of Military Justice.

NAVAL DISTRICT: A geographically defined area in which one naval officer, designated commandant, is the direct representative of the Secretary of the Navy and the Chief of Naval Operations. The commandant has the responsibility for local naval defense and security and for the coordination of naval activities in the area.

NAVAL ESTABLISHMENT: As used in Navy Regulations, means the naval sea, air and ground forces—vessels of war, aircraft, auxiliary craft, and auxiliary activities, and the personnel who man them—and the naval agencies necessary to support and maintain the naval forces and to administer the Navy as a whole; the Marine Corps and, in time of war or when the President shall so direct, the Coast Guard, are parts of thhe Naval Establishment.

NAVAL EXAMINING BOARDS: Constituted to inquire into and report upon the mental, or moral, and professional qualifications of such candidates for appointment or promotion in the naval service as may be ordered to appear before them.

NAVAL HOME: A naval station maintained for providing an honorable and comfortable home for old, disabled, and infirm officers and enlisted men of the Navy, Marine Corps, and Coast Guard (if the personnel have served with this organization when it was attacted to the U. S. Navy).

NAVAL LAW: The body of rules prescribed by competent authority for the government and regulations of the naval forces.

NAVAL RESERVE TRAINING CENTER: Activities established for the procurement, training and administration of members of the Naval Reserve.

NAVAL STATION: A naval activity on shore, having a commanding officer, and located in an area having fixed boundaries, within which all persons are subject to naval jurisdiction and to the authority of the commanding officer.

NAVAL SUPPLEMENT TO THE MANUAL FOR COURTS-MARTIAL: Supplementary instructions related to matters of justice in the naval service.

NAVAL TRAINING CENTERS: Maintained to provide the training for newly enlisted personnel in the Recruit Training Commands and, for enlisted personnel other than recruits, in the various service schools which comprise the Service School Commands at the training centers.

NAVY: The Department of the Navy at the seat of Government; the headquarters, United States Marine Corps; the entire operating forces of the United States Navy, including naval aviation, and of the United States Marine Corps, including the reserve components of such forces; all field activities; headquarters, forces, bases installations, activities, and functions under the control or supervision of the Department of the Navy; and the United States

Coast Guard when operating as a part of the Navy pursuant to law.

NAVY REGULATIONS: Principles for the guidance of the Naval Establishment as to the duty, responsibility, authority, distinctions, and relations of the various bureaus, officials, and individuals each to the other.

NECROFETISHISM: Corpse fetish.

NECROPHILIA: Sexual intercourse with the dead.

NECROPSY: Autopsy.

NEGLECT: Omission or failure to do an act or perform a duty, or an omission or failure due to want of due care or attention.

NEGLECT OF DUTY: An offense constituted by failure to obey or carry out an order, to perform a legally assigned task or mission, or to comply with the responsibilities of one's rank, grade or assignment.

NEGLIGENCE: The omission to do something which a reasonable man, guided by those ordinary considerations which ordinarily regulate human affairs, would do, or the doing of something which a reasonable and prudent man would not do.

NEGLIGENCE PER SE: Conduct, whether of action or omission, which may be declared and treated as negligence without any argument or proof as to the particular surrounding circumstances.

NEGLIGENT HOMICIDE: Unlawfully causing the death of another by simple negligence; it is the unlawful killing of a person as a result of the failure to use due care and circumspection in the circumstances.

NEGLIGENTLY: A person acts negligently with respect to a material element of an offense when he should be aware of a substantial and unjustifiable risk that the material element exists or will result from his conduct. The risk must be of such a nature and degree that the actor's failure to perceive it, considering the nature and purpose of his conduct, the circumstances known to him and the care that would be exercised by a reasonable person in his situation, involves substantial culpability.

NEGOTIABLE: That which can be negotiated, transferred, or assigned.

NEGOTIABLE NOTE: A promissory note in such form that it may be transferred or negotiated, so that the holder may maintain an action thereon in his own name.

NEGOTIATED CONTRACT: A purchase or sales agreement made by a government agency without normally employing techniques required by formal advertising.

NEGOTIATED PLEA: A pre-trial agreement entered into between the convening authority and the accused setting out the maximum sentence to be approved and/or the portion of the charge to be dismissed in consideration of a plea of guilty by the accused.

NET OBLIGATIONS: Total obligations adjusted for increases or decreases resulting from renegotiation, termination, and cancellation of contracts and from correction of errors, from discounts and other causes.

NEURITIS: Inflammation of a nerve.

NEUROLOGIST: A physician specializing in the diagnosis and treatment of diseases and disorders of the nervous system (brain, spinal cord, etc).

NEUROPATHIC: Pertaining to a nervous disorder.

NEUROSIS: A set of symptoms due essentially to emotional conflict. The word has the same meaning as psychoneurosis. At one time a distinction was drawn between "neuroses," which were supposed to be mechanical or structural disturbances of organs due to emotional conflict, and "psychoneuroses," which were supposed to be wholly of emotional origin and manifestation. Today the two words (neurosis and psychoneurosis) are treated as synonyms.

NEUROTIC: As a noun "neurotic" means a person who has a neurosis. As an adjective "neurotic" means having the characteristics of a neurosis, that is, due to emotional conflict. If a symptom is described as "neurotic," the implication is that the symptom is due primarily to emotional conflict. It is not "imaginary," of course; it is real enough, and is mediated through actual changes in body organs. "Neurotic" in modern usage is a synonym of "psychoneurotic." Some doctors use the word "neurotic" as a synonym for functional.

NEUTRAL: Not taking an active part in the hostilities of either of two belligerent states.

NEUTRAL PERSONS: The nationals of a State which is not taking part in the war are considered neutrals.

NEUTRALITY: The status of a nation which takes no part in a war between two or more nations.

NEUTRALIZATION: A permanent state of neutrality, usually imposed by treaty.

NEUTRALIZED STATE: A state which is permanently neutral.

NEW TRIAL: Petition for new trial on grounds of newly discovered evidence or fraud, may be filed by the accused with The Judge Advocate General within one year after approval by the convening authority of a sentence extending to death, dismissal, dishonorable or bad-conduct discharge, or confinement for a year or more. If the case is still pending before a board of review or the Court of Military Appeals, The Judge Advocate General shall refer the petition to the board or court for action, otherwise he shall act upon it.

NEXT OF KIN: Persons most nearly related to decedent by blood.

NOLLE PROSSE: An entry made on the record by which the prosecutor declares that he will proceed no further.

NOLO CONTENDERE: I do not wish to contest; a plea whereby the accused does not directly admit himself to be guilty, but tacitly admits it by throwing himself on the mercy of the court.

NONACCOUNTABLE OFFICER: Officer not under bond and not accountable for public property.

NONAGE: Legal minority.

NONAPPROPRIATED FUNDS: The monies which support certain revenue producing, welfare, and sundry activities which are not provided for in congressional appropriations but are necessary adjuncts to the Armed Forces.

NONBATTLE CASUALTY: A person who is not a battle casualty, but who is lost to his organization by reason of disease or injury, including persons dying from disease or injury, or by reason of being missing where the absence does not appear to be voluntary or due to enemy action or to being interned.

NON-COMBATANT: A person connected with an armed force, but for purposes other than fighting, such as surgeons or chaplains; sometimes used to denote the entire civilian population.

NONCOMMISSIONED OFFICER: An officer other than a commissioned or warrant officer; i.e. in the AF, an airman in the grade of staff sergeant, technical sergeant, or master sergeant.

NON COMPOS MENTIS: Not of sound mind, memory, or understanding.

NON CONSTAT: It does not appear.

NONDUTY STATUS: Status of an officer or enlisted man who, for any reason, such as arrest, leave, sick, confinement, or absence without leave, is not available for duty with the organization to which he belongs.

NON EST FACTUM: A plea denying execution of an instrument.

NONFEASANCE: The neglect or failure of a person to do some act which he ought to do.

NONJUDICIAL PUNISHMENT: Light punishments and other corrective measures imposed by a commanding officer upon any military person who does not demand trial by court martial.

NONPAY STATUS: Status of an officer or enlisted man who is not entitled to receive pay during the time that he is in a nonduty status, that is, when he is not available for duty with his organization because of his own fault or neglect. Absence without leave and time lost from duty because of illness due to the soldier's fault are cases in which the soldier is placed in a nonpay status.

NON-RATED MAN: An enlisted man below the rating of a petty officer.

NONRESTORABLE PRISONER: Prisoner deemed unsuitable for return to honorable duty status in the Army.

NON SUI JURIS: Without capacity to manage his own affairs.

NONSUIT: A judgment given against the plaintiff when he is unable to prove a case or when he refuses or neglects to proceed to the trial of a cause after it has been put in issue. Only the defendant may move for a nonsuit. The directed verdict is a bar to another action, whereas a nonsuit is not.

NOTARY OR NOTARY PUBLIC: A public officer whose duty it is to attest and take acknowledgments to the genuineness of deeds or writings, etc.

NOTES: Formal diplomatic or official written communications.

NOVATION: An agreement whereby an original party to a contract is replaced by a new party. In order for his substitution to be effective, it must be agreed to by all of the parties. The remaining contracting party must agree to accept the new party and at the same time consent to release the withdrawing party. The latter consents to withdraw and permits the new party to take his place. The new party agrees to assume the burdens and duties of the retiring party because of some consideration which he receives. Provided none of these essentials is missing, the withdrawing party is discharged from the old agreement.

NUDUM PACTUM: A nude pact; a promise that can not be enforced, either at law or in equity.

NUISANCE: A condition of things which is prejudicial to the health, comfort, safety, property, sense of decency, or morals, of the citizens at large, resulting either 1. From an act not warranted by law, or 2. From neglect of a duty imposed by law.

NUNC PRO TUNC: Now for then; refers to an entry made now of something which was actually previously done, to have effect as of the former date.

NUNCUPATIVE: Oral, not written.

NUNCUPATIVE WILL: A will that is not in writing and exists only when the testator has declared it orally before witnesses and afterwards reduced to writing and attested to by the same witnesses.

NYMPHOMANIA: Excessive sexual desire in a female. The corresponding disorder in the male is called satyriasis.

O

OATH: Includes an affirmation when an affirmation is authorized in lieu of an oath.

OBITER DICTUM: "A remark by the way." Statements and comment in an opinion concerning some rule of law or legal proposition not necessarily involved nor essential to determination of the case in hand and lacking the force of an adjudication.

OBLIGATE: To reserve funds for the liquidation of a specific commitment.

OBLIGATION: The dollar amount specifically reserved against an appropriation or fund for expenditure in payment of an order placed, contract awarded, or service received.

OBLIGATION AUTHORITY: Authorization from allotted funds making a designated portion available for obligation at another installation and in respect to which accounting records are not required to be maintained by the recipient.

OBLIGATION OF FUNDS: Amount of an order placed, a contract awarded, a service received, or any other transaction which legally reserves an appropriation or fund for expenditure.

OBLIGATIONS INCURRED: Total amount of obligations which have been established against an appropriation or fund during a given period of time.

OBSCENE LIBELS: An obscene writing, book, or print. To publish such a libel, or otherwise expose the same to public view, is a public nuisance, and a misdemeanor at common law.

OBSESSION: An absurd idea which seizes the person's mind and which keeps hold of him even though he recognizes that it is foolish. A compulsion is really an obsession. So is a phobia. So is the persistence of a tune, or some fixed thought. If the patient defends the idea as sensible, it is probably a delusion rather than an obsession. A subject knows that the obsession is foolish.

OBSTRUCTING JUSTICE: To obstruct public or private justice, as by resisting or obstructing an officer in the exercise of his duty, or preventing attendance of witnesses.

OBTAINING BY FALSE PRETENSE: Included in larceny (wrongful obtaining with intent permanently to defraud).

OCCUPATION: Takes place only after the invasion of any particular area has been successfully completed, and the invader has taken effective control of the area.

OEDIPUS COMPLEX: Sexual desire of the son for his mother, with hostility to the father.

OFFENSES IN CONNECTION WITH ELECTIONS: Frauds and obstruction in connection with public elections are misdemeanors at common law.

OFFER OF PROOF: A concise statement of the substance of expected testimony or other evidence which the court has excluded or refused to hear. It is made for the purpose of assisting reviewing agencies in determining whether the action of the law officer (president of a special court-martial) was proper in excluding the evidence in question; it is not to be considered by the court as proof of the matters therein contained. An offer of proof is properly made immediately after an objection has been sustained to the admissibility of offered evidence. If it appears to the law officer that the offer of proof may contain matter prejudicial to the rights of the Government or the accused, he may direct that it be made at an out-of-court hearing.

OFFERS ANY VIOLENCE AGAINST HIM: Comprises any form of battery or of mere assault not embraced in the more specific terms "strikes" and "draws or lifts up".

OFFICE: A public station, or employment, conferred by the appointment of government; the terms embraces areas of tenure, duration, emolument and duties.

OFFICE OF SPECIAL INVESTIGATION: An activity under the Inspector General, USAF, providing a centrally directed criminal, counter-intelligence, and special investigative service for all AF activities.

OFFICER: One who holds an office or position of authority or command, esp. a commissioned officer, warrant officer, or noncommissioned officer; A commissioned officer.

OFFICER CANDIDATE SCHOOLS: Include the United States Service Academies, Officer Candidate; and the various Reserve Officer Training Corps program conducted at civilian colleges and universities.

OFFICER IN CHARGE: An officer assigned the responsibility of directing special units under the direction of a commanding officer.

OFFICER IN COMMAND: An officer may be in command either because he is so detailed by competent authority or because he has succeeded to command by operation of law.

OFFICER OF THE DAY: Officer acting directly under the commanding officer, who is responsible on a given day for the performance of the guard, preserving order, protecting property, enforcing inspection regulations, and guarding prisoners at a military installation.

OFFICER OF THE GUARD: A commissioned officer assigned as commander of the guard for a given base.

OFFICER OF THE NAVAL SERVICE: Officers of the line, officers of the staff corps, commissioned warrant officers.

OFFICIAL: Made or done by an officer of the Government.

OFFICIAL CORRESPONDENCE: Correspondence on properly authorized military matters or business. It may be legally sent through the mails in official envelopes without prepayment of postage if four pounds or less.

OFFICIAL DOCUMENTS AND OFFICIAL STATEMENTS: Include all documents and statements in the line of duty.

OFFICIAL DUTY: Any duty to which military personnel on active duty may be assigned in connection with civilian personnel any duty included in their "job description", or additional duties to which they may be detailed by their superiors.

OFFICIAL STATEMENTS: See **OFFICIAL DOCUMENTS AND OFFICIAL STATEMENTS.**

OFFICIAL VISIT: Construed to mean a formal visit of courtesy requiring special honors and ceremonies.

OFF LIMITS: 1. Place or locality, usually outside military areas, which military personnel are forbidden to enter, except on official business. An off limits area may be patrolled by military police. 2. Being in such a forbidden place.

OLOGRAPHIC WILL: See **HOLOGRAPHIC WILL.**

OMISSION: A failure to act.

ON DUTY: When in the actual exercise of command, the commanding officer of a post, or of a command, or of a detachment in the field is constantly on duty; the commanding officer on board a ship is constantly on duty; in the case of other officers or enlisted persons the term "on duty" relates to duties of routine or detail, in garrison, at a station, or in the field, and does not relate to those periods when, no duty being required of them by orders or regulations, officers and men occupy the status of leisure known as "off duty" or "on liberty".

ONUS: A burden or responsibility; duty.

ONUS PROBANDI: The burden of proof.

OPEN ALLOTMENT: Allotment which designates a specific appropriation and project account without limiting the amount that may be obligated.

OPEN END CONTRACT: Agreement for the supply of goods or services which contains no or varying limits of time and quantity and which usually involves recurring orders and charges in varying degree.

OPERATING A VEHICLE: Includes not only driving or guiding it while in motion, either in person or through the agency of another, but also the setting of its motive power in action or the manipulation of its controls as to cause the particular vehicle to move.

OPERATING FORCES: The several fleets, seagoing forces, sea frontier forces, district forces, Fleet Marine forces, and such shore activities of the Navy and other forces and activities as may be assigned to the Operating Forces by the President or Secretary of the Navy.

OPHTHALMIA: Severe inflammation of the eye or of the conjunctiva.

OPHTHALMOSCOPE: A perforated mirror used in inspecting the interior of the eye.

OPINIONS: Depending upon the nature of the inquiry and the provisions of the appointing order, these opinions may include inferences drawn from facts; opinions as to performance of duty by individuals concerned or as to the performance of functions by equipment involved; and conclusions of law, e.g., opinions as to the questions of line of duty and misconduct in cases of death or injuries of personnel of the naval establishment. Also an impression upon the mind brought about by an accumulation of facts.

OPTHAMOLOGGIST: A physician specializing in the study, diagnosis of disorders and diseases of the eye.

ORAL DEPOSITION: A deposition taken on oral examination.

ORALISM: Sexual pleasure obtained through the use of the mouth on the sexual organs.

ORAL TESTIMONY CANNOT BE OBTAINED: If the person is dead, insane, too ill or infirm to attend the trial, beyond the reach of process, or cannot be found.

ORAL WILL: **See NUNCUPATIVE WILL.**

ORCHIDECTOMY: Excision of one or both testicles.

ORDER: A communication, written, oral, or by signal, in which a superior enjoins or commands a subordinate to do or accomplish something; Any of several publications, or single issues thereof, issued by order or command of a competent authority, as General Orders, Special Orders, etc.

ORDINANCE: An established rule; a public enactment; law passed by a municipal corporation.

ORDINARY LEAVE: The usual kind of leave, as distinguished from sick leave, emergency leave, or other special kinds of leave.

OROPHARYNGEAL: Pertaining to the mouth and pharynx.

OSSICULECTOMY: The excision of a small bone.

OSTEOMYELITIS: Inflammation of the bone caused by a pyrogenic organism.

OS UTERI: The mouth of the uterus.

OVARY: The female sexual gland in which the ova are formed.

OVERT ACT: An open act: a physical act, as distinguished from an act of the mind; an act done pursuant to a formed intent, design, plan, or conspiracy.

OVUM: The female reproductive cell.

P

PACIFIC BLOCKADE: Pacific blockade is a form of reprisal or constraint which consists in the blockading by one or more states of certain ports of another state without declaring or making war upon that state.

PACIFIC SETTLEMENT: Peaceful settlement.

PACT: An international agreement.

PANCREATITIS: An inflammation of the pancreas.

PARACENTESIS: Surgical puncture of a cavity; tapping.

PARAMNESIA: A derangement of the memory.

PARANOIA: Mental disease characterized by systematized delusions.

PARDON: An act of the President which exempts the individual on whom it is bestowed from the punishment the law inflicts for the crime he has committed. A pardon may be in the form of an individual pardon or of a general amnesty.

PARENTERAL: Not through the alimentary canal.

PARESIS: A paralysis.

PARI DELICTO: Equally at fault.

PAROL: By word of mouth; not in writing.

PAROLE: A method of conditional release of persons sentenced or committed to penal or correctional institutions after serving a portion of the sentence or term imposed by the court. The usual conditions attached to this form of release are that the person will maintain good conduct and that he will remain under the custody of the paroling or some other designated authority, subject to reincarceration upon violation of the conditions of the release.

PAROLE ADVISOR: An officer of the Federal Probation Service who acts as a guidance counselor to, and has supervision over, a prisoner on parole.

PAROLE OFFICER: Disciplinary barracks officer whose duties are to investigate applications for and to conduct the necessary correspondence relating to home parole.

PAROL EVIDENCE RULE: All prior negotiations between the parties to a written contract are superseded by, and merged in, the written instrument itself when finally executed. Therefore, evidence of talk or negotiations between the parties to a complete, valid written instrument, either prior to, or at the time of, its execution is inadmissible to contradict, vary, add to, or subtract from its terms.

PAROLE VIOLATOR TERM: The unexpired term of the sentence to be served by a prisoner who violated parole.

PARTIAL JURISDICTION: Applied in those instances wherein the Federal Government has been granted for exercise by it over an area in a State all of certain of the State's authority, but where the State concerned reserves to itself the right to exercise, by itself or concurrently with the United States, other authority constituting more than merely the right to serve civil or criminal process in the area.

PARTICEPS CRIMINIS: A partner in crime.

PARTIES TO THE TRIAL: Includes, when appropriate, the law officer and members of the court as well as counsel, the accused, the reporter and the interpreter; it also includes a witness who was not excused prior to the adjourning, recessing, or closing of the court.

PARTURITION: Childbirth.

PARTY: Any person subject to the UCMJ or employed by the Department of Defense who has a direct interest in the subject of inquiry shall, upon his own request, be designated a party to the inquiry by the convening authority, or by the court if request is made to it after proceedings have commenced.

PASS: 1. Authorized absence from military duty for officers and for enlisted personnel during which no ration allowance accrues. A pass may not exceed 3 days in duration. 2. Written authority for such an absence.

PASSING HONORS: Those honors, other than gun salutes, rendered on occasions when ships or embarked officials or officers pass, or are passed, closed aboard.

PASSPORT: A written permission, given by the belligerent government or by its authorized agent to the subject of the enemy state, to travel generally in belligerent territory.

PASSWORD: A secret word or distinctive sound used to reply to a challenge.

PAST RECOLLECTION RECORDED: Notwithstanding the fact that a witness' recollection is not refreshed or revived by an inspection of a writing so as to enable him to testify from memory, yet the writing may be used, subject to certain limitations in connection with, and as auxiliary to, the testimony of the witness.

PATELLA: The kneecap.

PATHOGENIC: Producing disease.

PATHOLOGIC LIAR: A psychopath who repeatedly tells lies because of some inner compulsion even though such lies are easily exposed, and even though they serve little useful purpose.

PATHOLOGIST: One versed in pathology—the study of the morbid processes taking place in organs, systems and tissue. A specialist in pathology.

PAY AND ALLOWANCES: The total pay of a military or civilian person, including base pay, incentive pay, etc., and all authorized allowances.

PAY GRADE: The grade of an enlisted man or officer reevaluated by consideration of his cumulative years of service, used as a basis for ascertaining base pay.

PAYING GUEST: One who commits himself to pay a definite amount as rent for space occupied; guests who simply contribute to the payment of direct and additional expenses incurred as the result of their presence, such as food and laundry, that are personal to the householder and not furnished by the Government, are not "paying guests".

PECULATION: The unlawful appropriation by a depository of public funds, of the property of the Government instructed to his care, to his own use or that of others.

PEDERASTY: (Sodomy.) Insertion of the penis in the anus for the purpose of sexual gratification. This term has been used for the practice of the act of sodomy upon children by adults.

PEDIATRIC: Pertaining to the diseases of children.

PEDIGREE: Pedigree as the subject of legal inquiry involves a question of parentage or relationship. Before hearsay evidence can be received, it must be determined that the fact to be proved is one of pedigree or is one of the collateral facts of family history to which the exception has been extended. If it be one of pedigree, it may be quickly and easily recognized, since it will involve parentage or relationship.

PEDOPHILIA: Erotic craving for children; sexual attraction to children, or gratification from sexual intimacies with children.

PELLAGRA: A disease said to be due to vitamin deficiency.

PENAL SERVITUDE: Punishment which consists in confinement and hard labor.

PENDENTE LITE: Pending the continance of an action; while litigation continues.

PENTAGON: Usually written 'The Pentagon'; A relatively low, massive, five-sided building on the Virginia side of the Potomac, in which are located the principal executive offices of the Department of Defense, including those for the Army, Air Force, and the Navy. Also called the 'National Defense Building'; The seat of authority in matters of the Army, Air Force, and the Navy. Often personified, as in 'The Pentagon says', 'The Pentagon ordered'.

PER ANNUM: By the year.

PER CAPITA: In descent, denotes that method of dividing an intestate estate by which an equal share is given to each of a number of persons, each of whom stand in equal degree to the decedent.

PER CURIAM: By the court.

PER DIEM: By the day; An allowance or amount of so much a day either for extradionary expenses at a station or for temporary duty away from the permanent station.

PEREMPTORY CHALLENGE: A challenge that does not require any reason or ground therefor to exist or to be stated. It may be used before, during, or after challenges for cause, or against a member unsuccessfully challenged for cause, or against a new member if not previously utilized in the trial. Each accused and the trial counsel shall be entitled to one peremptory challenge. A member challenged peremptorily will be excused forthwith.

PERINEUM: The area at the lower end of the trunk between the thighs.

PERJURY: The willful and corrupt giving, in a judicial proceeding or course of justice and upon a lawful oath or in any form allowed by law to be substituted for an oath, any false testimony material to the issue or matter of inquiry.

PERMANENT GRADE: That grade of an officer or enlisted man below which he cannot be reduced, except for cause, during service within the military component that authorized such grade to him.

PERMANENT PARTY: A person, or persons, with continuing duty at a base or other station, distinguished from personnel being processed or on duty for a special purpose.

PERPERTRATORS: Those who commit the overt acts constituting the crime in naval law, there is no distinction between principals in the first degree and principals in the second degree.

PER SE: Taken alone, in itself; by itself.

PERSON: As used in referring to one from whose possession property has been taken, obtained, or withheld, and to any owner of property, includes (in addition to a natural person) a government, a corporation, an association, an organization, and an estate.

PERSONAL KNOWLEDGE: Information which the witness has acquired as a result of the exercise of his physical senses (sight, hearing, taste, smell, and feeling).

PERSONAL PROPERTY: Includes both tangible and intangible property (including motor vehicles).

PERSONALITY: Personal property.

PERSONA NON GRATA: (Latin—not welcome person) A person not acceptable (for reasons peculiar to himself) to the court or government to which it is proposed to accredit him in the character of an ambassador or minister.

PERSONS OF HIS COMMAND: Include not only enlisted persons but also warrant officers and commissioned officers.

PER STIRPES: Method of dividing an intestate estate where a class or group of distributees take the share which their deceased would have been entitled to, taking thus by their right of representing such ancestor.

PERVERSION: The deviation of the sexual impulse from its normal goal.

PERVERT: One who indulges in unnatural sexual acts or fantasies.

PETITION: A complaint; a statement of a cause of action.

PETIT MAL: A form of epilepsy characterized by transient spells of unconsciousness without convulsions.

PETTY OFFICER: The non-commissioned officers of the Navy, these individuals are also called rated men or ratings. The petty officer grades are: chief petty officer (CPO), petty officer first class (POL1c), petty officer second class (PO2c), petty officer third class (PO3c). The chief petty officer ranks immediately after warrant officers, and above all other petty officers, the PO1c outranks a PO2c and PO3c, and the PO2c outranks a PO3c, and the PO3c ranks immediately above all non-rated men.

PHALANGES: Any bones of the fingers or toes.

PHANTOM ORDER: A draft contract with an industrial establishment for wartime production of a specific product with provisions for necessary preplanning in time of peace and for immediate execution of the contract upon receipt of proper authority.

PHARMACOPOEIA: A collection of formulae and methods for the preparation of drugs.

PHLEBITIS: Inflammation of a vein.

PHOBIA: A morbid fear which the patient himself knows is groundless, but which, nevertheless, seizes his mind. This is a form of obsession.

PHYSICAL DISABILITY APPEAL BOARD: Composed of two medical officers, three nonmedical officers, and a recorder appointed by the Secretary of the Navy to review certain records of proceedings of Physical Evaluation Boards in the light of the action taken by the Physical Review Council and the contentions of the individual concerned.

PHYSICAL EVALUATION BOARDS: Consist of three commissioned officers as members, two of whom shall be non-medical members and one of whom shall be a medical members, and a recorder; constituted to evaluate the physical fitness of certain members of the Armed Forces whose cases have been referred by competent authority.

PHYSICAL REVIEW COUNCIL: Composed of three members, convened by the Secretary of the Navy; function is to review the records of proceedings of Physical Evaluation Boards in the light of established medical, legal, and personnel policies, and to express its views for the information of the Secretary of the Navy.

PHYSICIAN: One who has received the degree of doctor of medicine from an incorporated institution; one lawfully engaged in the practice of medicine. The practice of medicine may be said to consist of three things: first, in judging the nature, character, and symptom of the disease; second, in determining the proper remedy and third, in giving or prescribing the application of the remedy to the disease.

PILLAGE: **See Plunder or Pillage; Looting or Pillaging.**

PIMP: A procurer; one who provides for others the means of gratifying lust.

PIQUERS: Sexual sadists who stab their victims, usually girls or women, with sharp instruments.

PIRACY: Robbery and depredation upon the high seas. It is an offense against the law of nations, and a felony, punishable by death, except where a different punishment is prescribed by statute. Piracy has, from the earliest times, been regarded as a crime against the law of nations.

PLACE OF DUTY: Includes any place of duty, whether permanent or temporary, fixed or mobile.

PLAGIARISM: The act of appropriating the ideas and language of another and passing them for one's own.

PLEADING: As used in the terminology of criminal law, does not refer to oratory used by counsel, but to the written formal indictment by which an accused is charged with an offense; in military law, the "pleadings" are called "charges" and "specifications".

PLEA IN ABATEMENT: The situation in which counsel for the accused may utilize a plea in abatement is when the indictment or information mis-states or mis-names the accused. The plea in abatement must be made prior to pleading to the indictment or information or else it is waived.

PLEA IN BAR: By entering a plea of not guilty the accused may raise any defense that would prevent a rendition of judgment against him. Prior to entering a plea, the accused may file a plea in bar stating former jeopardy, pardon, discharge for want of prosecution, or that the statute of limitations has run. The plea in bar should tender an issue of law and not an issue of fact, such as the identity of the crime or the identity of the accused, and on demurrer by the State the court disposes of the plea in bar.

PLEBISCITE: Vote of the entire population of a country or area expressing choice for or against a proposed law; in international law: expression of choice as to sovereignty.

PLENARY: Full; entire; complete.

PLUNDERING ON SHORE: The wrongful taking of the property of an inhabitant while on shore, abuse and maltreatment connected with such taking, and injury to property occasioned thereby.

PLUNDER OR PILLAGE: To seize or appropriate public or private property unlawfully.

POLICE: To clean up and put in order an area, building, or the like by picking or sweeping up refuse, polishing, etc.

POLICE POWER: The power vested in the legislature to make, ordain and establish all manner of wholesome and reasonable laws statutes, and ordinances, either with penalties or without, not repugnant to the Constitution, as they shall judge to be for the good and welfare of the commonwealth and of the subjects of the same.

POLY: A prefix meaning many.

PORT AREA: The area coming within the authority of a given port committee or, in the absence of such a committee, another administrative agency with similar powers.

PORT CALL: A notice to proceed to a port of embarkation or port of aerial embarkation.

PORT COMMANDER: An officer who is responsible for and has authority over all activities at the marine port, and who commands all personnel assigned or attached to the marine port organization.

POSSE COMITATUS ACT: The entire manpower of a county, which the sheriff may summon to aid him in keeping the peace and in pursuing and arresting criminals. The expression using the Army as a possee comitatus, means that the Army is being used to assist in the enforcement of the civil laws. This is expressly prohibited in the Possee Comitatus Act, which provides in part: It shall not be lawful to employ any part of the Army of the United States as a posse comitatus, or otherwise, for the purpose of executing the laws, except in such cases and under such circumstances as such employment of said force may be expressly authorized by the Constitution or by Act of Congress.

POSSESSION: Physical control over tangible objects.

POST: Not limited by an imaginary line, but includes, according to orders or circumstances, such surrounding area as may be necessary for the proper performance of the duties for which the sentinel or lookout was posted.

POST DIEM: After the day.

POST-MORTEM: After death.

POST REM: After the occurrence of the act.

POWER OF ATTORNEY: An instrument authorizing another to act as one's attorney.

PREAMBLE: 1. One of the components contained in the heading of a message whose elements include the degree of precedence, the date time group, and message instructions. 2. In intercept messages, the heading actually transmitted by the original station. 3. Loosely, the heading of a message. 4. Clause at the beginning of a constitution or statute explanatory of the reasons for its enactment and the objects sought to be accomplished.

PRECEDENT: An adjudged case or decision of a court of justice considered as furnishing an example or authority for an identical or similar case afterward arising or a similar question of law.

PREFERRING CHARGES: Signing and swearing to specific charges against an accused.

PREJUDICIAL ERROR: Error materially affecting appelant's legal rights and obligation.

PREJUDICE, GENERAL: General prejudice occurs when the accused has been denied a substantial right accorded to him by either the Constitution or the UCMJ i.e., a denial of due process.

PREJUDICE, MATERIAL: Material prejudice—the error had, or reasonably might have had, an effect upon the decision of the court.

PREJUDICE, SPECIAL: Specific prejudice occurs when there is a reasonable probability that an error had a substantial adverse effect upon the minds of the members of the court.

PRELIMINARY CONTRACTUAL AGREEMENT: Temporary contractual instrument to enable contractors to start work immediately upon war contracts prior to the time when information is available upon which a definitive contract can be negotiated and without the delay incident to contract negotiation. Such contractual instruments include letters of intent, letter contracts, letter orders, and letter purchase orders.

PRELIMINARY HEARING: It is the right of every person under arrest to be brought before a court without unnecessary delay for a preliminary hearing. Where upon the whole examination it appears to the court that no criminal offense has been committed, and where there is no probable cause for charging the prisoner with such an offense, then he shall be discharged; but when the offense charged amounts to a felony and there is probable cause for so charging the defendant, then he should be held to the grand jury, and if it is a bailable offense, the court will set the amount of bail. However, in the event the offense charged amounts to a misdemeanor and is within the jurisdiction of the court, a trial on the merits may be held and the issues determined.

PRELIMINARY INQUIRY: Looking into all the facts surrounding the report to be determine if there is evidence that an offense has been committed and gathering all matters in aggravation, extenuation and mitigation of the offense.

PREMEDITATED MURDER: Murder committed after the formation of a specific intent to kill someone and consideration of the act intended.

PREMEDITATION: A design formed to commit a crime or do some other act before it is done. Deliberation.

PREPONDERANCE OF EVIDENCE: Evidence which is of greater weight or more convincing than that which is offered in opposition to it.

PRESCRIPTION: The acquisition of territory by virtue of long-continued possession.

PRESCRIPTIVE TITLE: A title acquired by long-continued use and enjoyment.

PRESENT RECOLLECTION REVIVED: The rule which holds that any paper whatsoever may be used to refresh the recollection of a witness, provided it actually serves that purpose, so that, after inspecting the paper, the witness is able to recall the facts sufficiently to testify to them from memory.

PRESIDENT: The senior in rank among the members appointed to a general or special court-martial is the president; however, the senior member present at a trial, whether or not he is the senior member appointed to the court, is president of the court for the trial of that case.

PRESUME: Justifiably infer.

PRESUMPTION: A deduction which the law expressly directs to be made from particular facts. There is a presumption that a letter which has been mailed has been received by the addressee, but there is no presumption that the letter was mailed.

PRESUMPTION OF FACT: Arises out of the evidence offered, and may or may not become an element of proof.

THE PRESUMPTION OF INNOCENCE: A cardinal and important rule of the law of evidence that the defendant in a criminal trial, however degraded or debased he may be, and no matter what may be the enormity of the crime charged against him, must always be presumed innocent of the crime for which he is indicted until his guilt is proved beyond a reasonable doubt.

PRESUMPTIONS OF LAW: A rule of law which requires that a certain fact must be inferred by the court from the existence of certain other facts. It is a definite conclusion of law which must invariably be drawn as soon as a given set of facts is established, even though it may be thereafter rebutted by evidence offered in opposition to it.

PRE-TRIAL AGREEMENT: An agreement between the accused and the convening authority that the convening authority will approve only a certain sentence upon conviction or that the accused will be tried only upon certain charges and specifications—in return for the accused's plea of guilty.

PRIMA FACIE: At first view or appearance; prima facie evidence of fact is in law sufficient to establish the fact unless rebutted.

PRIMA FACIE CASE: A case which is established by sufficient evidence and can be overthrown only by rebutting evidence adduced on the other side.

PRIMA FACIE EVIDENCE: Such evidence as is sufficient to establish the fact, and if not rebutted, becomes conclusive of the fact.

PRIME CONTRACT: A contract, agreement, or purchase order entered into by a contractor with the United States Government.

PRINCIPAL: One who counsels, commands, or procures another to commit an offense subsequently perpetrated in consequence of such counsel, command, or procuring is a principal whether he is present or absent at the commission of the offense; one who voluntarily associates himself in the execution of an unlawful design so desperate that it ordinarily involves a hazard to life; the perpetrator.

PRINCIPALS: Any person punishable under the UCMJ who— 1. commits an offense punishable by this code, or aids, abets, counsels, commands, or procures its commission; or 2. causes an act to be done which if directly performed by him would be punishable by this code; is a principal.

PRINCIPALS IN THE FIRST DEGREE: One who actually commits the crime, either by his own hand, or by an inanimate agency, or by an innocent human agent.

PRINCIPALS IN THE SECOND DEGREE: One who is present when a felony is committed by another, and who aids or abets in its commission.

PRISON BREACH: The breaking and going out of his place of confinement by one who is lawfully imprisoned.

PRISONER: 1. One who is deprived of his liberty; one who has been placed in confinement or custody and has not been set at liberty by proper authority. 2. A category of personnel transferred or dropped from the rolls of their permanent organization but carried in a disciplinary or prisoner status.

PRISON GUARD: An individual or group assigned or detailed to a place of confinement for military prisoners for the purpose of maintaining the custody and control of the prisoners confined therein.

PRISON OFFICER: Officer, appointed by the commanding officer at a military installation, who is responsible for the custody, control, and training of military prisoners committed to his charge.

PRISONER OF WAR: With certain exceptions provided by international law or agreements, every person captured or interned by a belligerent power because of the war.

PRISONER ON PAROLE: One who has been released from the physical restraint of confinement upon certain conditions or for a specified purpose.

PRIVATE: In the US Army, the lowest enlisted rank in either of two classes, the lower class of private corresponding to basis airman in the AF, and the higher class corresponding to airman 3rd Class; In the Marine Corps, the lowest enlisted rank, immediately below private first class, and corresponding to basic airman. A person holding the rank of private; a title applied to such a person.

PRIVATE FIRST CLASS: In the US Army, an enlisted rank immediately below that of corporal, corresponding to airman 2nd class in the AF; In the Marine Corps, an enlisted rank immediately above private, corresponding to airman 3rd class in the AF; A person holding the rank of private first class.

PRIVILEGED COMMUNICATION: 1. A communication between parties to a confidential relation such that the recipient cannot be legally compelled to disclose it as a witness, as a communication between attorney and client, husband and wife, physician and patient, etc. 2. A defamatory communication the making of which does not expose the party making it to the civil or criminal liability that would follow from it if not privileged. Such communications may be absolutely privileged, as statements made by a judge in his judicial capacity, or conditionally privileged, as where a statement is made by one person to another who is in a confidential relation or who has an interest therein—bad faith with actual malice deprives this type of communication of its privileged character.

PRIVILEGE OF ORDINARY WITNESS AGAINST INCRIMINATION: No witness, in any legal proceeding, can be required to answer questions which will tend to show that he is guilty of a crime. The matters that are privileged include everything which would tend to subject the witness to: 1. A fine or imprisonment; 2. A forfeiture or confiscation of land; or 3. A penalty.

PRIVILEGES WITHHELD: Those that are within the prerogative of the commanding officer to grant or withhold, for example, leaves of absence, passes, the right to utilize recreation facilities, etc.

PRIVITY: Mutual or successive relationship to the same right of property. Privity of contract and estate between lessor and lessee.

PRIZE: A ship or cargo, belonging to one of two belligerent powers, forcibly captured at sea by the other belligerent.

PROBABLE CAUSE: A fact or facts which induce a belief in a reasonable man; it is not necessary to convince beyond a reasonable doubt.

PROBATE COURT: A court having jurisdiction of the estates of deceased persons and persons under guardianship.

PROBATION: Conditional release from committment to a penal institution, under supervision of a probationary officer.

PROBATIONARY OFFICER: A regular or nonregular commissioned or warrant officer who has completed less than three years of continuous active service since acceptance of his current appointment.

PROBATIONER: Prisoner assigned to a military training company.

PROBATIVE: Having the effect of proof; tending to prove or actually proving.

PRO BONO PUBLICO: For the public good.

PROCEDURAL LAW: The rules of pleading and practices by which rights are enforced, generally not considered to include the rules of evidence.

PROCESS: Written notice to a person formally and officially notifying or informing him of some court proceeding in which he is interested or concerned, and commanding him to take some action —usually appearance for a particular purpose.

PROCESS, LEGAL: A writ; any means of acquiring jurisdiction of person or property by the court.

PROCES VERBAL: A statement in writing; an official report relating to the commission of a crime.

PROCLAMATION: A document published to the inhabitants of an area which sets forth the basis of authority and scope of activities of a commander in a given area and which defines the obligations, liabilities, duties and rights of the population affected.

PROCURE: To cause to bring about, to effect, or to cause.

PROCUREMENT: Process of obtaining personnel, services, supplies (including construction), and equipment, including, as they relate to the above, design, specification, standardization, conservation, selection of contractors, contract forms, pricing, re-negotiation, financing, contract termination, and similar functions.

PRO FORMA: As a matter of form.

PROGRESSIVE JUVENILISM: A condition in which the subject is usually of the senile pedophile type, revealing juvenile tendencies in his habits of thought and action and in his desire for the companionship of adolescents and juveniles.

PROGRESS PAYMENT: A payment made as work progresses under a contract upon the basis of either costs incurred before deliveries, percentage of completion accomplished, or a particular stage of completion.

PRO HAC VICE: For this occasion.

PROMISSORY NOTE: An unconditional promise in writing made by one person to another, signed by the maker, engaging to pay on demand or at a fixed or determinable future time a sum certain in money to order, or to bearer.

PROMOTION: An act or instance of promoting, or the state of being promoted.

PROMOTION LIST: A list of all commissioned regular officers, indicating the order in which they are to be considered for permanent promotion.

PROOF: Comprehends everything, aside from mere argument, that may be adduced at a trial, within the legal rules, for the purpose of convincing the court; it is the result of, and is generated by and flows from, the production of evidence in court, but it also includes presumptions of law.

PROPERTY: The right of ownership; The thing owned. In this sense it is (a) real, or (b) personal.

PROPHYLAXIS: Measures preventing the development or spread of disease.

PROPRIETARY ARTICLE: Article manufactured and marketed under patent that is obtainable only from a single source of supply.

PROPRIETARY INTEREST ONLY: Applied in those instances wherein the Federal Government has not been granted, by the State concerned, any measure of the State's authority over an area.

PRO RATA: In proportion.

PRO RE NATA: For the occasion as it may arise.

PROSTHETIC: Pertaining to the replacement of an absent part by an artificial one.

PROSTITUTE: A female who promiscuously submits to sexual intercourse with men for hire.

PRO TANTO: For so much.

PROTECTED PERSONS: Civilian or military persons entitled to benefits under any convention or treaty relating to the conduct of hostilities to which the opposing belligerents are parties. All protected persons described in the Geneva Conventions of 1949 are included within this term.

PROTECTING POWER: A neutral nation entrusted by a belligerent with the protection, in the territory of or occupied by the enemy, of the interests of the belligerent and its nationals.

PROTECTORATE: A state which has transferred the management of its more important international affairs to a stronger state.

PRO TEMPORE: For the time being.

PROTOCOL: A document serving as the opening of a diplomatic transaction.

PROVOCATION: That treatment by another which arouses anger or passion; which produces in the minds of persons ordinarily constituted the highest degree of exasperation, rage, anger, sudden resentment, or terror.

PROVOKING AND REPROACHFUL: As used in UCMJ Article 117, describe those words or gestures which are used in the presence of the person to whom they are directed and which tend to induce breaches of the peace.

PROVOST COURT: Military tribunal of limited jurisdiction convened in occupied territory under military government and usually composed of one officer.

PROVOST MARSHALL: A staff officer at command or subordinate level who advises on, and exercises supervision and inspection over, the maintenance of discipline, enforcement of security, and the confinement of prisoners. Sometimes capitalized when specific reference is intended.

PROVOST SERGEANT: Noncommissioned officer who directs a group of military policemen in the performance of their duties and assists the prison officer in the management of the organization prison. A provost sergeant supervises prisoners, instructs and supervises the military police unit, and keeps the records of the unit.

PROXIMATE CAUSE: That cause which produces an effect directly as distinct from remotely. One is not liable for remote and indirect consequences; he is liable for proximate and direct consequences; there must be a close connection between the act and the injury, so close that it can be said that the act produced the result. There must be a continuous chain of events so linked together as to form a natural whole.

PROXY: Authority to act for another in some matter.

PSEUDOLOGISTS: Certain psychopathic personalities belonging to the hysterical group, whose chief role in life is deception, lying and cheating, and to whom fabrication is an art.

PSYCHIC: The mental system; the mind.

PSYCHOLOGIST: A nonphysician trained in the understanding of mental mechanisms. His field includes testing of mental capacities, determination of personality structure, vocational and personal guidance, experimental and animal psychology, and attempts at the correction of intellectual and emotional disabilities by use of psychological methods. A psychologist who has been trained to practice psychoanalysis is known as a "lay analyst," because he is not a physician and therefore is not a psychiatrist.

PSYCHONEUROSIS: A functional disorder of the mind and nerves, as opposed to organic nervous disease.

PSYCHOPATH: A shorthand term for "psychopathic personality," or, as it is called in some nomenclatures, "pathologic personality." A psychopath is a person who has trouble getting along because of some long-standing personality oddity, but who is not insane and not feeble-minded. There are a dozen kinds of psychopathic personality, but the one that the law is most disturbed about is the "asocial" or "antisocial." This describes a person who, though neither insane nor mentally defective, never seems to be willing to conform to normal standards of behavior; who engages in repeated criminal acts without learning from experience that crime doesn't pay.

PSYCHOPATHIC: As used in the phrase "psychopathic ward," a generic term for mental or emotional illness (a psychopathic ward is a place for mentally ill patients). Also the adjective of the word "psychopath" as above defined. Thus, psychopathic behavior, is not insane behavior; but a psychopathic ward can house insane patients.

PSYCHOPATHIC PERSONALITIES: 1. Those abnormal personalities who suffer from their abnormalities, and from whose abnormalities society suffers. 2. Those personalities whose striving and effort is impaired by quantitative deviations in the ego, and foreign valuation leading to the establishment of pseudo-values and to striving toward pseudo-goals.

PSYCHOPATHOLOGY: An explanation of the mental mechanisms which account for a patient's emotional or mental condition.

PSYCHO-SEXUAL INFANTILISM: A condition in which a chronologically adult individual remains sexually fixed at an infantile stage.

PSYCHOSIS: A mental disorder functional and organic; the term is applied to the major psychoses (dementia praecox, paranoia, and manic-depressive insanity).

PSYCHOSOMATIC: The combined influence of emotional and physical factors. Thus, high blood pressure is a psychosomatic disorder because it has both emotional and physical components. The blood pressure is measurably high, the arteries become hard to resist the rising blood pressure, and changes in the size of the heart may then occur: these are mechanical or physical factors in high blood pressure. However, emotion may raise the blood pressure; a sudden emotional experience may shoot up the blood pressure so fast that it causes a blood vessel to burst; and continued suppressed hostility may cause a slowly mounting pressure: these are emotional factors. So it is with a great many disorders—they have both physical and emotional components; they are "psychosomatic" disorders.

PSYCHOSURGERY: An operation on the brain done for the purpose of relieving tension or improving behavior.

PSYCHOTHERAPY: Treatment by psychologic methods.

PSYCHOTIC: The adjective of psychosis. Insane.

PUBLIC ADMINISTRATOR: A public official who administers the estate of any person dying intestate, without known heirs.

PUBLICIST: A writer in the field of public law such as government or International Law.

PUBLIC DOCUMENTS: All writings or records made by public officers in any of the three departments of government, setting forth facts which such officers are required, in the performance of duties of their office, to record.

PUBLIC OFFICE: Includes a military office, even though only military personnel, or certain military personnel, have access thereto.

PUBLIC PLACE: A place frequented by the public, or some of the public, or as a place open to public view. It need not, however, be a place available to the whole public without discrimination.

PUBLIC POLICY: That principle of law which holds that no subject can lawfully do that which has a tendency to be injurious to the public or against the public good.

PUBLICLY UTTER: To make, to state, to publish, to put forth, or to put in circulation openly, generally, or notoriously as distinguished from doing so privately or in secret.

PUERPERAL INSANITY: A type of mental derangement occurring in women at the time of childbirth or immediately thereafter.

PULMONARY: Pertaining to the lungs.

PUNISHMENT BOOK: Record book kept by a company or similar unit commander, in which an account is given of all minor offenses committed by soldiers and the punishment awarded under the Uniform Code of Military Justice, Article 15, in each case.

PUNITIVE ADMONITION: An admonition given as punishment under the Uniform Code of Military Justice.

PUNITIVE ARTICLES: Those articles of the UCMJ, which define an offense; which tells what is necessary to make up a particular crime.

PUNITIVE REPRIMAND: A reprimand given as punishment the Uniform Code of Military Justice.

PURCHASE RESPONSIBILITY: That function of procurement which consists of contracting for and may include final acceptance of a given item or class of items or manufacturing items in Government owned establishments.

PURCHASING OFFICE: Central office of a technical service whose primary function is to contract for commodities and direct their shipment to agencies requiring them.

PYGMALIONISM: The sexual desire for a statue or statues; a statue fetish.

PYKNIC: (Cyclothymic.) Refers to certain body types or physiques whose psychic tempo swings toward the cycloid or manic-depressive group.

PYKNOLEPSY: Recurrent, frequent, but very brief episodes of mental blankness.

PYROMANIA: An uncontrollable impulse to set fires.

PYROPATH: A psychopathic individual who sets fires.

PYROPATHIA: A condition also known as psychopathic incendiarism.

Q

Q CLEARANCE: A security clearance granted by the Atomic Energy Commission, based upon an investigation conducted by the Federal Bureau of Investigation.

QUAERE: Query; a word frequently used to denote that an inquiry ought to be made of a doubtful thing.

QUALIFICATION CARD: A card or form maintained on an enlisted person setting forth his name, birthplace, and other vital statistics, and listing briefly his skills, hobbies, occupation, record of current service, test scores, arms qualification, and the like.

QUALIFICATION RECORD: A record or form maintained on an officer or warrant officer, giving his name, citizenship status, and other vital statistics, and setting forth a record of education, occupational specialty, source of commission, promotions, foreign service data, etc.

QUANTUM: Amount.

QUARTERMASTER: A staff officer of an Army unit or post who is responsible for furnishing food, clothing, and certain other supplies and services.

QUARTERMASTER CORPS: An Army corps providing certain supplies and services, and consisting of the Quartermaster General, his deputies, assistants, and such other members of the Army as may be assigned.

QUARTERS: Lodgings or accommodations for one or more military persons, or for a military person or persons and dependents; the structure or shelter affording such lodgings or accommodations, or the place where they are located. Always construed as a plural.

QUARTERS ALLOWANCE: A basic allowance for quarters.

QUASH: To overthrow or annul; to vacate by judicial action.

QUASI: As if; almost; a term used to mark a resemblance and which supposes a difference between two objects.

QUESTIONS OF FACT: The question of the existence or nonexistence of a physical object, act, state of things, or condition.

QUESTIONS OF LAW: Wherever the thing to be determined involves the application of some principle of the statute or common law.

QUID PRO QUO: Something for something; an equivalent.

QUI FACIT PER ALIUM FACIT PER SE: He who acts through another acts himself.

QUOAD HOC: As to this; with respect to this; a term frequently used to signify, as to the thing named, the law is so and so.

QUORUM: The minimum number, e.g. five for a general court-martial; three for a special court-martial.

QUO WARRANTO: A proceeding requiring a person to show by what right he exercised any office or liberty.

R

RANK: The status of a person as determined by the grade to which he belongs; also the relative status of a person within a grade; The line grade to which an officer belongs.

RAPE: Rape is sexual intercourse by a man with a female, not his wife, by force and without her consent. The penalty is death or such other punishment as a court-martial may direct.

RATIFICATION: Approval or sanction of a treaty by the President with the advice and consent of Congress.

RATING: The designation of an occupation in the United States Navy which calls for basically related aptitudes, skills, knowledge and experience. Just petty officers are considered to have ratings and because of this petty officers are frequently referred to as "ratings"; This designation in the other services often refers to a specialist grade held by an individual such as a gunner, pilot, observer, etc.

RATIO LEGIS: The reason behind the rule.

RE: With respect to.

REAL ESTATE: Lands and interests therein, leaseholds, buildings, improvements, and appurtenances, owned by the United States and under control of the Department of the Army, real propetry. It also includes piers, docks, warehouses, rights-of-way, and easements, whether temporary or permanent, and improvements permanently attached and ordinarily considered real estate. It does not include machinery, equipment, or tools which have not been affixed to, have been removed from land or buildings or may be removed without destroying the usefulness of the structure.

REAL ESTATE PROGRAM: Acquisition and disposal of real property or interests therein for the Department of the Army. Acquisition is accomplished by obtaining fee title by purchase, condemnation, transfer, or donation, and leasehold interests are obtained through voluntary lease, donation or, condemnation. Disposal is accomplished by sale, transfer to other agencies, or cancellation of leasehold interests.

REAL EVIDENCE: Consists of physical objects such as clothing, jewelry, weapons, etc. Such evidence is admissible if relevant to an issue in the case. Prior to admission in evidence the object must be identified and a connection established with the crime alleged. This is usually accomplished by establishing a chain of custody; however, another method is to have a witness identify the object as being the particular one in question.

REAL PROPERTY: Land, including any right, title or interest therein and buildings, fixed improvements, utilities or other permanent additions to land.

REASONABLE CARE: The degree of care that the ordinary, prudent man would exercise when acting in the same similar circumstances.

REASONABLE DOUBT: One where the state of mind of the jurors is such that they can not say that they feel an abiding conviction to a moral certainty that the defendant is guilty, and the phrase "to a moral certainty" applicable to the quality or quantity of proof is synonymous with "beyond reasonable doubt." It is the property of the defendant, and is his substantial right.

REBUT: To rebut is to defeat or take away from the effect of something. Thus, when a plaintiff in an action produces evidence which raises a presumption of the defendant's liability and the defendant adduces evidence which shows that the presumption is ill-founded, he is said to "rebut it."

REBUTTABLE PRESUMPTONS: Those which arise and continue until they are overcome by evidence or by some stronger presumption.

REBUTTAL: Testimony intended to deny or to contradict.

RECEIVING STATE: A nation, party to an international agreement, which pursuant thereto accepts within its territory the presence of military personnel of another nation party to the agreement.

RECEIVING STATION: An activity established to receive, process, house, mess, clothe, pay and transfer transient enlisted personnel; to provide, when necessary and consistent with economy of operation, logistic support to other naval activities as may be prescribed by a district commandant or the Chief of Naval Personnel; to process naval personnel destined for separation from the service and to assure that they are fully advised of their rights and obligations under existing legislation.

RECEIVING STOLEN GOODS: The offense of receiving stolen goods, knowing them to have been stolen, with the intent to deprive the owner of them.

RECEPTION PERIOD: The initial portion of confinement devoted to the indoctrination and integration of newly arrived prisoners at correction installations. This period is also used for determining whether newly arrived prisoners have a contagious disease.

RECESS: The time between terms of court within which the court is not in session; or the time during a term when the session is temporarily discontinued.

RECIPROCITY OF STATES: Full faith and credit given by a state to the acts and judicial decisions of another state.

RECKLESS: The operation of a vehicle when the operator exhibits a culpable disregard of foreseeable consequences to others from the act or omission involved.

RECKLESSLY: A person acts recklessly with respect to a material element of an offense when he consciously disregards a substantial and unjustifiable risk that the material element exists or will result from his conduct. The risk must be of such a nature and degree that, considering the nature and purpose of the actor's conduct and the circumstances known to him, its disregard involves culpability of high degree. (Alternative: its disregard involves a gross deviation from proper standards of conduct.)

RECOGNITION: The formal acknowledgement by one country of the independence and sovereignty of another.

RECOGNIZANCE: An obligation of record entered into before a court by an accused in which he promises to return to the court at a designated time to answer the charge against him.

RECORDER: A person whose duty includes or consists of keeping accurate record of data, information, etc; specifically the person making a record of the proceedings of a court-martial or board of inquiry.

RECORDING ACTS: Statutes enacted in the several states relative to the official recording of deeds, mortgages, bills of sale, chattel mortgages, etc. and effect of such records as notice to creditors and others interested.

RECORDS: Any papers, photographs (including film), photographic copies, or maps, regardless of physical form or characteristics, accumulated or maintained in filing equipment, boxes, or on shelves and occupying office or storage space, but exclusive of publications or blank forms maintained for supply purposes. This term has the same meaning as files, except that it is a more inclusive term and has a more generalized meaning.

RECOUPMENT: Usually a payment to an individual for expenses; may be a payment to the Government by an individual for losses that are his fault or are due to his carelessness. Repayment or recovery of money.

RECRUIT: An enlisted person newly entered in military or naval service, esp. such a person who has voluntarily entered.

REDEPLOYMENT: The transfer of an individual, a unit, or supplies in an overseas theater of operations to another place with that theater to another theater.

REDRESS: Receiving of satisfaction for an injury sustained.

REDUCE IN GRADE (RANK): To deprive a person of his military rank and place him in a lower grade.

REDUCTIO AD ABSURDUM: Reduction to an absurdity; proof of a proposition by showing the absurdity of assuming the truth of its contradictory.

REDUCTION IN GRADE OR RATE: It is a punishment that takes from the accused his present grade or rate and substitutes therefore a lower rate or grade. It does not become effective until it has been ordered executed by a reviewing authority.

RE-EXAMINATION: Further examination by a party of his own witnesses, after cross-examination, redirect examination.

REFUGEE: A civilian who by reason of real or imagined danger has left his home to seek safety elsewhere. **See displaced person.**

REGIONAL ORGANIZATION: An organization embracing the nations of a certain geographical region or having interests in that region.

REGISTERED MATTER: Classified matter to which a registered number is assigned, and which is accounted for at prescribed intervals and upon specified occasions.

REGULAR OVERHAUL: As applied to work on naval ships, an availability for the accomplishment of general repairs and alterations at a naval shipyard or other shore based repair activity, normally scheduled in advance and in accordance with an established cycle.

REGULATION: An official order issued by a military service or command setting forth or prescribing rules, procedures, policies, or the like considered general in application and permanent in nature; a publication promulgating such an order.

REHABILITATION CENTER: Army correctional installation used in periods of national emergency as a vehicle for rehabilitating and restoring prisoners to duty. Oversea detention and rehabilitation centers, disciplinary training centers, and disciplinary training companies are included.

RELEASE: A written contract by which some claim or interest is surrendered to another person.

RELEASE OF A PRISONER: A removal of restraint by the custodian rather than by the prisoner. Circumstances which justify charges against the custodian for release of a prisoner without proper authority will not justify charges against the prisoner for escape from confinement.

RELEVANCY: Anything which tends to create in the mind a persuasion or belief as to the existence or non-existence of some fact in issue is said to be relevant.

RELEVANT EVIDENCE: Evidence is relevant when it is not too remote or farfetched to prove a particular fact.

REMAND: To remand a case brought into an appellate court or removed from one court into another is to send it back to the court from which it came so that further proceedings in the case, if any, may be taken there.

REMIT: Means to do away with entirely.

RENEGOTIATION: Proceeding under the Renegotiation Act to determine the existence of and secure the repayment to the Government of excessive profits, if any, for a fiscal year or other period, received or accrued under contracts and subcontracts subject to statutory renegotiation.

RENEGOTIATION AGREEMENT: Voluntary agreement resulting from renegotiation, which provides for the repayment of that portion of the profits found to be excessive, or for price reductions, or both.

REPAIR: As applied to work on naval ships, work necessary to restore a ship to serviceable condition without change in design, materials, number, location or relationship of the component parts.

REPATRIATES: Persons who are returned to their own countries with or without their consent.

REPATRIATION: 1. Return or being returned to one's own country; return of refugees to their own locality. 2. Return of sick and wounded enemy prisoners of war to the country they were serving at the time of their capture or to a neutral country prior to the cessation of hostilities. 3. Return of enemy prisoners of war, after the conclusion of peace to the country they were serving at the time of their capture, or to the country of their allegience. 4. Return of the bodies of deceased personnel from theaters of operations to the United States.

REPORT: 1. Official statement of facts, written or oral. 2. Make such a statement. 3. Present oneself; appear for duty. 4. Disclose a crime, misdemeanor, or offense.

REPORT OF INVESTIGATION: An official written record of all pertinent information obtained in an inquiry concerning a crime, offense, accident, allegation, or personal background.

REPORT OF SURVEY: Official report used to record the circumstances concerning the loss, unserviceability, or destruction of property, and serves as, or supports, a voucher for droppage of items from the property records on which they are listed. It also serves to determine all question of responsibility (pecuniary or otherwise) for the absence or condition of the articles.

REPRIEVE: A temporary postponement of the execution of a sentence, generally for the purpose of further investigation of the guilt of the prisoner. It is used in connection with the death penalty.

REPRIMAND: A reproof, either oral or written, more severe than an admonition, given to an officer or enlistedman, and carrying a strong implication of official censure.

REPRISAL: Measures, otherwise illegal, taken by one state to suppress illegal action by another.

REPUTATION: The repute in which a person is generally held in the community in which he lives or pursues his business or profession.

RES: A thing, meaning property of all kinds.

RES ADJUDICATA: Any issue of fact or law put in issue and finally determined by a court of competent jurisdiction cannot be disputed between the same parties in a subsequent trial.

RESCUE: The forcible delivery of a prisoner from lawful custody.

RES GESTAE: The transaction or thing done. Declarations or statements which accompany an act and which tend to elucidate and explain the character and quality of the act are admitted in evidence as part of the res gestae.

RESIDE: To live permanently in a fixed abode. It generally means actual physical presence in a particular place, as distinguished from domicile, which ordinarily deals with a place considered by a person as his home whether he is there or not. Temporary sojourn or casual presence in transit—even if for a substantial time—is usually not called residence.

RESIDENCE: A place of one's abode. **See Reside.**

RESIDUARY CLAUSE: Clause in will by which that part of property is disposed of which remains after satisfying bequests and devises.

RES IPSA LOQUITUR: Occurrences wholly within the control of the defendant, having to do with situations or things the character of which is matter of general knowledge, if productive of injury, will in themselves be prima facie proof of negligence.

RESISTING APPREHENSION: An active resistance to the restraint attempted to be imposed by the person apprehending.

RES JUDICATA: Any issue of fact or law put in issue and finally determined by a court of competent jurisdiction cannot be disputed between the same parties in a subsequent trial even if the second trial is for another offense.

RESPECTABLE MINORITY RULE: Where there is more than one recognized and approved method of treatment applicable to the case, the physician or surgeon is not liable for honest mistake of judgment in selecting a method. A charge of negligence in choice of treatment is refuted by showing that a respectable minority of expert physicians approved the method selected.

RESPONDEAT SUPERIOR: "Let the master answer." This maxin means that a master is liable in certain cases for the wrongful acts of his servant and a principal for those of his agent.

RESPONDENT: The defendant in an action; the party adverse to an appellant in an appeal.

RESPONSIBILITY: 1. The obligation to carry forward an assigned task to a successful conclusion. With responsibility goes authority to direct and take the necessary action to insure success. 2. The obligation of an individual for the proper custody, care, and safekeeping of property or funds entrusted to his possession or under his supervision. **See accountability.**

RESPONSIBLE: 1. To be charged with accomplishment of a task. 2. In army usage, to be liable for the protection and preservation of property and funds and for the payment for neglectful loss of, or damage to, property and funds that have been entrusted to one. **See accountable.**

RESPONSIBLE OFFICER: Officer answerable by law or regulations for the discharge of a duty. He may or may not be accountable in the supply sense. **See accountable officer.**

RESTORABLE PRISONER: Prisoner deemed suitable for return to honorable duty status in the Army.

RESTORATION: Return to honorable duty status in the Army.

RESTRICTED DIET: Meals given prisoners as a disciplinary measure and under medical supervision which consist of not less than 2,100 calories daily, including portions of all components of daily ration, less meat, butter, eggs, sweets, desserts, and condiments.

RESTRICTION: Punitive restraint imposed on a person subject to military law by nonjudicial punishment or a military court which restricts the person to limits prescribed in the order. **See administrative restriction.**

RESTRICTION IN LIEU OF ARREST: An officer authorized to arrest may, within his discretion and without imposing arrest, restrict an accused person of his command, or subject to his authority, to specified areas of military command with the further provision that he will participate in all military duties and activities of his organization while under such restriction.

RESTRICTION TO LIMITS: This form of punishment is a deprivation of privileges.

RETIREMENT: 1. Orderly withdrawal of troops according to their own plan and without pressure by the enemy. 2. Release from active service of an individual because of age, disability, or other cause, in accordance with service regulations and applicable laws.

RETROACTIVE: Operating in a backward direction; affecting acts and conditions prior to enactment.

RETORTION: Legal measures taken by one state in retaliation for legally permissible acts of another state which are cruel, unfair, harassing, or otherwise objectionable.

REVIEW: A formal inspection of an organization, during which a formation of the members of the organization is held; A ceremony to honor a person or persons, or to honor an event.

REVIEWING AUTHORITY: 1. Person or appellate agency who must approve and affirm the findings and sentence of a court-martial before sentence may be carried out. 2. Office authorized to take final action on Reports of Survey by authority of the Secretary of the services.

REVISION: A publication rewritten to include all amendments, changes, additions, and deletions, reprinted to supersede the basic publication.

REVOKE: In connection with published directives to denote repeal or cancellation from the beginning in whole or in part, producing effect of never having existed.

RIGHT: That which a man is entitled to have, or to do, or to receive from others within the limits prescribed by law.

RIGHT OF SEARCH: The right of a war vessel of a belligerent nation to board a ship of a neutral nation and to search it for weapons, contraband, etc.

RIOT: Any use of force or violence, disturbing the public peace, or any threat to use such force or violence, if accompanied by immediate power of execution, by two or more persons acting together, and without authority of law.

ROBBERY: The taking of anything of value, with intent to steal it, from the person or presence of another, against his will, by force or putting him in fear of immediate or future injury to his person or property, or the person or property of a relative or any one in his company at the time. It is punishable as a court-martial may direct.

RORSCHACH TEST: A method of determining the structure of personality by noting the patient's reaction to a set of cards containing standardized ink-blots.

ROTATION: A regulated process in which military personnel, crews, units, or the like perform duties in overseas areas, in combat or in hardship environments with interim periods of less exacting service in the ZI or elsewhere.

ROUT: Where three or more persons, who have assembled in such a way as to constitute an unlawful assembly, make some advance towards doing an unlawful act. It is a misdemeanor at common law.

ROUTINE ORDER: Order covering matters not connected with, or affected by, operations in the field. Routine orders include general and special orders, court-martial orders, bulletins, circulars, or memorandums.

RULES OF THE ROAD: The traffic laws of the sea, made up of International Rules (applying to ships outside of territorial waters), Inland Rules and Pilot Rules (applying to ships in territorial waters). These are rules for methods of maneuvering in passing, the display of lights at night, etc. so that collisions may be prevented and the safety of navigation may be guaranteed.

RUNNING AWAY: An unauthorized absence under conditions disclosing that the leaving was with the requisite intent to avoid some sort of combat action by or with the enemy.

S

SADISM: A perversion in which the libido becomes misdirected or perverted, so that the act of inflicting pain becomes in itself an object of sexual gratification.

SAFE CONDUCT: Document similar to a passport, issued by a military authority, which a person must have if he wishes to enter or remain in a restricted area. A safe conduct may also enable the holder to move goods to or from places within the area and to engage in trade, which would otherwise be forbidden.

SAFEGUARD: A detachment, guard or detail posted by a commander for the protection of persons, places or property of the enemy, or of a neutral affected by the relationship of belligerent forces in their prosecution of war or during circumstances amounting to a state of belligerency; the term also includes a written order left by a commander with an enemy subject or posted upon enemy property for the protection of the individual or property concerned.

SALARY: See Hire.

SALVAGE: A compensation allowed to persons by whose assistance a ship or its cargo has been saved from impending danger or recovered from actual loss in cases of ship-wreck.

SANCTION: 1. Solemn or ceremonious ratification; confirmation 2. penalty or punishment provided as a means of enforcing obedience to law.

SANS PEUR ET SANS REPROCHE: Without fear and without reproach.

SAPPHISM: Titillation of the clitoris through mutual masturbation or cunnilingus practiced by females.

SATISFACTORY EVIDENCE: That amount of evidence which is necessary to lead the jury to a conclusion.

SATYRIASIS: Excessive sexual drive in a male. The male equivalent of nymphomania.

SCHIZOID: A term used to distinguish certain psychopathic types in the mid-zone between the healthy schizothymic and the sick schizophrenic.

SCHIZOID PERSONALITY: Long-term difficulty in adjustment because of unsociability, excessive intraversion, shyness, autistic thinking, or seclusiveness.

SCHIZOPHRENIA: A psychosis characterized by various degrees of withdrawal from reality, autistic thinking, delusion formation, bizarre behavior, and/or hallucinations. Also called "dementia precox."

SCHIZOTHYMIC: A term referring to physical habitus comprising physique, physiognomy, temperamental and characterological qualities.

SCIENTER: A term used in reference to pleading signifying the accused's previous knowledge of certain facts.

SCOPTOPHILIA: Synonymous with voyeurism.

SEA LAWYER: Navy slang for one who questions and twists regulations and orders in his favor.

SEAMAN: A non-rated enlisted man in the U.S. Navy. Ranks below petty officers and above apprentices.

SEAMAN APPRENTICE: A non-rated enlisted man in the U.S. Navy. Ranks below seaman and above seaman recruit.

SEAMAN RECRUIT: A non-rated enlisted man in the U.S. Navy. Ranks below all other navy personnel.

SEARCH: In military police usage, an examination authorized by law of a person's house or other buildings or premises, or of his person, for the purpose of discovering contraband, illicit, or stolen property, or some evidence to be used in the prosecution of criminal action.

SEARCH WARRANT: A warrant requiring the officer to whom it is addressed to search a house or person specified for property alleged to have been stolen or unlawfully held and secreted there.

SEAWORTHINESS: The sufficiency of a vessel in materials, construction, equipment, officers, men and outfit, for the voyage, or service, in which it is employed. It is an implied condition of all policies of marine insurance, unless otherwise expressly stipulated, that the vessel shall be seaworthy.

SEBASTOMANIA: Religious insanity.

SECOND LIEUTENANT: A commissioned rank or person in the AF, Army, or Marine Corps, immediately below first lieutenant, the lowest of commissioned ranks or persons.

SECRET: Defense information or material the unauthorized disclosure of which could result in serious damage to the Nation, such as by jeopardizing the international relations of the United States, endangering the effectiveness of a program or policy of vital importance to the national defense, or compromising important military or defense plans, scientific or technological developments important to national defense, or information revealing important intelligence operations.

SECRETARY OF THE AIR FORCE: The civilian head of the Department of the Air Force.

SECRETARY OF THE ARMY: The civilian head of the Department of the Army.

SECRETARY OF DEFENSE: The civilian head of the Department of Defense and the second ranking member of the President's cabinet; the title of this officer.

SECRETARY OF THE NAVY: The civilian head of the Department of the Navy.

SECURITY CLASSIFICATION: A category or grade assigned to defense information or material which denotes the degree of danger to national security that would result from its unauthorized disclosure and for which standards in handling, storage, and dissemination have been established.

SECURITY CLEARANCE: A clearance given a person permitting him access to classified material, equipment, or information up to and including a given classification, provided he can establish a need-to-know.

SE DEFENDENDO: Defending himself.

SEDITION: Willful making or conveying of reports or statements with the intent to interfere with the operation or the success of the United States Armed Forces or to promote the success of its enemies; the willful causing of insubordination, disloyalty, mutiny, or refusal of duty in the Armed Forces, or willful obstruction of recruiting or enlistment service of the United States. See **Mutiny.**

SEDITIOUS CONSPIRACY: A conspiracy to overthrow the government by force or otherwise to oppose force to its lawful exercise of authority. An overt act is necessary to constitute the crime. The statutes of the United States define a number of other similar offenses of lesser degree.

SEIZURE: The taking of the thing into possession, the manner of which and whether it is actual or constructive depending upon the nature of the thing seized. As applied to subjects capable of manual delivery, the term means capture, the physical taking of the thing into custody. It also contemplates a forcible dispossession of the owner, and it is not a voluntary surrender.

SELF-SERVING DECLARATION: An oral or written statement made, or an act done, by a party to an action, or by his agent on some prior occasion, which supports a claim of that party at the time of the trial.

SENDING STATE: A nation, party to an international agreement, which pursuant thereto orders its military personnel to enter and remain in the territory of another nation party to the agreement.

SENILE DEMENTIA: The madness of old age caused by the weakening of the mind from the decay of old age.

SENIOR OFFICER PRESENT AFLOAT: Unless some other officer has been so designated by competent authority, the "senior officer present afloat" is the senior line officer of the Navy, on active service, eligible for command at sea, who is present and in command of any unit of the Operating Forces in the locality or within an area prescribed by competent authority, whether afloat or based ashore, except such units as may be assigned to shore commands by competent authority.

SENTENCE: The judgment formally pronounces by the court or Judge upon the defendant after his conviction in a criminal prosecution, awarding the punishment to be inflicted.

SENTENCED PRISONER: A prisoner whose sentence to confinement has been ordered into execution.

SENTRY: A guard, esp. one who stands guard at a point where only properly authorized and identified persons are permitted to pass.

SEPARATE: A squadron, battalion, or corresponding unit or command is "separate" or "detached" when isolated or removed from the immediate disciplinary control of a superior in such a manner as to make its commander primarily the one to be looked to by superior authority as the officer responsible for the discipline of the persons composing the command.

SEPARATE OR DETACHED COMMANDS: Any flag or general officer in command or the senior officer present, may designate organizations which are separate or detached commands within the meaning of UCMJ Article 23.

SEPARATION: The living apart of husband and wife, in pursuance of a mutual agreement. The agreement is set aside by subsequent cohabitation. An agreement for future separation is invalid.

SERGEANT: The title given to a sergeant in any grade; In the Army, a noncommissioned officer between corporal and sergeant first class, corresponding to staff sergeant in the AF; In the Marine corps a noncommissioned officer above corporal and below staff sergeant.

SERIATIM: In a series; severally; as, the judges delivered their opinions seriatim.

SERVICE CRAFT: Comprising generally the waterborne utilitarian craft not classified as vessels or boats.

SERVICE OBLIGATION: An obligation incurred under the Universal Military Training and Service Act, as amended, by those men who enter military service for the first time while under 26 years of age. The obligation dates from induction, initial enlistment, or appointment. It may be for either 6 or 8 years service, active and reserve combined, depending on the time of entry into service and other factors.

SERVICE OF PROCESS: The law compels the giving of notice of a suit to a defendant, so as to make him a party to the suit, and compels him to appear in court or suffer Judgment by Default. The means of compelling a defendant to appear in court is called "process"; the giving of the notice is known as "service of process."

SERVICE PERSONNEL: Means the commissioned, appointed, enrolled, and enlisted personnel of the Armed Forces.

SERVICE RECORD: A form on which the record of an individual's military service is maintained. It is begun upon enlistment or induction, is kept current during the period of service, and at separation is forwarded to Headquarters, Department of the Army for filing as a permanent record.

SERVITUDE: A right by which a thing is subject to a certain use or enjoyment by another person.

SEXUAL DEVIATION: Preference for a unconventional method of sexual gratification. As used in current nomenclatures, the term is applied to a personality disorder (not a psychosis or psychoneurosis) in which the patient derives major satisfaction from one of the less conventional modes of sexual intercourse.

SHIPPING ARTICLES: The agreement between the Government and a naval recruit, covering the terms of his enlistment.

SHIPPING CONTRACT: Contract between an appropriate government agency and a commercial operator providing for the shipment of cargo at special rates per cubic foot of cargo on regularly scheduled commercial ships in certain established trade routes. (Formerly called space charter.)

SHOAL: A sand, mud, or gravel bank or bar that makes the water shallow.

SHOCK THERAPY: Treatment of certain mental disorders by inducing convulsions, coma, or other sudden reactions, accomplished by electricity, inhalant gases, or by the injection of chemicals.

SHOP BOOK RULE: A rule of evidence allowing the admission in evidence of a party's account books of original entry.

SHORE BASED REPAIR ACTIVITIES: As employed in connection with repairs and alterations to ships, shall be construed to include naval repair activities under the management control of the Bureau of Ships or Chief of Naval Operations, and commercial ship repair yards under contract to the Navy.

SHORE ESTABLISHMENT: All activities of the Naval Establishment not assigned to the Operating Forces and not a party of the Navy Department.

SHORT TERM OF SENTENCE: The full term of sentence as reduced by credit for abatements.

SHORT TERM RELEASE DATE: The day preceding the date arrived at by adding the term of the sentence as reduced by abatements to the beginning date of the sentence.

SIBLINGS: Brothers and sisters having the same father and mother.

SIC: Such; so; thus a word inserted in brackets after an erroneous or astonishing statement, to indicate that the quotation is a literal transcript.

SIGNAL CORPS: A corps of the US Army, charged with the development, maintenance, and operation of communications systems within the Army.

SIMPLE ARSON: The willful and malicious burning or setting fire to the property of another under circumstances not amounting to aggravated arson.

SINE DIE: Without a specified day for further consideration.

SINE QUA NON: Without which not; an indispensable requisite or condition.

SITUS: Situation, location.

SLANDER: The utterance of defamatory words intended to prejudice the reputation or business of another.

SMUGGLING: The offense of importing goods without paying the duties imposed by the laws of the customs and excise. This was made a felony by statutes in England when committed clandestinely. It is also punished in this country by acts of congress.

SODOMY: Sodomy is unnatural carnal copulation with another person of the same or opposite sex or with an animal. It is punishable as a court-martial may direct.

SOLDIER'S AND SAILORS' CIVIL RELIEF ACT: Federal statute enacted to give civil and legal protection to members of the armed forces by suspending the enforcement of certain civil liabilities; Civil Relief Act.

SOLICITATION: Any act or conduct which reasonably may be construed as a serious request or advice to commit desertion, mutiny, misbehavior before the enemy, or sedition.

SOLICITING ANOTHER TO COMMIT A CRIME: The act of the least magnitude which is punishable by the common law. In such offenses the actor does nothing himself but he urges others to violate the law. The necessity for punishing such persons is obvious, and such conduct is generally punished as a substantive crime, notwithstanding the solicitation does not move the party solicited to commit the offense.

SOLITARY CONFINEMENT: The physical restraint of a person (in a brig, or retraining command) by himself where he can not communicate with any unauthorized person.

SOMNAMBULISM: Commonly called "sleep-walking."

SOVEREIGN: A person or state in which independent or supreme authority is rested.

SPACE CHARTER: Agreement made between the government and the owner of a vessel which provides that a specified number of cubic feet of shipping space is allocated by means of voyage commitment orders for use on specified voyages from and to designated ports. **See shipping contract.**

SPECIAL COURT-MARTIAL: The intermediate court-martial; composed of three or more members, a trial counsel (and his assistants, if any), a defense counsel (and his assistants, if any), and a reporter.

SPECIAL ORDERS: Orders normally used to promulgate directives affecting the status of individuals, such as appointment, assignment, reassignment, detail, transfer, promotion, reduction, relief from active duty, discharge, retirement, and for appointment of boards of officers, courts-martial, and courts of inquiry.

SPECIAL OWNER OF PROPERTY: One, such as a borrower or hirer, who does not have title but who does have possession, or the right to possession, of the property.

SPECIFICATIONS: It is a statement in simple and concise language of the facts constituting the offense.

SPHERE OF INFLUENCE: A sort of attenuated protectorate in which the aim was to secure rights without obligations.

SPIES: Those who, in disguise acting under false pretenses, collect or seek to collect information in the districts occupied by the enemy, with the intention of communicating it to the opposing force. Such agents are not forbidden, but are liable to such treatment as the laws of the capturing army may prescribe. This may be death by hanging, though a spy is always entitled to a trial. The office of spy is not necessarily dishonorable.

SPONTANEOUS EXCLAMATION: An utterance concerning the circumstances of a startling event made by a person while he was in such a condition of excitment, shock, or surprise, caused by his participation in or observation of the event, as to warrant a reasonable inference that he made the utterance as a spontaneous and instinctive outcome of the event, and not as a result of deliberation or design.

SPYING: A clandestine dissimulation of the true object sought, which object is an endeavor to obtain information with the intention of communicating it to the hostile party.

STAFF: Construed to mean those officers assigned to a commander to assist him in the administration and operation of his command.

STAFF SERGEANT: A noncommissioned officer with the lowest rank of sergeant in the AF, immediately above airman first class and immediately below technical sergeant; the rank or grade of this person; Staff sergeant in the AF corresponds to sergeant in the US Army.

STANDING ORDERS: Interpreted to include orders ranging from those issued by a Department down to those promulgated by the commander of a post, ship or station.

STARE DECISIS: Let the decision stand—If a competent authority has decided the question once—the same reasoning and decision should be reached in a similar case.

STATE: In international law a sovereign political unity. It is of the relations of states that public international law mainly treats. These states may vary greatly. The unity, must, however, 1. be political, i.e., organized for public ends as understood in the family of nations and not organized for private ends as in the case of a commercial company, a band of pirates, or a religious organization, 2. possess sovereignty, i.e., supreme political power beyond and above which there is no political power.

STATELESS PERSON: A person who is destitute of nationality.

STATE SECRETS: Communications between public officers, transactions in public bodies, acts of the executive department, information obtained in the course of, or for the purpose of, the enforcement of the criminal law, and other like matters.

STATUS QUO: The existing state of things at any given date.

STATUTE LAW: The law expressly promulgated by the law-making power,—in England, by parliament; in the United States, by congress for the federal government and for the District of Columbia, by the legislatures or general assemblies for the states, and by congress and the territorial legislatures for the territories.

STATUTE OF FRAUDS: A statute which requires that certain contracts and transactions affecting realty be in writing.

STATUTE OF LIMITATIONS: Amounts to a surrender by the government of its sovereign right to punish for the commission of certain offenses under its laws once a specified period of time has elapsed subsequent to the date of the offense.

STATUTORY LAW: Rules that have been formulated into law by legislative action.

STERILIZATION OPERATION: The act of making one incapable of reproducing.

STIPULATION: Is a concession by both parties to the existence or non-existence of a fact, to the contents of a document or to the testimony of a witness. A stipulation may be oral or written and ordinarily is employed to expedite the trial when there is mutual agreement as to the matters stipulated and both parties are willing to dispense with actual proof of such matters.

STOCK ACCOUNTING: The establishment and maintenance of formal records of materiel in stock reflecting such information as quantities, values, condition, or other information as required.

STOCKADE: A confinement facility used for the confinement of military prisoners and under the jurisdiction of an installation commander.

STOCK CORPORATION: A private corporation with a capital stock divided into shares.

STRAGGLER: A soldier who has become separated from his organization without authority. Straggling is most prevalent in the area of combat. The control of straggling, and the prompt return of stragglers to their organization, is a primary function of the military police.

STRAIGHT LEGAL CASE: One that, upon review, is found to be legally sufficient in all respects.

STRANDED: Run aground so that the vessel is fast for a time; if a vessel "touches and goes" she is not stranded; if she "touches and sticks", she is.

STRANDING: The running of a ship on shore accidentally, or voluntarily. When accidental, or done voluntarily to avoid a worse fate, the loss is one within the terms of an ordinary policy of marine insurance.

STRATAGEM: A deception, either by words or actions, in time of war in order to obtain an advantage over an enemy; a ruse. Stratagems are legal, whereas treacherous acts are illegal.

STRICTI JURIS: Of strict right or law; according to strict law.

STRICTISSIMI JURIS: The most strict right or law.

STRIKE: An intentional blow with anything by which a blow can be given.

STRUCTURE: As used in UCMJ Article 130, refers only to those structures which are in the nature of a building or a dwelling—examples of such structures are a stateroom, hold or other compartment of a vessel, an inhabitable trailer, an enclosed goods truck or freight car, a tent, and a house-boat.

SUA SPONTE: Of his or its own will or motion; voluntarily.

SUBCONSCIOUS MIND: That portion of the psychic where thoughts are formed, impulses and impressions consolidated; it is here, through the facilities of reason and judgment, a conclusion is reached.

SUB JUDICE: Under or before a judge or court; under judicial consideration; undetermined.

SUBLETTING: A leasing by a tenant of the whole or a portion of the leased premises for a term less than the original lease. An assignment of a lease is not a subletting, because it is a transfer of the lessee's entire right in the premises. In general, the lessee may sublet the premises for a term of years less than his lease, unless there is a covenant against subletting or a statute prohibiting such subleases. A subletting does not relieve the original lessee of his duty to his lessor for the payment of rent or for the performance of any of the covenants in the lease. Similarly, a tenant may assign his lease unless there is some stipulation against it, and the assignment will not release the assignor of responsibility for the terms of the lease.

SUBLIMATION: The mechanism by which the energy in primitive or unacceptable impulses is transformed and directed to socially useful goals.

SUBORDINATE COMPELLING SURRENDER: Any person subject to this code who compels or attempts to compel the surrender to the enemy by the commander of any place, vessel, aircraft, or other military property, or body of troops, or who "strikes" the colors to an enemy without proper authority, is punishable by death or such other punishment as a court-martial may direct.

SUBORNATION OF PERJURY: The procuring by one person of another person to commit perjury.

SUBPOENA: A written order requiring attendance of a person in court at a particular time and place to testify as a witness.

SUBPOENA AD TESTIFICANDUM: A process to compel a witness to appear and give testimoney, commanding him to appear before a court or magistrate therein named, at a time therein mentioned, to testify for a party named, under a penalty therein mentioned.

SUBPOENA DUCES TECUM: In addition to requiring the attendance of a witness, requires such person to produce certain materials such as documents, books, etc. In order for the witness to comply with the subpoena, it must clearly describe the material desired. Unless the material desired is not clearly described, or unless there exists a privilege for not producing, the witness must comply with the directions of the subpoena and he cannot refuse on the ground that he believes the documents are not material or that producing them is too expensive.

SUBROGATION: The substitution of one person for another with reference to lawful claim or right.

SUBSCRIBE: To write one's name under a written instrument for the purpose of adopting its terms as his own expression.

SUBSEQUENT CONDITIONS: Those whose effect is not produced until after commencement of the obligation.

SUBSISTENCE: Food or provisions; also, a monetary allowance given a military person in lieu of food.

SUBSTANTIAL RIGHTS: Not imaginary or illusive; but instead real, solid, firm rights.

SUBSTANTIVE LAW: That portion of the body of the law which contains the rights and duties and the regulations of the Government, as opposed to that part which contains the rules and remedies by which the substantive law is administered.

SUBSTITUTED SERVICE: The service of process by leaving a copy at the defendant's residence in his absence, or by posting or publishing notice of the suit and mailing of the notice to the defendant.

SUCCESSION: The taking over of one state of the rights and sovereign duties of another.

SUICIDE: Self destruction. The deliberate termination of one's existence, while in the possession and enjoyment of his mental faculties.

SUFFER: To allow or to permit.

SUI GENERIS: Of its own kind; unique.

SUI JURIS: Of his own right; possessing full social and civil rights.

SUIT MONEY: An allowance which is required to be paid by the husband to the wife pending suit for divorce, for the expenses for such suit.

SUMMARY COURT-MARTIAL: A court-martial given an enlisted person for a minor offense, authorized to impose sentences such as confinement up to one month, forfeiture of two-thirds of pay for a like period, etc.

SUMMARY PROCEEDING: A form of legal proceedings in which the established procedure is disregarded, especially in the matter of trial by jury. The term is applied to the process by which a landlord may dispossess a tenant instead of having to resort to eviction, which is a long drawn-out proceeding.

SUMMONS: Written notice to a person that court proceedings have been commenced against him, and that he is required to appear, on a day named, and to answer the complaint against him.

SUPERIOR COMPETENT AUTHORITY: As used in UCMJ Articles 22b and 23b, any superior in the tactical or administrative chain of command authorized to convene a special or general court-martial, as appropriate.

SUPERIOR OFFICER: Not only the commanding officer of the accused, whatever may be the relative rank of the two, but any other commissioned officer of rank or command superior to that of the accused.

SUPRA: As cited above.

SURETY: A person who binds himself for the payment of a sum of money or for the performance of something else for another person.

SURVEILLANCE: Covert observation of an individual, a place, or an activity.

SUSPEND: Deprive an officer of some of the privileges of his rank, such as sitting as a member of a court-martial, selecting quarters, or exercising command, as a punishment for some offense. Suspending an officer does not deprive him of his right to promotion. To withhold the execution.

SUSPENSION: Act of suspending an officer as a punishment for an offense; or the act of suspending the execution, in whole or part, of the sentence of a court-martial.

SUSPENSION FROM COMMAND: Merely deprives the officer of authority to exercise military command and, consequently, his authority to give orders to his juniors and to perform any duty involving the exercise of command; it does not affect his right to promotion.

SUSPENSION OF ARMS: Short truce arranged by local commanders for a special purpose, such as to collect the wounded, to bury the dead, or to arrange for an exchange of prisoners.

SURVEYING OFFICER: Officer authorized to make an inquiry and fix responsibility for damage, destruction, or loss (not due to fair wear and tear) of Government property.

SUZERAIN: A state which exercises political control over another state.

SYLLABUS: A headnote; a note prefixed to the report of an adjudged case, containing an epitome or brief statement of the rulings of the court upon the point or points decided in the case.

SYMBOLIC SADISM: The condition in which the subject expresses his sadistic impulse by acts of mutilation of some symbol that has specific meaning for him.

SYNDROME: A group of symptoms; an assembly of signs and symptoms which together spell out a specific pattern of disease.

SYMBOLISM: The use of, or representation by, symbols; the process in which one thing stands for something else.

T

TABLE OF EQUIVALENT PUNISHMENTS: Table that permits a court-martial to determine the maximum punishment that may be imposed for a particular offense in terms of some punishment other than forfeiture of pay and confinement at hard labor.

TABLE OF MAXIMUM PUNISHMENTS: Table that prescribes a maximum punishments that a court-martial may impose for the various offenses under the UCMJ.

TALESMAN: A person summoned to act as a juror.

TAXATION: Includes but not limited to licenses, fees, or excises imposed in respect of motor vehicles or the use thereof, provided that the license, fee or excise required by the State, Territory, possession or District of Columbia of which the person is a resident or in which he is domiciled has been paid.

TECHNICAL AVAILABILITY: As applied to work on naval ships an availability for the accomplishment of specific items of work by a repair activity, with the ship not present.

TECHNICAL CONTROL: The specialized professional guidance and direction exercised by authority of the Naval Establishment in technical matters.

TECHNICAL ERRORS IN CHARGES AND SPECIFICATIONS: Also known as errors in form; those which would be sufficient to sustain an objection by the accused, such as uncertainty as to time or place of occurence of the alleged offense, name of accused misspelled, etc.

TEMPORARY DUTY: Duty performed away from the organization or station to which assigned or attached, usually extending over a limited period of time.

TEMPORARY GRADE: A grade held by a military person in accordance with a special schedule extablished during a period of emergency or special circumstance.

TEMPORARY OFFICER: An officer commissioned in an armed service, but without status in either the regular component or the reserve.

TEMPORARY PROMOTION: Promotion to a temporary grade.

TENANCY AT SUFFERANCE: Where a tenant holds over after the expiration of a definite period, the landlord may treat him as a tenant at sufferance. Likewise, a tenant at sufferance is created if the original entry by the tenant was otherwise than by lease, and such person continues in possession at the option of the landlord. If the owner accepts the payment of rent due after the expiration of a term, the acceptance is evidence of his intention to treat the party in possession as a tenant, and such act creates a new tenancy from month to month or for a period for which the rent was received. A tenancy at sufferance may be terminated at any time by the landlord.

TENANCY AT WILL: Where the lease is for no definite period, but at the will of the lessor, it is said to be a tenancy at will. A tenancy at will may be either express or implied, and, if the landowner permits a person to occupy his premises an indefinite period of time, without demanding rent, a tenancy at will is said to be created by implication. Such a tenancy may be terminated at any time by either the lessor or the lessee, and their death terminates such tenancy. Under some jurisdictions, it is necessary to give reasonable notice of such termination; whereas, under others, the landlord may terminate the tenancy at any time.

TENANCY FOR LIFE: An estate for life is usually created by deed. However, a lease may be made to hold for the term of the grantee's life or for the life of another, with an agreement to pay rent or other consideration. In the absence of a definite agreement with respect to rents and services to bind the grantee to the grantor, a conveyance will be made, in which an estate for life is created. Under such circumstances, the grantor is not a landlord and the grantee is not a tenant.

TENANCY FROM PERIOD TO PERIOD: When a tenant holds over after the termination of a lease for a definite period and remains in possession, and the landlord accepts rent, a tenancy from period to period is created.

TENDER: An unconditional offer of payment of the amount alleged due.

TERMINATED: As used in the sense of UCMJ Article 44, means a final conclusion of the hearing, and not a mere continuance for the purpose of obtaining additional evidence or for any other purpose.

TERMINATED PORTION OF CONTRACT: That portion of a terminated contract which does not relate either to completed work or material delivered and accepted under the contract or to any continued portion of the contract.

TERMINATION CLAIM: Any claim or demand by a prime contractor or subcontractor for compensation arising out of the termination of a contract or subcontract.

TERMINATION INVENTORY: Any materials properly allocable to the terminated portion of a war contract, except any machinery or equipment subject to separate contract or contract provision specifically governing its use or disposition.

TERRITORIAL PERSONNEL: All individuals who at time of entry in the military service of the United States were residents of territories or possessions of the United States, including Canal Zone, Guam, the Commonwealth of Puerto Rico, United States Samoa, and the United States Virgin Islands. For certain purposes, persons who at the time of entry into service were residents of the republic of the Philippines are included in this category.

TERRITORIAL SEAS: The belt of water immediately adjacent to a state's land mass and subject to its sovereignty; territorial waters.

TERRITORY: The definite area of land over which a sovereign exercises jurisdiction.

TESTATOR: One who makes or has made a testament or will; one who dies leaving a will.

TESTIMONY: Evidence given by a competent witness under oath or affirmation.

THEOMANIA: A form of religious insanity in which the afflicted individual believes that he is the Deity or is inspired.

THERAPIST: One who treats.

THIRD STATE NATIONAL: A non-United States citizen who is not a citizen of the country in which he is employed and who has been imported into the country for employment by the U. S. Army under special employment conditions.

THREAT: A declaration of one's purpose or intention to work injury to the person, property, or rights of another, with a view of restraining such person's freedom of action.

THROMBOSIS: The clotting of blood within the heart or blood vessels.

THROUGH NEGLECT: Means the omission by a person to take such measures as are appropriate under the circumstances or his doing of some act without giving attention to its probable consequences.

TIC: An involuntary twitch.

TIME CHARTER: Lease of a vessel, for a stipulated period of time, the customary arrangements being that the shipowner supplies the crew, their food, and maintenance, and keeps the ship in repair, while the charterer furnishes the fuel and pays port and terminal charges. Time charter rates generally are paid on the dead weight tonnage of the vessel employed.

TITLE: Is the means whereby the owner of lands has the just possession of his property and is the union of all the elements which constitute ownership.

TO GIVE UP TO AN ENEMY: To surrender.

TOLL THE STATUTE: To stop the running of statute of limitations.

TOP SECRET: Defense information or material which requires the highest degree of protection. The Top Secret classification shall be applied only to that information or material the defense aspect of which is paramount, and the unauthorized disclosure of which could result in exceptionally grave damage to the Nation such as leading to a definite break in diplomatic relations affecting the defense of the United States, an armed attack against the United States or its allies, a war, or the compromise of military or defense plans, or intelligence operations, or scientific or technological developments vital to the national defense.

TORT: A private or civil wrong or injury other than a breach of contract.

TORT-FEASOR: One who commits or is guilty of a tort. To be "joint tort-feasors," the parties must either act together in committing the wrong; or their acts, if independent of each other, must unite in causing a single injury.

TO STRIKE THE COLORS OR FLAG: To haul down the colors or flag in the face of the enemy or to make any other offer to surrender.

TO SUFFER: To allow or permit.

TO THE PREJUDICE OF GOOD ORDER AND DISCIPLINE: Refers only to acts directly prejudicial to good order and discipline and not to acts which are prejudicial only in a remote or indirect sense.

TOUCHERISM: An irresistible impulse to touch the body of another person. Toucheurs are frequently encountered in large crowds. They obtain considerable sexual excitement by touching the breasts of women inadvertently or pinching of the buttocks or merely by casual contacts. If they rub against the other individual, they are known to be frotteurs.

TOXICOLOGIST: An expert in the science of poisonous drugs.

TRACHEA: Windpipe.

TRADE ACCEPTANCE: Type of bill of exchange, used largely by manufacturers and merchants, is the trade acceptance. A trade acceptance is taken by the seller as payment for goods purchased at the time of the sale. The seller draws on the purchaser to his own order for the goods sold. When the draft is accepted by the purchaser, it becomes his primary obligation. The seller usually discounts trade acceptances at the bank, or uses them as collateral for loans. The buyer, having acknowledged the debt by his acceptance, cannot later dispute the debt as against a holder of the trade acceptance.

TRAFFIC CONTROL POLICE: A traffic control policeman is any person ordered by a Military Commander and/or by National Authorities to facilitate the movement of traffic and to prevent and/or report any breach of road traffic regulations.

TRAFFIC PATROL: Mounted military police whose primary duty is the enforcement of traffic laws and regulations and to implement the traffic circulation plan within a given area.

TRAITOR: A person in a place or district under martial law who, unauthorized by the military commander, gives information of any kind to the enemy, or holds intercourse with him.

TRANSFERENCE: Displacement of emotion from one person or idea to another.

TRANSFER ORDER: Order by the Secretary of Defense to the Secretary of the Army, Secretary of the Navy and/or Secretary of the Air Force generally transferring certain functions, powers, and duties from one to the other.

TRANSIENT: A person stopped temporarily at a station with destination elsewhere; also a transient aircraft.

TRANSVESTISM: The wearing of clothing of the opposite sex with the erotic desire of simulating attributes thereof. The practice is not uncommon among homosexuals and is seen in its full-fledged state in male individuals who make themselves up as females and parade the streets in open solicitation.

TRAUMA: In general medicine, an injury, blow, or hurt. In psychiatry, a hurtful or damaging emotional experience.

TRAUMATIC INSANITY: That form of mental derangement resulting from an injury to the brain, such as skull fracture or concussion of the brain.

TRAUMATIC NEUROSIS: A psychoneurosis precipitated by injury, generally by head injury.

TRAUMATIC PSYCHOSIS: Insanity due to injury to the brain; not now official in any widely used nomenclature, though it is the common term among doctors and lawyers.

TRAVEL ORDER: An official order authorizing an individual to travel by railway train or otherwise.

TREACHERY: Acts of deceit of a perfidious character involving breach of faith; perfidy. Acts of treachery are illegal under international Law. Example: Treacherous use of flag of truce.

TREASON: Treason consists in levying war against the government, or in adhering to its enemies, giving them aid and comfort. No person may be convicted of treason except upon the testimony of two witnesses, or upon confession in open court.

TREATMENT: A broad term covering all steps taken to effect cure of injury or disease.

TREATY: An agreement, generally in writing, and always in conformity with law, between two or more states or political unities having treaty making capacity. A treaty may establish, modify, or terminate obligations. As distinguished from other forms of international agreement, a treaty in the technical sense is usually concerned with matters of high state importance, with a considerable number of questions, or with matters involving several states.

TREATY BILATERAL: Agreement between two sovereign states.

TREATY, MULTILATERAL: An agreement between several sovereign states.

TRESPASS: An unlawful act, committed with violence, actual or implied, causing injury to the person; any offense done to another; to enter upon the property of another without authority.

TRIAL: A regular and formal examination by a competent court or judicial officer into the material facts of a controversy in issue, in order to determine and enforce the respective rights of the contestants. Some trials may be conducted by the judge alone, and others with the assistance of a jury.

TRIAL COUNSEL: Officer appointed for each general or special court-martial who prosecutes in the name of the United States, and under the direction of the court, prepares the record of its proceedings.

TRIBADY: Intimate homosexual relationship between females (lesbians); the active individual assumes the male character towards the female partner in the sexual acts.

TRIBUNAL: A judicial court.

TRIBUNAL, INTERNATIONAL: An international court usually established by treaty.

TRIOLISM: A form of exhibitionism in which the subject desires to perform the sexual act with several partners or in the presence of several persons.

TRUE COPY: Transcript, word for word, of any military document; authentication as a correct and accurate duplicate by an officer or by some other person authorized by regulations.

TRUE OWNER: Refers to the person who, at the time of the taking, obtaining, or withholding, had the superior right to possession of the property in the light of all conflicting interests therein which are involved in the particular case.

TRUSTEESHIP INTERNATIONAL: A system established by the United Nations by which certain countries whose inhabitants are not sufficiently advanced for self-government, and are administered by other countries which remain responsible to the United Nations.

TRUTH SERUM: A drug used to obtain an uninhibited expression of repressed material by the subject.

TRY: To investigate judicially, as question of fact.

TURPITUDE: Inherent baseness; depravity; everything done contrary to justice, honesty, modesty, or good morals is said to be done with turpitude.

U

ULTIMATE ISSUE: In any criminal trial, the guilt or innocence of the accused.

ULTRA VIRES: An act of a corporation which is beyond the powers conferred upon it.

UNAUTHORED BELLIGERENTS: Men or units not recognized as lawful combatants under the rules of land warfare, and so not entitled to be treated as prisoners of war if captured.

UNCLASSIFIED: Not having a security classification. Said of documents, information, lectures, equipment, etc.

UNDESIRABLE DISCHARGE: Form of discharge given a soldier under conditions other than honorable, usually given for misconduct, fraud, undesirable habits or traits of character, etc.

UNIFIED COMMAND: A joint force under a single commander which is composed of significant assigned or attached components of two or more services, and which is constituted and so designated by the Joint Chiefs of Staff or by a commander of an existing unified command which was established by the Joint Chiefs of Staff.

UNIFORM CODE OF MILITARY JUSTICE: The law (Public Law 506 of the Second Session of the 81st Congress, signed by President Truman on May 5, 1950) that has been in effect since May 31, 1951, controling and governing the conduct of all members of all branches of the Armed Services, providing for judiciary procedures and punishments applying to all branches alike. In this sense this Code supersedes the Army's Articles of War, the Articles for the Government of the Navy, and the Disciplinary Laws of the Coast Guard.

UNIFORMED SERVICES CONTINGENCY OPTION ACT: An act which gives a member of the Uniformed Services the opportunity to elect prior to retirement a reduced monthly retired pay in order to provide a steady income for his eligible dependents after his death.

UNIT: Any regularly organized body as defined by the Secretary of the Department, but in no case shall it be a body larger than a company, a squadron, or a ship's crew, or than a body corresponding to one of them.

UNITED STATES AIR FORCE: An official name given the air arm of the United States military forces, responsible for the development, training, equipment, and employment of aviation forces both combat and service.

UNITED STATES ARMED FORCES: Collectively, the regular components only of the Air Force, Army, Navy (including the Marine Corps), and Coast Guard.

UNITED STATES ARMY: The land military forces of the US, including the Regular Army, the National Guard of the United States, and the Army Reserve.

UNITED STATES COAST GUARD: A military or police force responsible for certain duties along the coasts of the US, esp. in enforcing customs, immigration, and navigational laws, and for maintenance of the International Ice Patrol.

UNITED STATES MARINE CORPS: A corps of soldiers in the US Navy.

UNITED STATES NAVY: The naval establishment of the United States.

UNIVERSAL MILITARY TRAINING: A proposed program for the common defense and security of the US that would provide for the drafting into military service of all men in the US as each becomes of a certain age, subject to certain physical and mental examinations, and for the training and service of such men for a period of time determined by law.

UNLAWFUL ASSEMBLY: When three or more persons assemble with intent to commit a crime by open force, or with intent to carry out any purpose in such manner as to cause reasonable apprehension of a breach of the peace.

UNLAWFUL DETENTION: Any person subject to the UCMJ who, except as provided by law, apprehends, arrests, or confines any person is guilty of unlawful detention.

UNLAWFUL ENLISTMENT, APPOINTMENT, OR SEPARATION: Any person subject to the UCMJ who effects an enlistment or appointment in or a separation from the armed forces or any person who is known to him to be ineligible for such enlistment, appointment, or separation because it is prohibited by law, regulation, or order shall be punished as a court-martial may direct.

UNLAWFULLY: The taking possession of or the exercise of dominion over property without authorization or justication. As used in a specification "unlawfully" means without justification or excuse.

UNNATURAL CARNAL COPULATION: It is unnatural carnal copulation for a person to take into his or her mouth the sexual organ of another person or of an animal; or to place his or her sexual organ in the mouth or anus of another person or of an animal; or to have carnal copulation in any opening of the body, except the sexual parts, with another person; or to have carnal copulation in any opening of the body of an animal.

UNNEUTRAL SERVICE: Differs from the carriage of contraband, particularly in being hostile in its nature and involving a participation in the contest by the neutral rendering the service. Such service involves assistance in the performance of warlike acts. While the destination is a question of vital importance in the case of contraband, the nature of the act is a matter of highest importance in cases of unneutral service.

UPKEEP PERIOD: As applied to work on naval ships, a period of time assigned a ship, while moored or anchored, by competent authority for the uninterrupted accomplishment of work by the ship's force or other forces afloat.

URANISM: The condition of homosexuality.

URNIDS: Female homosexuals.

URNINGS: Male homosexuals.

UROLAGNIA: A condition found in sado-masochism and fetishism in which the person is sexually aroused through the sight and odor of urine.

UROPHILIA: A psychopathic condition in which the individual has a fetish for urine.

USAGE: Consists merely of a repetition of acts; it refers to a general habit, mode, or course of procedure.

USURY: The act of intentionally taking or reserving by contract a greater compensation or rate of interest for the loan of money than the highest rate of interest the law allows.

UTILE PER INUTILE NON VITIATUR: What is useful is not vitiated by the useless.

UT SUPRA: As above.

UTTER: To offer; to put out; to pass off; to sell; to vend; to emit at large or publish.

UTTERING FORGED INSTRUMENT: To offer it, directly or indirectly, by words or actions, as good. This, if done with intent to defraud, and with knowledge of the falsity of the instrument, being an attempt to cheat, is a misdemeanor at common law.

V

VACATE: To annul; to make void.

VALUE: The legitimate market value at the time and place of the act.

VASECTOMY: A cutting through the excretory duct of the testis to produce sterility.

VEHICLE: Not restricted to motor driven or passanger carrying vehicles nor does it describe only types of land transportation.

VENUE: The county where the facts of a case were alleged to have occurred, and in which the trial is held. If it can be shown that justice requires trial in another county, the case is removed by change of venue.

VENUE, MOTION FOR CHANGE: If an accused can demonstrate that there exists at the place of trial where the prosecution is pending so great a prejudice against him that he cannot obtain a fair and impartial trial in that place, he is entitled to be tried in some other place. Objection to trial on this ground should be raised by a motion for change of venue. When such a motion is granted by the law officer, the case shall be returned to the convening authority for arraignments for trial elsewhere.

VERBATIM: In the exact words, word for word.

VERBIAGE: Use of many words without necessity; wordiness.

VERDICT: The definitive answer given by the jury to the court concerning the matters of fact committed to the jury for their deliberation and determination.

VERTIGO: Dizziness.

VESSELS: Comprising generally the ocean-going ships and craft of the Navy, and such other water-borne craft as may be assigned this classification.

VETO: The non-approval of an act or a resolution in the Security Council of the United Nations by the decisive negative vote of one of its permanent members.

VICE ADMIRAL: A person in the US Navy, corresponding to a lieutenant general in the Army or AF; the rank held by this person.

VIDE: See.

VI ET ARMIS: With force and arms.

VIOLATION OF SAFE-CONDUCTS OR PASSPORTS: It is an offense against the law of nations to violate safe-conducts or passports expressly granted by the sovereign or chief executive of a nation or his ambassadors to the subjects of a foreign power in time of mutual war, or to commit acts of hostility against such as are in amity, league, or truce, and are in the country under a general implied safe-conduct, and one who committed such an offense was indictable at common law. In this country, under the power to define and punish offenses against the law of nations, congress has passed an act expressly punishing, by imprisonment and fine, any person "who violates any safe-conduct or passport duly obtained or issued under authority of the United States."

VIRAGINITY: A condition found in female homosexuals analogous to the effeminate in males.

VISA: An endorsement made on a passport by the proper authorities, denoting that it has been examined and that the bearer may proceed on his trip into the country concerned.

VIVA VOCE: With the living voice; by word of mouth.

VOID: Entirely null and of no effect.

VOIDABLE: Capable of being avoided or confirmed.

VOIDABLE CONTRACTS: One which, for some reason satisfactory to the court, may be set aside at the request of one of the parties. It is sometimes incorrectly said that such a contract is void. It differs, however, from a contract which is void, in that the latter cannot be enforced by either party, while the former may be binding unless the injured party sees fit to avoid the agreement.

VOIRE DIRE: To speak the truth; refers to an oath administered to a proposed witness or juror (or member of a court-martial), and also to the examination itself, to ascertain whether he possesses the required qualifications, he being sworn to make true answers to the questions about to be asked him concerning the matter.

VOLENTI NON FIT INJURIA: "He who consents to an act is not wronged by it."

VOLUNTARY MANSLAUGHTER: An intentional homicide in sudden passion or heat of blood caused by a reasonable provocation, and not with malice aforethought.

VOYAGE REPAIRS: As applied to work on naval ships, emergency work necessary to enable a ship to continue on its mission and which can be accomplished without requiring a change in the ship's operating schedule or the general steaming notice in effect.

VOYEUR: One who obtains sexual gratification by witnessing sexual intercourse.

VOYEURISM: (Peeping Tom) The derivation of sexual excitement and satisfaction through viewing the genitalia or the nude body of an individual.

W

WAIVE: To forego, to decline to take advantage of, e.g., a legal right, or an omission or irregularity of another person.

WAIVER: The voluntary relinquishing of a known right.

WANTON: Includes "reckless", but in describing the operation of a vehicle, may, in a proper case, connote willfulness, or a disregard of probable consequences, and thus describe a more aggravated offense.

WANTONNESS: An act committed in disregard of the rights of others, in a reckless spirit, or under circumstances which evince a lawless, wicked, or mischievous intent.

WARD: A person over whom or over whose property a guardian has been appointed by the court.

WARRANT ARRESTS: An arrest made upon the authority of a warrant by an officer or even by a private person where he has been authorized by order of court to execute the warrant. Any judge or justice of the peace is authorized to issue a warrant where a complaint is made charging the person to be apprehended with some criminal offense.

WARRANT OF ATTACHMENT: An authorization to arrest the witness and bring him before the court to testify.

WARRANT OFFICER: An officer, senior to all noncommissioned officers and junior to all commissioned officers, who derives his authority from a warrant issued by the Secretaries of the Services.

WARRANTY: Affirmation of a material fact or promise by the seller, which acts as an inducement for the buyer to make a purchase.

WASTES AND SPOILS: Wrongful acts of voluntary destruction such as burning down buildings, burning piers, tearing down fences, or cutting down trees. To be destroyed, property need be only sufficiently injured to be useless for the purpose for which it was intended. "Damage" consists of any physical injury to the property.

WATCH OFFICER: A watch officer, within the meaning of the Navy Regulations, is one regularly assigned to duty in charge of a watch or of a portion thereof.

WILL: A written instrument, executed with the formalities of law, whereby a person makes disposition of his property to take effect after his death.

WILLFULL: Means something more than voluntary or intentional.

It implies a guilty mind. It implies, at least, that the act is done without justification or excuse, and it generally implies, to some extent, an evil mind or intent.

WILLFUL DISOBEDIENCE: Is such as shows an intentional defiance of authority.

WILLFUL FAILURE IN PERFORMANCE OF DUTIES: When nonperformance is with full knowledge of the duty and an intention not to perform it.

WILLFULLY: The doing of an act knowingly and purposely, specifically intending the natural and probable consequences thereof.

WING: An AF unit or establishment on a level of command below the level of an air force or of an air division and above a group.

WRIT: A process issued out of a court.

WRITTEN DEPOSITION: Deposition taken on written interrogatories.

WRITTEN INTERROGATORIES: Questions, propounded by the prosecution or defense, or both, which are reduced to writing prior to submission to a witness whose testimony is to be taken by deposition on written interrogatories; the answers, reduced to writing and property sworn to, constitute the deposition of the witness.

WRONGFUL APPROPRIATION: The taking or withholding the property of another with intent temporarily to deprive or defraud another of its use or benefit, or to appropriate the same to his own use or the use of some one other than the true owner. **See Larceny.**

WRONGFULLY: As used in UCMJ Article 110, means contrary to law, regulation, lawful order, or custom.

Y

YEAR: In a sentence means 12 calendar months.

YEOMAN: A navy petty officer who performs clerical and secretarial duties.

Z

ZOOPHILIA: A passion for animals, often fetishistic in nature; erotic sexual relationship with animals.

A

A: Army.

AAA: Army Audit Agency.

AACS: Airways and Air Communications Service.

AAD: Admission and disposition.

AADA: Advanced Air Depot Area.

AAF: Army and Air Force; Army air field.

AAFCE: Allied Air Force, Central Europe.

AAFCWF: Army and Air Force Central Welfare Fund.

AAFEMPS: Army and Air Force Exchange and Motion Picture Service.

AAFES: Army and Air Force Exchange Service.

AAFMPS: Army and Air Force Motion Picture Service.

AAFNE: Allied Air Force, Northern Europe.

AAFPS: Army and Air Force Postal Service.

AAFSE: Allied Air Force, Southern Europe.

AAFWB: Army and Air Force Wage Board.

AAG: Air Adjutant General.

AAGR: Air to air gunnery range.

AAHA: Awaiting action higher authority.

AAM: Air to air missile.

AAML: Artic Aeromedical Laboratory.

A & B: Assault and battery.

AAOC: Anticraft Operations Center.

AAR: Aircraft Accident Report.

AARS: Army aircraft repair ship.

AB: Air Base; Aviation Boatswain's Mate.

ABC: Atomic, Biological, and chemical.

abbr: Abbreviation.

ABCD: Awaiting bad conduct discharge.

ABMA: Army Ballistic Missile Agency.

ABMC: American Battle Monuments Commission.

abn: Airborne.

abs: Absent.

ABSAP: Airborne search and attack plotter.

acad: Academic.

ACAN: Army Command and Administrative Network.

AC&SC: Air Command and Staff College.

AC&W: Aircraft control and warning.

ACB: Airmen Classification Battery; Army Classification Battery.

ACC: Air Coordinating Committee; Allied Control Commission; Air control center; Allied Control Council.

ACCA: Ad hoc Crypto-coordinating Agency.

accom: Accommodate.

accomp: Accomplish.

acct: Account.

acd: Accord.

acdt: Accident.

ACDUTRA: Active duty for training.

ACE: Allied Command Europe.

acft: Aircraft.

ACI: Air combat information; Air - controlled interception.

ACIC: Aeronautical Chart and Information.

ack: Acknowledge.

ACL: Allowable cabin load.

ACLant: Allied Command, Atlantic.

ACLV: Accrued leave.

ACM: Air court-martial; American Campaign Medal; Decision of the board of review of the United States Air Force.

acmp: Accompany.

ACMS: Special court-martial (U.S. Air Force).

ACMYS: Airman has completed seven or more years service.

ACofS: Assistant Chief of Staff.

ACOG: Aircraft on ground.

ACP: Allied communication publication.

ACPATT: All commands through which this shipment passes will process personnel as attached.

ACP DIR: Army Current Procurement Directive.

acpt: Accept.

acq: Acquittal.

ACQT: Aviation Cadet Qualification Test.

ACS: Alaskan Communication System.

ACSC: Air Command and Staff College.

ACSF: Attack Carrier striking force.

ACSI: Assistant Chief of Staff, Intelligence.

ACSRC: Assistant Chief of Staff for Reserve Components.

ACST: Army Clerical Speed Test.

ACT: Air Control Team.

act: Active, acting, or action.

ACTB: Aircrew Classification Test.

ACTMC: Army Clothing and Textile Material Center.

actv: Activate; activity.

ACW: Aircraft control warning.

AD: Active duty; air defense.

ad: Advice.

ADA: Air defense area.

ADAVAL: Advise availability.

ADC: Air Defense Command; Aide-de-camp.

ADCC: Air defense control center.

ADCOC: Area Damage Control Center.

ADCON: Advise all concerned.

add: Addition.

ADDC: Air defense direction center.

adee: Addressee.

ADep: Air depot.

ADF: Air direction finder.

ADGRU: Advisory group.

ADHCA: Advise this headquarters complete action.

ADI: Alien declared intention.

ADiv: Air division.

ADIZ: Air identification zone.

adj: Adjutant; adjust.

ADJFCUSA: Adjusted on basis of photostat or reviewed copy of temporary pay record from Finance Center, U.S. Army.

ADLATAD: Advise latest address, military if on duty, home if not on active duty.

Adm: Admiral.

ADMCEN: Administration Center.

ADMIN: Administrative Instructions.

admin: Administrate.

ADMINO: Administrative orders.

ADMSG: Advise by message.

ADSHIPDA or ADSHIPDAT: Advise shipping date.

ADSM: American Defense Service Medal.

ADTIC: Arctic, Desert, Tropic Information Center.

adv: Advance.

ADVON: Advanced echeleon.

ADW: Air defense warning; Assault with dangerous weapon.

ADWKP: Air defense warning key point.

A-E: Architect-Engineer.

AEC: Atomic Energy Commission.

AEF: Aviation engineer force.

AEOP: Amend existing orders pertaining to.

AER: Airman effectiveness report; Abbreviated effectiveness report; Army Emergency Relief.

AERNO: Aeronautical Equipment Reference Number.

aero: Aeronautics.

AEW: Airborne early warning.

AEWRon: Airborne early. warning squadron.

AF: Air Force with specific reference to the United States Air Force; Aviation Photographer's mate.

AFA: Army Flight Activity.

AFAC: Air Force Armament Center.

AFAS: Air Force Aid Society.

AFB: Air Force Base.

AFBU: Air Force base unit.

AFC: Army Finance Center; Automatic frequency control.

AFCE: Automatic flight control equipment.

AFCent: Allied Forces, Central Europe.

AFCRC: Air Force Cambridge Research Center.

AFCS: Active Federal Commissioned service.

AFDCCO: Air Force Departmental Catalog Coordinating Office.

AFEB: Armed Forces Epidemiological Board.

AFES: Armed Forces Examining Station.

AFF: Army Field Forces.

AFFC: Air Force Finance Center.

affd: affirmed.

affg: affirming.

AFFTC: Air Force Flight Test Center.

AFIED: Armed Forces Information and Education Division.

AFIP: Air Force Information Program; Armed Forces Institute of Pathology.

afirm: Affirmative.

AFIS: Armed Forces Information School.

AFJKT: Air Force Job Knowledge Test.

AFL: Air Force Letter.

afld: Airfield.

AFM: Air Force Manual.

AFMed: Allied Forces Mediterranean.

AFMTC: Air Force Missile Test Center.

AFNA: Air Force with Navy.

AFNC: Air Force Nurse Corps.

AFNGUS: Air National Guard of the United States.

AFNorth: Allied Forces, Northern Europe.

AFOQT: Air Force Officer Qualifying Test.

AFORD: Air Force Overseas Replacement Depot.

AFORG: Air Force Overseas Replacement Group.

AFOSCR: Air Force Organization Status Change Report.

AFOUAR: Air Force Outstanding Unit Award Ribbon.

AFP: Air Force Pamphlet.

AFPC: Air Force Procurement Circular.

AFPG: Air Force Personnel Processing Group.

AFPI: Air Force Procurement Instructions.

AFPP: Air Force Procurement Procedures.

AFPR: Air Force plant representative.

AFPS: Armed Forces Press Service.

AFPTRC: Air Force Personnel Training and Research Center.

AFPU: Air Force postal unit.

AFQT: Armed Forces Qualification Test.

AFQTVA: Armed Forces Qualification Test, Verbal Arithmetic.

AFR: Air Force Regulation.

AFRB: Air Force Retiring Board.

AFRCSTC: Air Force Reserve Combat Support Training Center.

AFRCTC: Air Force Reserve Combat Training Center.

AFResM: Armed Forces Reserve Medal.

AFRFTC: Air Force Reserve Flying Training Center.

AFRO: Air Force Reserve Orders.

AFROIC: Air Force Resident Officer in Charge.

AFROTC: Air Force Reserve Officers Training Corps.

AFRS: Armed Forces Radio Service.

AFRSTC: Air Force Reserve Specialist Training Center.

AFRTC: Air Force Reserve Training Center.

AFRTS: Armed Forces Radio and TV Service.

AFS: Air Force Specialty.

AFSA: Armed Forces Security Agency.

AFSC: Air Force Specialty Code; Armed Forces Staff College.

AFSMAAG: Air Force Section, Military Assistance Advisory Group.

AFSN: Air Force service number.

AFSouth: Allied Forces, Southern Europe.

AFSS: Air Force service statement.

AFRes: Air Force Reserve.

AFSWP: Armed Forces Special Weapons Project.

AFT: Air freight terminal.

AFTRC: Air Force Training Command.

AFUS: Air Force of the United States.

AFV: Armored Force vehicle.

AFVA: Air Force Visual Aid.

AFWAR: Air Force personnel on duty with Army.

AFWN: Air Force personnel on duty with Navy.

AFWST: Armed Forces Women's Selection Test.

AG: Adjutant General.

AGARD: Advisory Group for Aeronautical Research and Development.

AGC: Adjutant General's Corps.

AGCT: Army General Classification Test.

agcy: Agency.

AGF: Army Ground Forces.

AGN: Articles for Government of Navy.

AGO: Adjutant General's Office.

AGOS: Air-ground operations system.

AGP: Aircraft grounded for lack of parts.

AGRS: American Graves Registration Service.

AGS: Army General Staff.

ahd: Airhead.

AHP: Allied Hydrographic Publication.

AIF: Army Industrial Fund.

AIFUC: Assignment instructions were furnished your command.

AII: Army intelligence interpreter.

AirA: Air Force attache.

aja: Adjacent.

ALD: At a later date.

ALG: Advanced landing ground.

ALNAV: A general message having wide standard distribution in the Navy, originated by the Navy Department or fleet commander. Usually serially numbered, as an ALNAV.

aloc: Allocate.

alot: Allotment.

alt: Altitude.

altn: Alternate.

alw: Allowance.

AM: Air medal.

AMAS: American Military Assistance Staff.

amb: Ambulance.

AMBLADS: Advise method, bill of lading, and date shipped.

ambt: Ambulatory.

AMC: Air Material Command; Army Medical Center.

amdt: Amendment.

AMEDS: Army Medical Service.

AMG: Allied Military Government of Occupied Territory.

ammo: Ammunition.

AMOS: Alternate military occupational specialty.

amph: Amphibious.

AMS: Army Map Service.

AMSC: Army Medical Specialist Corps.

AMSS: Army Medical Service School.

AN: Army-Navy; Air Force-Navy.

ANC: Army Nurse Corps.

ANCR: Aircraft not combat ready.

ANDB: Air Navigation Development Board.

ANEXGOVT: At no expense to the government.

ann: Annotated; announce.

ANO: Above named officer.

ans: Answer.

ANSIA: Army-Navy Shipping Information Agency.

anx: Annex.

AO: Male Air Force Reserve and USAF Officer when used with a service number as in AO335464.

AOCM: Aircraft out of commission for maintenance.

AOCP: Aircraft out of commission for parts.

AOM: Army of occupation medal.

AP: Air police; Armour-piercing; ammunition point.

apar: Apparatus.

APC: Army Procurement Circular.

APCM: Asiatic-Pacific Campaign Medal.

APG: Air Proving Ground; Army Planning Group.

APIC: Army photo interpretation center.

APID: Army photo interpretation detachment.

APM: Air Provost Marshal.

APMA: Advanced payment of mileage authorized.

APMALTA: Advance payment of monetary allowance in leiu of transportation authorized.

APO: Air Force post office or Army post office.

APOD: Aerial port of debarkation.

APOE: Aerial port of embarkation.

APP: Army Procurement Procedure.

app: Appendix; apprehend.

appl: Applicable; applicant; application.

appr: Approve; apprenticeship.

APR: Air Priority.

aprop: Appropriate.

aprx: Approximate.

APS: Army Postal Service.

APSQ: Advance payment of subsistence and quarters.

APT: Airman Proficiency Test.

apt: Appoint; aptitude.

APTPDA: Advance payment of travel per diem authorized.

APU: Army postal unit.

APWI: Air prisoner of war interrogation.

AQB: Army Qualification Battery.

AQE: Airman Qualifying Examination.

AR: Army Regulations; Army; Arithmetic Reasoning Test; Airman recruit.

AR&D: Air Research and Development.

ARC: American Red Cross; Army Radio Code Aptitude Test.

ARCS: Air resupply and communication service.

ARDC: Air Research and Development Command.

ARI: Authority is requested inter the remains of.

ArLo: Army Liaison Officer.

armd: Armored.

armgrd: Armed guard.

armt: Armament.

ARNA: Army with Navy.

ARNG: Army National Guard.

ARNGUS: Army National Guard, of the United States.

arr: Arrive.

ARS: Air Rescue Service.

ARSIP: Arrears in pay.

art: Article.

ARTL: Awaiting results of trial.

arty: Artillery.

arv: Armored recovery vehicle.

ASA: Army Security Agency.

ASAP: As soon as possible.

ASBCA: Armed Services Board of Contract Appeals.

asg: Assign.

ASGS: Assistant Secretary of the General Staff.

aslt: Assault.

ASM: Air to surface missile.

ASMPA: Armed Services Medical Procurement Agency.

ASP: Ammunition supply point.

ASPA: Armed Services Procurement Act of 1947.

ASPB: Armed Services Petroleum Board.

ASPPA: Armed Services Petroleum Purchasing Agency.

ASPR: Armed Services Procurement Regulations.

ASR: Airport survellance radar; Airsea rescue; Available supply rate.

assoc: Associate.

asst: Assist.

assy: Assembly.

ASTIA: Armed Services Technical Information Agency.

ASTP: Army Specialized Training Program.

ASU: Area service unit.

ASW: Antisubmarine warfare.

ASWAF: Arms and Services on duty with Air Force.

ATA: Actual time of arrival.

ATAF: Allied tactical air force.

ATAG: Air Training Advisory Group.

ATB: Air Transportation Board.

ATC: Air Training Command; Air Traffic Control.

ATCC: Atlantic Division Transport Control Center.

atch: Attach.

ATD: Armament Test Division; Actual time of departure.

ATF: Air task force; Actual time of fall.

ath: Athletic.

ATI: Air technical intelligence.

atk: Attack.

ATO: Aircraft transfer order; Assist takeoff.

ATP: Allied Tactical Publication; Army Training Program.

ATRC: Air Training Command.

ATS: Air Tactical School.

ATSC: Air Technical Service Command.

ATT: Army Training Test.

attn: Attention.

attnd: Attendant.

AU: Air University; Army unit; Female Air Force Reserve and USAF Warrant Officer when used with a service number.

aug: Augment.

AUS: Army of the United States.

auth: Authority.

AUTHGR: Authority granted.

autmv: Automotive.

auto: Automatic.

Aux: Auxiliary.

aval: Available.

AV: Female Air Force Reserve and USAF Warrant Officer when used with a service number.

AVC: Automatice volume control, Aviation Cadet.

AvCad: Aviation cadet.

AVCS: Assistant Vice Chief of Staff.

AVFR: Available for reassignment.

avg: Average.

avn: Aviation.

AW: Automatic weapons; Article of War; Air warning in combination only; Male Air Force Reserve and USAF Warrant Officer when used with a service number.

AWC: Army War College; Air War College.

AWCO: Area Wage and Classification Office.

AWDISCOM: Awaiting disciplinary action this command.

AWOL: Absent without leave.

AWS: Air Weather Service.

awt: awaiting.

Az: Azmuth; Azores.

B

b: Base; bomber.

BABS: Blind approach beacon system.

BACU: Battle area control unit.

BAD: Berlin airlift device.

BADA: Base air deport area.

BAFCom: Basic Armed Forces Communication Plan.

bag: Baggage.

BAL: Base authorization list.

bal: Balance.

BAMO: Bureau of Aeronautics material officer.

B&G: Buildings and grounds.

B&GR: Bombing and gunnery range.

BAO: Budget and Accounting Officer.

BAPREPT: Beds and patients report.

BAQ: Basic allowance for quarters.

BAR: Browning automatic rifle; Bureau of Aeronautics representative.

BAS: Basic allowance for subsistence; Basic airspeed.

BASO: Base accountable supply officer.

bat: Battle; battleship.

BCD: Bad conduct discharge.

bcst: Broadcast.

BCT: Basic combat training.

bd: Board.

bdry: Boundary.

BG: Battle group; beach group.

BGR: Bombing and gunnery range.

bhd: Beachhead.

BI: Background investigation.

BIF: Bombardier's Information File.

bil: Billet.

biowar: Biological Warfare.

biv: Bivouac.

BIW: Battle injury or wound.

bks: Barracks.

BL: Bill of lading; bombline.

bloc: Blockade.

BLT: Battalion Landing Team.

BM: Bench mark.

bmbdr: Bombardier.

bmr: Bomber.

bn: Battalion.

BOI: Basis of issue.

BOQ: Bachelor officers quarters.

BP: Basic pay; Base point; Beach party.

BPED: Basic Pay Entry Date.

BPO: Base Post Office.

BR: Board of Review Decisions.

br: Branch.

Brit: British.

BR-JC: Army Board of Review and Judicial Counsel Decisions.

BSM: Bronze Star Medal.

btry: Battery.

btwn: Between.

BuAer: Bureau of Aeronautics.

BUDOCKS: Bureau of Yards and Docks (Navy).

bul: Bulletin.

BUMED: Bureau of Medicine and Surgery (Navy).

BUORD: Bureau of Ordnance (Navy).

BUPERS: Bureau of Naval Personnel.

BUSANDA: Bureau of Supplies and Accounts (Navy).

BUSHIPS: Bureau of Ships (Navy).

BUWEPS: Bureau of Weapons (Navy).

BW: Biological warfare.

BX: Base exchange.

C

C: Chief.

CA: Civil Affairs; Convening authority; Court of Appeals.

CAB: Civil Aeronautics Board.

CADF: Central Air Defense Force.

CADO: Central Air Documents Office.

CAG: Carrier air group.

CAirC: Caribbean Air Command.

cal: Caliber.

CAM: Commercial air movement.

CAMG: Civil Affairs/Military Government.

can: Cancel.

cand: Candidate.

C&GSC: Command and General Staff College.

CAP: Civil Air Patrol; Combat air control.

cap: capacity.

Capt: Captain.

cas: Casualty.

cat: Category.

CAtk: Counterattack.

Cau: Caucasian.

CB: Control brach; Construction battalion.

CBCC: Conviction by civil court.

CBNC: Collective Bargaining Negotiations and Contracts.

CBI: Complete background investigation.

CBR: Chemical, biological and radiological warfare.

CBTI: Combat intelligence.

CC: Combat command; Control center; Common carrier; Channel Command.

CCF: Contract Cases Federal.

CCH: Commerce Clearing House.

CCmlO: Chief Chemical Officer.

CCN: Contract change notification.

CCPO: Central civilian personnel office.

CCr: Combat crew.

CD: Corpus delicti.

Cdr: Commander (U.S. Navy)

cdt: Conduct.

CE: Corps of Engineers.

CEC: Civil Engineer Corps.

cel: Celestial.

cem: Cemetery.

cen: Center.

cens: Censor.

CER: Commanders Evaluation Report.

cert: Certificate.

cert. den.: Writ of certiorari denied.

cfm: Confirm.

CFR: Code of Federal Regulations.

CFSSB: Central Flight Status Selection Board.

CG: Comanding General; Coast Guard.

CGAS: Coast Guard Air Station.

CGCM: Decision of the board of review of the United States Coast Guard.

CGR: Coast Guard Regulations.

cgo: Cargo.

chan: Channel.

chg: Charge.

chmn: Chairman.

CI: Counter Intelligence.

CIA: Central Intelligence Agency.

CIC: Counterintelligence corps; Combat information center; Commander in Chief.

CID: Criminal Investigation Division.

CIIC: Counter Intelligence interrogation center.

CIL: Certificate in lieu of.

CINC: Commander in Chief, used only in combinations.

CINFO: Chief of Information.

cir: Circular.

circ: Circumstance.

cit: Citation; citizen.

civ: Civil; civilian.

CJTF: Commander Joint Task Force.

CL: Clerical Aptitude Area.

cl: Class; carload.

clas: Classify.

CLL: Chief of Legislative Liaison.

CLMA: Clothing monetary allowance.

cln: Colon.

clnc: Clearance.

clo: Clothing.

clr: Clearing.

CLUS: Continental limits United States.

CM: Court-martial; Decision of a board of review of the United States Army.

CMA: Court of Military Appeals.

cmbt: Combat.

CMC: Commandant of the Marine Corps.

CMF: Court-martial forfeiture.

CmlC: Chemical Corps.

cmm: Comma.

CMMR: Hereby confirmed and made a matter of record.

CMO: Court-Martial Orders.

cmo: Commodore.

cmpl: Complete.

CMR: Court-Martial Reports.

cmt: Comment.

CNA: Chief of Naval Air.

cncr: Concurrent.

cnf: Confine.

CNGB: Chief, National Guard Bureau.

CNM: Chief of Naval Material.

CNO: Chief of Naval Operations.

cntn: Contain.

cntr: Contribute.

cnvt: Convict.

CO: Commanding Officer; Chain Overseas.

CoA: Comptroller of the Army.

CofCh: Chief of Chaplains.

CofEngrs: Chief of Engineers.

CofF: Chief of Finance.

CofOrd: Chief of Ordnance.

CofS: Chief of Staff.

CofT: Chief of Transportation.

COG: Convenience of the Government; Commander of the guard.

CoGard: Coast Guard.

Col: Colonel.

coll: Collect.

colm: Column.

Com. or Comm.: Department of Commerce.

com: Commission; complement; committee.

COMATS: Commander Military Air Transportation Service.

comb: Combine.

COMCM: Communication countermeasures and deception.

cmd: Command.

Comdt: Commandant.

coml: Commercial.

CommCen: Communications center.

comp: Component; composite.

compate: Compassionate.

compen: Compensate.

Comp Gen: Comptroller General of the United States.

Compt: Comptroller.

COMSTS: Commander, Military Sea Transportation Service.

comsy: Commissary.

con: Conversation; consul; consulate; control.

ConAC: Continental Air Command.

Cong: Congress.

CONAD: Continental Air Defense.

conc: Concentrate.

cond: Condition.

conec: Connection.

conf: Confidential conference.

Cong: Congress.

cons: Consider; consist.

const: Constitute; construct.

constab: constabulary.

consv: Conserve.

cont: Continue.

contem: Contemplate.

contl: Continental.

contr: Contract.

ConUS: Continental United States.

conv: Convalescent.

convl: Conventional.

convn: Convenient.

coord: Coordinate.

COR: Contracting Officer's Representative.

corr: Correspond.

COR: Combat Operations Report.

COS: Civilian Occupation Speciality.

CP: Command post; copilot.

CPA: Combat pay.

cpbl: Capable.

CPD: Civilian Personnel Division.

CPFF: Cost-plus-fixed-fee.

Cpl: Corporal.

CPPC: Cost-plus-percentage-of-cost.

CPX: Command post exercise.

CQ: Charge of quarters; By extension a person in charge of quarters.

CR: Commendation ribbon; Crossroads.

CRD: Chief of Research and Development.

crim: Criminal.

CRPL: Central Radio Propagation Laboratory.

CRT: Combat Readiness training.

crt: Correct.

crypto: Cryptographer; cryptographic; or cryptography.

CSC: Civil Service Commission.

CSigO: Chief Signal Officer.

CSJAGA: Military Affairs Division, Office of the Judge Advocate General of the Army.

CSPM: Communication Security Publication Memorandum.

Ct: Court.

Ct Cl: Court of Claims Reports.

curr: Current; currency.

cust: Custody.

cvn: Convene.

CW: Chemical warfare.

CWO: Chief warrant officer.

cy: Copy.

CZ: Combat Zone.

D

DA: Department of the Army.

DAF: Department of the Air Force.

DAI: Death from accidental injuries.

DALVP: Delay enroute authorized chargeable as ordinary leave provided it does not interfere with reporting on date specified and providing individual has sufficient accrued leave.

dam: Damage.

DAR: Daily Activity Report.

DATO: Disbursing and transportation officer.

DB: Disciplinary barracks.

DC: Dental Corps; Defense counsel or District of Columbia.

DCG: Deputy Command General.

DCofS: Deputy Chief of Staff.

DCS: Deputy Chief of Staff, used in combination: DCS/C, Deputy Chief of Staff Controller, etc.

DCSLOG: Deputy Chief of Staff for Logistics.

DCSOPS: Deputy Chief of Staff for Military Operations.

DCSPER: Deputy Chief of Staff for Personnel.

DD: Dishonorable discharge.

DDALV: Days delay en route authorized chargeable as leave.

DDD: Deadline delivery date.

debk: Debark.

dec: Decrease, decision.

decd: Deceased.

decn: Decision.

ded: Deduct.

def: Defense; defend.

del: Delegate or delegation.

DELACCT: Delinquent acount.

DEML: Detached enlistmen's list.

demob: Demobilize or demobilization.

den: Dental, dentist, or dentistry.

dep: Depot.

depn: Dependent or dependency.

dept: Department.

DEROS: Date eligible for return from overseas.

dest: Destroy; destination.

destn: Destination.

det: Detach or detachment.

detm: Determine.

dev: Develop.

DF: Direction finding (er); disposition form; defensive fire.

DFC: Distinguishd Flying Cross.

DIA: Date of initial appointment.

DID: Daily Intelligence Digest.

Dig Ops: Digest of Opinions—The Judge Advocates General of the Armed Forces.

DIR: Depot inspection and repair.

dir: Direct.

disap: Disapprove.

disch: Discharge.

discrm: Discriminate.

disem: Disseminate.

dism: Dismiss.

disqual: Disqualify.

disre: Disregard.

dist: District.

distr: Distribute.

DK: Disbursing clerk.

dlvr: Deliver or delivery.

DMO: Defense Mobilization Order.

DMOS: Duty military occupational specialty.

DN: Department of the Navy.

dn: Denied.

DO: Defense Order.

DOA: Dead on arrival.

DOB: Date of birth.

doc: Document.

DOCA: Date of current appointment.

DOCE: Date of current enlistment.

DOCG: Date of rank in current grade.

docu: Document.

DOD: Department of Defense; Died of disease.

DOE: Date of enlistment.

DOP: Detachment of patients.

DOS: Date of separation.

DOW: Died of wounds.

DP: By direction of the President; Displaced person; Distribution point.

DPA: Defense Production Administration.

DPG: Date of permanent grade.

DPM: Designated for prompt mobilization.

DR: Date of rank; dead reckoning.

DROS: Date returned from overseas.

DS: Detached service; direct support; Date of service.

dsabl: Disable or disability.

DSC: Distinguished Service Cross.

DSM: Distinguished Service Medal.

dspln: Disciplinary or discipline.

DTG: Date-time-group.

DTO: District transportation officer.

DUCE: Distinguished Unit Citation Emblem.

DUE: Distinguished Unit Emblem.

dy: duty.

E

EAC: Eastern Air Command.

EDCSA: Effective date of change of strength accountability.

EDFR: Effective date of federal recognition.

EDRT: Effective date of relief from training.

EDS: Estimated date of separation.

EDSA: Effective date of change in station assignment.

EDT: Effect date of training.

educ: Education.

EEI: Essential elements of information.

EES: Enlisted Evaluation System.

EET: Education Equivalency Test.

EFD: Excused from duty.

eff: Effect.

effcy: Efficiency.

EG: Expert gunner.

EIT: Electrical Information Test.

EKG: Electrocardiogram.

EL: Education level.

elig: Eligible.

ELM: Eastern Atlantic and Mediterranean.

EM: Enlisted man or enlisted men; Education Manual.

EMCCC: European Military Communications Coordinating Committee.

emerg: Emergency.

EMR: Enlisted manning report.

EMT: Emergency medical tag.

en: Enemy; Engineman.

enl: Enlist.

enr: en route.

ens: Ensign.

EO: Executive Order.

EOA: Effective on or about.

EOD: Entry on duty; explosive ordnance disposal.

EOS: Eligible for overseas service.

EPD: Earliest practicable date.

EPTE: Existed prior to entry.

EPTS: Existed prior to service.

eqp: Equipment.

ER: Emergency rescue; Effectiveness report.

ERB: Equipment Review Board.

ERC: Enlisted Reserve Corps.

ERFA: European Radio-Frequency Agency.

ES: Eligible for separation.

esn: Essential.

ESPWO: Exigencies of the service having been such as to preclude the issuance of competent written orders in advance.

EST: Enlistment Screening Test.

ETA: Estimated time of arrival.

ETC: Estimated time of completion.

ETD: Estimated time of departure.

ETE: Estimate time en route.

ETN: Equipment table nomenclature.

ETO: European Theater of Operations.

ETR: Estimated time of return.

ETS: Expiration term of service.

ETSP: Entitled to severance pay.

eval: Evaluate or evaluation.

EW: Enlisted woman; or enlisted women; Early warning; Electronics warfare.

EWR: Early-warning radar.

exp: Expend, expense, or express.

explo: Explosive or explosion.

expr: Expire or expiration.

ext: Extend or extension.

F

FA: Family allowance; field artillery.

FAdm: Fleet Admiral.

FAir: Fleet Air.

fam: Family.

FBI: Federal Bureau of Investigation.

FC: Finance Corps.

FCC: Federal Communications Commission; Fighter control center.

FD: Finance Department.

FDP: Foreign duty pay.

FEAF: Far East Air Forces.

FEB: Flying Evaluation Board.

FEC: Far East Command.

Fed: Federal.

fgn: Foreign.

FICA: Federal Insurance Contributions Act.

1Sgt: First Sergeant.

fld: Field.

FLDO: Field officer.

FM: Field manual.

FMACC: Foreign Military Assistance Coordinating Committee.

FMASC: Foreign Military Assistance Steering Committee.

FMF: Fleet Marine Force.

FN: Flight nurse.

FNA: Following named airmen.

FNOA: Following named officers and airmen.

FO: Field order, finance officer or forward observer.

FOA: Foreign Operations Agency.

FOB: Free on board.

FofF: Field of fire.

fol: Follow.

FOLNOAVAL: Following items not available.

forf: Forfeit.

FP: Flight pay.

FPO: Fleet post office.

FPR: Field personnel record.

FR: Federal Register.

FRD: Federal Rules Decisions.

FRE: Field representative, Europe.

freq: Frequent or frequency.

f rev: **Further review.**

FRFE: Field representative, Far East.

FS:. Field Services; Film strip.

FSA: Federal Security Agency.

FSC: Foreign service credits.

FSP: Foreign service pay.

FSS: Federal Supply Schedule.

FSSD: Foreign service selection date.

ft: Feet; foot; fort.

FTAF: Flying Training Air Force.

FTC: Flying Training Command.

FUPOSAT: Follow up on supply action taken.

FUSA: First United States Army.

FUSAG: First United States Army Group.

FWPA: First War Powers Act.

FY: Fiscal Year.

FYI: For your information.

FYIG: For your information and guidance.

G

G1: Assist. Chief of Staff, G-1, Personnel.

G2: Assist. Chief of Staff, G-2, Intelligence.

G3: Assist. Chief of Staff, G-3, Operations.

G4: Assist. Chief of Staff, G-4, Logistics.

GAC: General agency check.

GAO: General Accounting

gar: Garrison.

GBL: Government bill of lading.

GC: Government contribution; General Counsel.

GCM: General court-martial; Good Conduct Medal.

GCMA: General Court-Martial Authority.

GCMO: General court-martial order.

GCT: General Classification Test.

GD: General discharge.

GEDT: General Education Development Test.

gen: General.

GERA: Guard's expense in returning absentee.

GFAE: Government furnished aircraft equipment.

GFE: Government-furnished equipment.

GFM: Government furnished material.

GFP: Government furnished property.

GH: General hospital when used with the name of the hospital.

GHQ: General Headquarters.

GI: Government issue.

gig: A demerit or penalty.

GIT: General Information Test.

GLSM: Gold Life Saving Medal.

GM: Guided missile.

GMS: General Military Science.

GMST: General Military Subjects Test.

GO: General Orders.

GOCO: Government-Owned Contractor-Operated.

Govt: Government.

GP: General purpose.

gp: Group.

GPLD: Government property lost or damaged.

GPO: Government Printing Office.

GPVEH: General purpose vehicle.

GR: Gunnery range.

gr: Granted.

grd: Guard.

grdhse: Guardhouse.

GRS: Graves registration service.

GS: General support; General Staff Officer.

GSA: General Service Administration.

GSC: General Staff Corps.

GSD: General supply depot.

GSS: General service school.

GSUSA: General Staff, US Army.

GT: General Technical Aptitude Area.

H

har: Harbor.

HD: Honorable discharge; Harbor defense; Historical Division.

HE: High explosive.

HEW: Department of Health, Education & Welfare.

HF: High frequency.

HHFA: Housing & Home Finance Agency.

HMG: Heavy machine gun.

HNG: Hawaiian National Guard.

HOI: Headquarters Office Instruction.

hon: Honor.

HOR: Home of record.

HPT: High-pressure test.

hq: Headquarters.

HRS: Honorary Reserve Section.

HV: High velocity.

hwy: Highway.

hyd: Hydraulic.

hydro: Hydrographic.

I

I&E: Information and Education.

I&M: Installation and Maintenance.

I&R: Intelligence and reconnaissance.

IAOD: In addition to other duties.

IAPO: Industrial accountable property officer.

IATR: Is amended to read.

IB: Incendiary bomb.

IC: In charge of; internal combustion.

ICAF: Industrial College of the Armed Forces.

ICAO: International Civil Aviation Organization.

ICBM: Intercontinental ballistic missile.

ICC: Interstate Commerce Commission.

ICFATCMUTAL: Individual is cleared for access to classified material up to and including.

ICUS: Inside continental United States.

ICW: In compliance with; Interrupted continuous wave.

ident: Identify; identification.

IE: Information and Education.

IFB: Invitation for bid.

IFF: Identification, friend or foe.

IFR: Instrument flight rules.

IFRB: International Frequency Registration Board.

IFT: In-flight test.

IG: Inspector general.

IGD: Inspector General's Department.

IHCA: In hands of civil authorities.

IHP: Indicated horsepower.

ILA: Instrument landing approach.

ILO: In lieu of.

ILOUE: In lieu of until exhausted.

ILS: Instrument landing system.

ILT: In lieu thereof.

IM: Interceptor missile.

imm: Immune or immunity.

immat: Immaterial.

immed: Immediate or immediately.

IMR: Individual medical record.

IMTP: Industrial Mobilization Training Program.

IN: Infantry Aptitude Area.

incl: Inclose or include.

incom: Incomplete.

indct: Induct or induction.

indef: Indefinite.

indiv: Individual.

indoc: Indoctrinate.

Ind. Rev. Reg.: Industrial Personnel Security Review Regulation, Department of Defense.

induc: Induction.

inf: Infantry.

InfoCen: Information center.

init: Initial.

inj: Injure.

inl: Initial.

INO: Issue necessary orders.

INOAVNOT: If not available notify this office at once.

InReq: Information request.

ins: Insure or insurance.

insp: Inspect.

inst: Instrument; Instruction; Instant.

Int: Department of Interior.

intel: Intelligence.

intcp: Intercept or interceptor.

interf: Interference.

intg: Interrogate or interrogator.

intl: International.

intmed: Intermediate.

intns: Intransit.

intpr: Interpret or interpreter.

IntRept: Intelligence Report.

IntSum: Intelligence summary.

InUS: Inside the United States.

inv: Invent; Invoice.

inves: Investigate or investigator.

IO: Investigating officer.

IOH: Item on hand.

IPW: Interrogation prisoner of war.

IRAC: Interdepartmental Radio Advisory Committee.

IRAN: Inspection and repair as necessary.

IRBM: Intermediate range ballistic missile.

IRC: International Red Cross.

IRO: International Refugee Organization.

ISL: Inactive status list.

ISO: Information Services Officer.

iss: Issue.

IWISTK: Issue while in stock.

J

JA: Judge Advocate.

JAAF: Joint action Armed Forces; Joint Army-Air Force.

JAAFAR: Joint Army-Air Force Adjustment Regulations.

JAAFCTB: Joint Army-Air Force Commercial Traffic Bulletin.

JAAFPC: Joint Army-Air Force Procurement Circular.

JADF: Japan Air Defense Force.

JAG: Judge Advocate General.

JAGA: Military Affairs Division Office of The Judge Advocate General of the Army.

JAGC: Judge Advocate General's Corps.

JAGO: Office of the Judge Advocate General of the Army.

JAGT: Opinions of the Procurement Law Division, JAGO.

JALS: Judge Advocate Legal Service (Army).

JAMAG: Joint American Military Advisory Group.

JAMMAT: Joint Military Mission for Aid to Turkey.

JAN: Joint Army-Navy.

JANAP: Joint Army-Navy-Air Force Publication.

JANAST: Joint Army-Navy-Air Force sea transportation message.

JANIS: Joint Army-Navy Intelligence Study.

JATO: Jet-assisted takeoff.

JBUSMC: Joint Brazil-United States Military Commission.

JCA: Joint communication activity.

JCEC: Joint Communications-Electronics Committee.

JCI: Joint communications instructions.

JCS: Joint Chiefs of Staff.

JIC: Joint Intelligence Center.

JICA: Joint Intelligence Collecting Agency.

JIG: Joint Intelligence Group.

JLFB: Joint Landing Force Board.

JLPC: Joint Logistics Plans Committee.

JMTC: Joint Military Transportation Committee.

JOC: Joint Operations Center.

JPR: Joint Procurement Regulation.

JSPC: Joint Strategic Plans Committee.

JSPG: Joint Strategic Survey Committee.

JSSC: Joint Strategic Survey Committee.

JTF: Joint Task Force.

JTR: Joint Travel Regulation.

juris: Jurisdiction.

JUSMAG: Joint United States Military Advisory Group.

JUSMAP: Joint United States Military Advisory and Planning Group.

JUSMG: Joint United States Military Group.

Justice: Department of Justice.

K

kd: Killed.

ki: Kitchen.

KIA: Killed in action.

KMAG: United States Military Advisory Group to the Republic of Korea.

KP: Kitchen police.

KSM: Korean Service Medal.

kw: Kilowatt.

L

LA: Low altitude; Labor Arbitration Reports.

lab: Laboratory.

Labor: Department of Labor.

LAM: Latin-American Mission.

LC: Legitimate child; Line of contact; Liaison cargo; Landing craft.

LCAVAT: Landing craft and amphibious vehicle assignment table.

lcdr: Lieutenant commander.

LCL: Less than carload lot.

LCT: Latest closing time; Local civil time; Landing craft, tank.

LD: Line of duty; Line of departure; landing.

LDC: Light direction center.

ldg: Landing.

LDO: Limited duty officer.

ldr: Leader.

ldry: Laundryman.

LE: Low explosive; Light equipment.

leg: Legislate, legislation, or legislative—in combination only.

LF: Low frequency.

lgth: Length.

lh: Lighthouse.

li: Lithographer.

LIO: Lesser included offense.

liq: Liquid.

LM: Legion of Merit.

LMF: Last meal furnished.

LMG: Light machine gun.

lmn: Lineman.

LMT: Local mean time.

lmt: Limit or limitation.

ln: Liaison.

LO: Law officer; Lubrication order; Letter order.

lo: 'local' in combination only.

LOA: Leave of absence.

LOC: Line of communication.

LOD: Line of duty.

log: Logistics.

LOP: Line of position.

LOS: Line of sight.

loy: Loyalty.

LP: Last paid; Litter patient.

LPD: Local procurement direct.

LR: Long range.

LRNA: Laws relating to the Navy Annotated.

LT: Landing team.

lt: Lieutenant; light.

LTA: Leave travel allowance; Lighter than air.

lt col or LTCOL: Lieutenant colonel.

ltd: Limited.

LTG: Lieutenant general.

lt gen also LTGEN: Lieutenant general.

lthr: Leather.

LtJG: Lieutenant junior grade.

LTL: Less than truckload.

ltr: Letter.

LtrO: Letter order.

lub: Lubricate.

lv: Leave.

lwop: Leave without pay.

LZ: Landing zone.

M

MAAG: Military Assistance Advisory Group.

MABRON: Marine air base squadron.

MAC: Major air command.

MACG: Marine air control group.

mach: Machine; machinist or machinery.

MACR: Missing aircrew report.

MAD: Marine air detachment.

MADAEC: Military Application Division of the Atomic Energy Commission.

MADW: Military Air Defense Warning.

MAE: Medical air evacuation.

MAF: Major academic field.

MAFS: Mobilization. Air Force Speciality.

MAFSC: Mobilization Air Force Speciality Code.

MAG: Marine aircraft group.

maj: Major.

maj gen also MAJGEN: Major general.

MAL: Material allowance list.

M&R: Maintenance and repair.

mand: Mandatory.

MANOP: Manual of operations.

MAP: Military Aid Program.

MAPAG: Military Assistance Program Advisory Group.

mar: march.

MAQ: Monetary allowance in lieu of quarters.

Mar also MAR: Marine, in combinations only.

MarAllWeaFiTraRon: Marine allweather fighter training squadron.

MarCor also MARCOR: Marine Corps in combination only.

MaritAdmin: Maritime Administration.

MaritCom: Maritime Commission.

MARS: Military Affiliated Radio System.

MAS: Monetary allowance in lieu of subsistence; Military Agency for Standardization.

MAT: Mechanical Aptitude Test.

matno: Material (requested) not available.

MATS: Military Air Transportation Service.

matso: Material requested being supplied.

MAW: Marine aircraft wing.

max: Maximum.

MB: Munitions Board; Missile bomber.

MBad: Medical badge.

MBI: May be issued.

mbl: Mobile.

mbr: Member.

MBRUU: May be retained until unserviceable.

MC: Medical Corps or Member of Congress.

MCA: Military Construction, Army.

MCAB: Marine Corps air base.

MCAF: Marine Corps air facility.

MCC: Military Coordinating Committee.

MCM: Manual for Courts-Martial.

MCO: Main civilian occupation.

MCR: Master change record.

MD: Movement directive; Medical department.

MDAA: Mutual Defense Assistance Act.

MDAP: Mutual Defense Assistance Program.

MDRS: Mobolization Designation Reserve Section.

MDW: Military District of Washington.

MEE: Minimum essential equipment.

MEMQ: Married enlisted men's quarters.

MEW: Microwave early warning.

MF: Medium frequency.

MFcT: Major fraction thereof.

mfg: Manufacturing.

MFHA: Medal for Humane Action.

mfr: Manufacture or manufacturer.

MG: Machine gun; Major general.

MGO: Military government officer.

mgr: Manager.

mgt: Management.

MH: Medal of Honor.

MI: Military Intelligence, Middle initial.

MIA: Missing in action.

MII: Military intelligence interpreter.

mil: Military.

milgovt: Military government.

MIPR: Military interdepartmental purchase. request.

mis: Missing.

misc: Miscellaneous.

miscon: Misconduct.

MISR: Major item status report.

MIT: Military intelligence translator.

mk: Mark.

mkm: Marksman.

ML: Military payroll money list, Military Laws of The U.S. (Army) annotated.

ml: Molder.

MLCAEC: Military Liaison Committee to the Atomic Energy Commission.

MLG: Main landing gear.

MLR: Main line of resistance.

MM: Medal for Merit.

mm: Millimeter.

MMSA: Military Medical Supply Agency.

MN: Magnetic north.

mntn: Maintain.

mo: Month.

MoARS: Mobilization Assignment Reserve Section.

mob: Mobilize.

mod: Modify or modification.

MOIC: Medical officer in command.

mon: Monetary.

montrg: Monitoring.

MOP: Mustering-out pay(ment).

MOPR: Manner-of-performing rating.

MOQ: Married officers quarters.

MOS: Military occupational specialty.

MOT: Month of travel.

mot: Motion.

mov: Movement.

MP: Military police.

MPC: Military payment certificate; Military Police Corps.

MPCI: Military Police Criminal Investigation.

MPerR: Master Personnel Record.

MPO: Military pay order; Military Permit Office.

MPR: Military pay record; Master personnel record.

MPSA: Military Petroleum Supply Agency.

MPV: Military Pay Voucher.

MR: Morning report; machine records.

MRC: Movement Report Center.

MRCC: Movement Report Control Center.

MRD: Material Redistribution Division.

MRO: Movement Report Office.

MRS: Military Railway Service.

MRU: Machine records unit; Mobile radio unit.

MS: Major subject; Ship station, as used by NATO.

MSA: Mutual Security Agency.

MSC: Medical Service Corps.

MS Comp. Gen.: Manuscript decisions of the Comptroller General.

MSF: Mobile striking force.

msg: Message.

msgcen: Message center.

msgfm: Messageform.

MSGp: Mobile support group.

msgr: Messenger.

MSgt: Master sergeant.

msl: Missile.

msn: Mission.

MSP: Mutual security program.

MSR: Main supply route.

mstr: Master.

MSTS: Military Sea Transport Service.

MSTSO: Military Sea Transportation Service Office.

MTCA: Ministry of Transport and Civil Aviation, British.

MTCC: Military Air Transport Service, Transport Control (Hq).

mtl: Material or materiel; Metal.

MTP: Mobolization training program.

mtr: Motor.

mtrcl: Motorcycle.

mtrg: Metering.

MTU: Mobile training unit.

MUE: Meritorious Unit Emblem.

mun: Munition.

muni: Municipal.

mux: Multiplex.

mvmt: Movement.

MWO: Modification work order.

M/Y: Marshaling yards.

N

N: Navy in combinations; Negroid.

NA: Not applicable; Naval Air, in combination only.

NAAFI: Navy-Army-Air Force Institute, the British counterpart of the USO.

NAC: National Agency Check; North Atlantic Council.

NACA: National Advisory Committee for Aeronautics.

NaDefCol: Nato Defense College.

NaDevCen: Naval Air Development Center.

NAF: Naval Air Facility.

NAMilCom: North Atlantic Military Committee.

NARS: Non-affiliated Reserve Section.

NAS: Naval Air Station.

NASA: National Aeronautics and Space Administration.

nat: National.

NatDefSm: National Defense Service Medal.

NATO: North Atlantic Treaty Organization.

nav: Navigate, navigation, navigational, or navigator.

NavCm: Navigation countermeasures and deception.

NaWAF: Navy with Air Force.

NaWAr: Navy with Army.

NCD: Notice of credit due.

NCM: Navy Board of Review Decision.

NCO: Noncommissioned officer.

NCOIC: Noncommissioned officer in charge.

NCS: Net control station.

NCW: Not complied with.

ND: Navy Department.

NDA: National Defense Act.

NDR: Normal daily requirement.

NDRC: National Defense Research Committee.

nec: Necessary.

neg: Negative.

NET: Not earlier than.

NF: Newfoundland.

NFC: Not favorably considered.

NFR: No further requirement.

NG: National Guard; Not guilty.

NGB: National Guard Bureau.

NGLO: Naval gunfire liaison officer.

NGLT: Naval gunfire liaison team.

NGR: National Guard Regulations.

NGUS: National Guard of the United States.

ni: Night.

NIS: Not in stock; National Intelligence Survey.

NLD: Not in line of duty.

NLF: Nearest landing field.

NLO: Naval Liaison Officer.

NLT: On or before but not later than.

NME: National Military Establishment.

nmi: No middle initial.

NOA: Not otherwise authorized.

NOAFIRM: Affirmative replies neither required nor desired.

nocost: This travel is authorized with the understanding that no expense to the government will be involved.

NODEL: Not to delay.

NOE: Notice of exception.

NOFORN: Special handling required. Not releasable to foreign Nationals. Used on classified materials.

NOIBN: Not otherwise indexed by name.

nom: Nominate.

nomen: Nomenclature.

noneg: Negative replies neither required nor desired.

Nor: Nonrated; North, used in combination only.

norm: Normal.

NOTAM: Notice to airmen. Pronounced and used as a word.

NP: Neuropsyciatry.

NPD: Navy Procurement Directives.

NPO: Navy Post Office.

NPOPR: Not paid on prior rolls.

NPR: Navy Procurement Regulations.

NPS: No prior service.

nr: Number.

NRA: No repair action.

NRFI: Not ready for issue.

NRL: Naval Research Laboratory.

ns: Nonstandard.

NSA: National Security Agency.

NSC: National Security Council.

NSI: Nonstandard item.

NSLI: National Service Life Insurance.

NSRB: National Security Resources Board.

NST: Not sooner than.

NTC: Normal tour of duty completed.

ntcaval: Notice of availability.

ntfy: Notify.

NTI: No travel involved.

NTIOC: No travel involved for officer concerned.

NTL: No time lost.

nur: Nurse or nursing.

NVAL: Not available.

NWC: National War College.

NYR: Not yet reported.

O

O: Officer or order, used in combinations only; Office.

OA: On or about. Often written o/a.

OA&S: Other Arms and Services.

O and R: Overhaul and repair.

OAR: Organized Air Reserve.

OB: Order of battle.

ob: Obsolete.

obj: Objective or object.

obl: Oblique.

oblg: Obligate or obligation.

obs: Obstacle.

obsn: Observation.

obsr: Observe or observer.

obsy: Observatory.

OC: Officer candidate.

OCAFF: Office, Chief of Army Field Forces.

occ: Occupation.

OCE: Officer conducting the exercise.

OCLUS: Outside continental limits United States.

OCMH: Office of the Chief of Military History (Army).

OCofF: Office of the Chief of Finance.

OComS: Office of Community Services.

OConUS: Outside Continental United States.

OCS: Office of Contract Settlement.

OD: Officer of the day; Olive drab.

ODM: Office of Defense Mobilization.

ofc: Office.

off: Officer.

ofl: Official.

OG: Officer of the guard.

OGC: Office of the General Counsel.

OIC: Officer in charge.

OICC: Officer in charge of construction.

OIR: Office of Industrial Relations.

OJT: On-the-job training.

OL: Operating location.

OLA: Office of Legislative Affairs.

OLC: Oak-leaf cluster.

OLF: Outlying field.

OM: Occupation Medal, as used with specific reference to Germany or Japan; Officer messenger.

OMA: Office of Military Assistance.

OMGUS: Office of Military Government, United States.

ONI: Office of Naval Intelligence.

ONM: Office of Naval Material.

ONR: Office of Naval Research.

OP: Observation post.

op or ops: Opinion or opinions.

Op Atty Gen: Opinions of the Attorney General.

OPlan: Operation plan.

OPLR: Outpost line of resistance.

Op Nav: Office of the Chief of Naval Operations.

opnl: Operational.

opord: Operations order.

opp: Opposite.

oppor: Opportunity.

ops: Operations.

opt: Optical.

OQR: Officer's Qualification Record.

OR: Overseas replacement.

ORC: Organized Reserve Corps.

ord: Ordnance, order.

OrdC: Ordnance Corps.

ordcan: Orders cancelled.

ordconcan: Orders considered cancelled.

ordcor: Orders are hereby corrected.

ordy: Ordinary.

org: Organize, organization, or organizational.

ORI: Operational readiness inspection.

orig: Origin, original, or originator.

ORT: Operational readiness test.

ortho: Orthopedic.

OS: Overseas or oversea.

OSA: Office of the Secretary of the Army.

OSAF: Office of the Secretary of the Air Force.

OSD: Office of the Secretary of Defense; Ordnance Supply Depot.

OS/D: Over, short and damaged report.

OSI: Office of Special Investigation.

OSN: Office of the Secretary of the Navy.

OSR: Overseas returnee.

OSSN: Other Specialty Serial Numbers.

OT: Observer-target.

OTC: Officer in tactical command.

OTS: Officer training school.

OTSG: Office of the Surgeon General.

OTT: One time tape.

OTU: Operational training unit.

OUTC: Ordnance unit training center.

ovhl: Overhaul.

ovpd: Overpaid.

oxy: Oxygen.

P

PAC: Pursuant to authority contained in.

Pac: Pacific.

PAD: Port of aerial debarkation.

P.A.D.: Passive air defense. British.

PADoc: Pay adjustment document.

PAE: Port of aerial embarkation.

PAF: Pacific Air Force.

PAFS: Primary Air Force Specialty.

pahel: Pay record and health record.

PAL: Personnel augmentation list; Prisoner at large.

palcru: Pay and allowance accrue from.

PAM: Personnel actions memorandum; Pulse amplitude modulation.

pam: Pamphlet.

PAMO: Port Air Materiel Office.

P&EML: Personnel and equipment modification list.

pandl: Pay and allowances.

para: Paragraph; parachute, or parachuting—used only in prefix combinations.

parec: Pay record.

paren: Parenthesis.

PAS: Professor of Air Science.

pas: Passage.

pasep: Being passed separately.

PAST: Professor of air science and tactics, now historical.

pat: Patrol used in combinations only.

pathol: Pathologist.

PAV: Personnel allotment voucher.

pax: Passenger or passengers.

PBR: Precision bombing range.

PBX: Private branch exchange.

PC: Port call; Prior conviction.

PCA: Permanent change of assignment.

pclk: Pay clerk.

PCS: Permanent change of station; Post, camp, or station.

pct: Percent.

PD: Port of debarkation.

pd: Paid; Period.

pdn: Production.

PDR: Philippine Defense Ribbon.

PE: Port of embarkation, when used in combinations.

pend: Pending.

pent: Penetrate or penetration.

per: Permission.

PerAM: Personnel action memorandum.

peref: Personal effects.

perf: Perform or performance.

PERG: Production equipment redistribution group.

peri: Perimeter.

perm: Permanent.

permr: Permanent residence.

pernogra: Permission not granted.

perp: Personnel processing.

pers: Personnel.

perscon: Personnel control. money.

persexp: Personal expense

pert: Pertain or pertinent.

pet: Petition.

pet. den.: Petition denied.

petrl: Petroleum.

PF: Pneumatic float; Proximity fuse.

PFBrg: Pneumatic float bridge.

pfc or PFC: Private first class.

PFD: Present for duty.

pfdr: Pathfinder.

PG: Permanent grade; Post graduate; Proving ground.

pgn: Pigeon.

pgnd: Propaganda.

p gr: Petition for review granted.

PH: Purple Heart.

ph: Phase.

pharm: Pharmacy or pharmacist.

phot: Photographer.

photo: Photograph.

phys: Physical.

PI: Photo interpreter or photo interpretation; Public information; Philippines.

PIB: Publishing Information Bulletin.

PIC: Pursuant to instructions contained in; Photo interpretation center.

pic: Picture.

PID: Public information division; Photo-interpretation department.

PIF: Pilots' Information File.

PIO: Public Information officer or public information office.

PIR: Philippine Independence Ribbon.

pkbd: Packboard.

pkdom: Pack for domestic use.

pkg: Package.

pkmr: Packmaster.

pkr: Packer.

pksea: Pack for overseas.

PL: Public Law; Phase line; Pipeline; Pay loss.

plat: Platoon.

plb: Plumber or plumbing.

plcy: Policy.

PLR: Philippine Liberation Ribbon.

PLS: Procurement Legal Service.

plt: Pilot.

Plt. Off: Pilot Officer, British.

PM: Provost marshall.

P.M.O.: Principal medical officer, British.

PMOS: Primary military occupational specialty.

PMST: Professor of Military Science and Tactics.

pmt: Payment.

PMW: Prompt mobilization designation withdrawn.

pndg: Pending.

PNFD: Present not for duty.

pnl: Panel.

PNMO: Provided no military objection exists.

PNS: Professor of Naval Service.

pnt: Patient.

PO: Post office; Petty Officer; Previous orders.

POA: Pacific Ocean Area.

POAE: Port of aerial embarkation.

POC: Privately owned conveyance.

POD: Port of debarkation.

POE: Port of embarkation.

POI: Programs of instruction.

POL: Petroleum, oil, and lubricants.

polit: Political.

POM: Preparation for oversea movement.

pon: Pontoon.

POR: Preparation for oversea movement of individual replacements.

PorDir: Port Director.

posit: Position.

poss: Possession.

pot: Potential or potentiality.

POW: Prisoner of war.

PP: Private property; Permanent-party; Parcel Post.

PPG: Personnel processing group.

PPI: Plan-position indicator.

PPO: Publications and printing office.

PPR: Permanent pay record.

PPSq: Personnel Processing Squadron.

PR: Procurement regulations; Parachute rigger; Puerto Rico; Purchase request.

P/R: Pay roll.

prchst: Parachutist.

PrchstBad: Parachutist Badge.

prcht: Parachute.

prec: Precedence or precision.

prej: Prejudice.

prelim: Preliminary.

prem: Premium.

prep: Prepare.

prev: Previous.

PRF: Pulse recurrence frequency.

prim: Primary.

prin: Principal.

pris: Prison or prisoner.

pro: Proceed or procedure; Procure or procurement; Prophylactic.

proc: Procure.

Proc Cir: Army Procurement Circular.

prod: Product.

produtas: Proceed on duty assigned.

proj: Project or projectile.

ProLT: Procurement lead time.

prom: Promote or promotion.

proml: Promulgate.

prop: Property; Propeller.

prov: Provide, provision, or provisional.

prpln: Propulsion.

PRS: Physically restricted status.

PRT: Personnel research test.

PSD: Promotion service date.

PSDS: Permanently separated from duty station.

pstl: Postal.

psych: Psychology or psychological.

psywar: Psychological warfare.

PT: Physical training.

pt: Point.

ptbl: Portable.

ptgt: Primary target.

PTO: Port transportation officer.

pty: Party.

pub: Publish, public, publication, or publicity.

PUC: Presidential Unit Citation.

pur: Pursuit, purchase, or pursuant.

pvnt: Prevent or preventive.

pvt: Private.

PWCen: Public works center.

PX: Army Exchange.

Q

QM: Quartermaster.

QMC: Quartermaster Corps.

QMG: Quartermaster General.

QPL: Qualified Products List.

qtr: Quarter or quarterly.

qty: Quantity.

quad: Quadruplicate.

qual: Qualify or qualification.

quar: Quarantine.

ques: Question.

quin: Quintuplicate.

R

RA: Regular Army.

RAD: Reported for active duty.

rad: Radio.

rada: Radioactive.

RADAR: Radio detection and ranging.

RADCM: Radar countermeasures and deception.

radl: Radiological.

radlic: Radio link.

radlo: Radiological defense officer.

radlsafe: Radiological safety.

radlwar: Radiological warfare.

RAdm: Rear admiral.

RadPropCast: Radio propagation forecast.

RadSO: Radiological survey officer.

R.A.E.: Royal Aircraft Establishment, British.

RAF: Royal Air Force, British.

RAl: Reenlistment allowance.

R&D: Research and development.

RaOb: Radiosonde observation.

RApCon: Radar approach control center.

RAPP: Registered air parcel post.

rat: Rations, rate, or rating.

RATO: Rocket assisted takeoff.

Ratt: Radioteletypewriter.

RB: Road bend; Relative bearing.

RC: Reception center.

RCAF: Royal Canadian Air Force.

RCC: Rescue control center.

RCM: Radar countermeasures.

RCN: Royal Canadian Navy.

RCP: Rotation combat personnel.

RCS: Reports control symbol.

RCT: Regimental combat team.

RCTSR: Radio code test, speed of response.

RD: Readiness date or radarman.

rd: Road.

RDF: Radio direction-finder or radio direction-finding.

RDT: Reserve duty training.

rdvu: Rendezvous.

rdy: Ready.

re: Regard.

rec: Receive, record, recreation, or receipt.

recm: Recommend.

RECNO: This office has no record of.

recog: Recognize.

recomp: Recommend completion.

recon: Reconnaissance or reconnoiter, reconsideration.

recond: Recondition.

reconst: Reconstruct.

recov: Recover or recovery.

recp: Reciprocal or reciprocating.

red: Reduce.

reefer: Refrigerator.

reenl: Reenlist.

ref: Refer or refresher.

refd: Refund.

ReFrAd: Release from active duty.

refrg: Refrigerate.

refrig: Refrigeration.

reg: Regulate, regulation, or regular.

RegAF: Regular Air Force.

regis: Register.

regt: Regiment.

reh: Rehearing.

reh. den.: Rehearing denied.

rehab: Rehabilitate.

reimb: Reimburse.

ReInCo: Report(ing) in compliance.

reinf: Reinforce.

rejn: Rejoin.

rel: Relief, relieve, or relation.

RelBy: When relieved by.

REle: Radio electrician.

rels: Release.

rem: Remanded.

remd: Remanded.

renv: Renovate.

reorg: Reorganize.

rep: Repair, represent, or reported.

repat: Repatriate.

RepCAT: Report corrective action taken.

RepDu: Reporting for duty.

RepIN: Reply if negative.

repl: Replace or replacement.

repln: Replenish.

repmt: Repayment.

repro: Reproduce.

rept: Report.

req: Request.

res: Reserve.

resc: Rescind.

resig: Resignation.

resp: Responsible or responsibility.

rest: Restrict.

resup: Resupply.

ret: Retire, returned.

retro: Retroactive.

rev: Reversed.

revd: Reversed.

revo: Revoke or revocation.

rew: Reward.

RFI: Ready for issue.

rfl: Refuel.

rfty: Reformatory.

RG: Reserve grade.

rg: Range.

rgn: Region or regional.

rgr: Rigger.

RH: Relative humidity.

rhd: Railhead.

RIF: Reduction in force.

RIO: Reporting in and out.

RIT: Radio Information Test.

RJ: Road junction.

rkt: Rocket.

rktr: Rocketeer.

RL: Rocket launcher.

RLTA: Reenlistment leave travel allowance.

rltv: Relative.

RM: Radioman; Receiver mobile.

RMM: Rifle marksman.

rnd: Round.

rngt: Renegotiate.

rngtn: Renegotiation.

ROCCM: Controlled devices countermeasures and deception.

ROCP: Radar out of commission for parts.

ROIC: Resident officer in charge.

ROICC: Resident officer in charge of construction.

ROK: Republic of Korea.

ROKPUCE: Republic of Korea Presidential Unit Citation Emblem.

ROPA: Reserve Officer Personnel Act.

ROS: Reduced operational status.

ROTC: Reserve Officers Training Corps.

rout: Routine.

RP: Release point; Rally point; Rocket projectile.

RPIO: Registered publication issuing office.

RPMIO: Registered publication mobile issuing office(r).

rpmn: Repairman.

RPS: Registered publication section.

RPSM: Registered publication shipment memorandum.

rpt: Repeat.

rptr: Repeater.

RPU: Registered publication unit.

rqn: Requisition.

rqr: Require or requirement.

RQS: Ready qualified for standby.

RR: Railroad.

RROTC: Executive for Reserve and ROTC affairs.

RRS: Retired Reserve Section.

RS: Road space; Regulating station; Reception station; Revised Statutes of the United States.

RSCR: Reserve Special Commendation Ribbon.

rsg: Reassign.

rsgmt: Reassignment.

rsn: Reason.

rspv: Respective.

rsq: Rescue.

RSS: Rifle sharpshooter.

RT: Ranger tab; Reduction table; Receive-transmit; Radiotelephone.

RTC: Replacement training center.

RtdA: Returned absentee.

rtn: Return or returnee; Retrain.

RTO: Rail transportation office(r).

RTST: Radio technician selection test.

RUQ: Rifle unqualified.

RUUR: Regrade unclassified upon receipt.

RV: Reading and vocabulary test.

rvw: Review.

RW: Radiological warfare.

RWR: Rail-water-rail.

rwy: Runway.

ry: Railway; Capitalized RY means Ryuku when used in combinations.

S

SA: Secretary of the Army; Small arms.

SAA: Senior Army Advisor.

SAC: Strategic Air Command; Supreme Allied Commander in combinations only; Senior aircraftman, British.

SACEur: Supreme Allied Commander, Europe.

SACLant: Supreme Allied Commander, Atlantic.

SAF: Secretary of the Air Force; Strategic air force.

SAFI: Senior Air Force Instructor.

SAFS: Secondary Air Force Specialty.

slav: Salvage.

SAM: Surface-to-air missile; School of Aviation Medicine; Special air mission.

S&B: Sterlization and bath.

SAR: Search and rescue.

sat: Satisfactory; Saturday.

SAtk: Strike attack.

SB: Supply bulletin.

SBA: Small Business Administration.

sbm: Submit or submission.

SBR: Standby reserve, used in Af accounts to designate tools and equipment in that category.

sbtg: Sabotage.

sby: Standby.

SC: Supply Corps; Statistical control; Service command as used in the Marine Corps; Stratocumulus; Seperate cover: Signal Corps. See SigC which is the authorized abreviation for Signal Corps.

SCARWAF: Special category Army personnel with Air Force.

SCC: Standard commodity classification.

SCCO: Security classification control officer.

SCEL: Signal Corps Engineering Laboratories.

sch: School.

SCM: Summary court-martial.

SCMO: Summary Court-Martial Order.

SCNAWAF: Special Category Navy with Air Force.

SCO: Statistical Control Office(r).

SCP: Survey control point.

SCPt: Security control point.

SCS: Signal communications system.

sct: Scout.

SDO: Special duty only.

SE: Single engine.

SEATO: Southeast Asia Treaty Organization.

sec: Section or security; Secretary in combinations only.

secd: Secondary.

SecNav: Secretary of the Navy.

secy: Secretary.

sel: Selectee.

SENL: Standard Equipment Nomenclature List.

sep: Separate.

SepRos: Separation processing.

ser: Serial.

SERTH: Satisfactory evidence received this headquarters.

serv: Service in combinations only.

sev: Sever.

SF: Standard form.

sfc: Sergeant first class.

sfgd: Safeguard.

SG: Surgeon General; Standing Group; Smoke generator, as part of a symbol.

sgd: Signed.

SGLO: Standing Group Liaison Officer to the North Atlantic Council.

SGN: Standing Group, North Atlantic Treaty Organization.

sgnr: Signature.

sgt: Sergeant.

SHAPE: Supreme Headquarters Allied Powers, Europe.

SHF: Super high frequency.

ShipDa: Shipping data.

ShipDTO: Ship on depot transfer order.

ShipgO: Shipping order.

ShipIm: Ship immediately.

shipmt: Shipment.

ShipReq: Ship to apply on requisition.

shp: Shaft horsepower.

ShpTArBy: Ship to arrive not later than.

shrtg: Shortage.

SIAM: Signal information and monitoring.

SIC: Survey information center.

sig: Signal.

SigC: Signal Corps.

SigO: Signal Officer.

SIOE: Special issue of equipment.

SIP: Standard Inspection Procedure.

siper: Request the following items be domestic packed and shipped to.

sipex: Request the following items be export packed and shipped to.

sit: Situation when used in combinations.

SitRep: Situation report.

SIW: Self-inflicted wounds.

SJA: Staff Judge Advocate.

skd: Skilled.

sked: Schedule.

SLO: Staff Legal Officer.

SLOE: Special list of equipment.

SLSM: Silver Life Saving Medal.

slt: Searchlight.

SM: Soldier's Medal; Strategic missile, as in SM-65.

SMA: Senior military attache.

SMaj: Sergeant Major.

smbl: Semimoble.

smcln: Semicolon.

SME: Standard Medical Examination.

SMG: Submachine gun.

SMLO: Senior military liaison officer.

SMM: Specialty Meritorious Medal.

SMO: So much of.

SMOP: So much of paragraph.

SMR: Special money requisition.

SMS: Subject matter specialist.

SMT: Shop mechanic's test.

SN: Service number.

SNL: Standard nomenclature list.

SO: Special orders; Shipment; Sonarman; Superior Officer.

SOA: Speed of advance.

SOFAR: Sound fixing and ranging.

SOI: Signal operation instructions; Standing operating instructions.

SOIC: Supply officer in command.

SOLog: Standardization of certain aspects of operations and logistics.

SONAR: Sound, navigation and ranging.

SOP: Standing operating procedure.

SOQ: Sick officer's quarters.

SP: Shore Police or shore party.

sp: Special.

spchgr: Supercharger.

SpCM: Special court-martial; Spanish Campaign Medal.

SPE: Subport of embarkation; Special purpose equipment.

spec: Specify or specification.

SpecDevCen: Special Devices Center.

specl: Specialist or specialize.

SpecDiaT: Special diary transcript.

spn: Sponsor.

SOP: Special Order.

SpS: Special Services.

SPTC: Special Period of Time Contract.

SptL: Support line.

sq: Squadron.

sqd: Squad.

SR: Service Record; Special regulations; Shipment request; Saudi Arabia. Nationaly Condesation Code; Short range when referring to radar sets.

S/R: Service record.

sr: Senior.

SrAvBad: Senior Army Aviator Badge.

SRB: Service record book.

SRC: Standard requirements code; Sound ranging control.

SrParaBad: Senior parachutist badge.

SS: Sworn statement; Steamship; Special Staff; Staff specialist; Surveillance station; Selective Service; Standard frequency station; Silver Star Medal.

SSB: Single side band.

SSgt: Staff sergeant.

SSI: Standing signal instructions.

SSIA: Specification serial of individual assigned.

SSM: Silver Star Medal; Surface-to-surface missile.

SSO: Statistical service office or statistical service officer.

SSS: Selective Service System; Strategic support squadron.

SSU: Statistical service unit.

SSvc: Selective Service.

st: Street; Statement.

sta: Station.

stat: Statistic; statute.

stbd: Starboard.

stc: Stepchild.

std: Standing or standard.

steno: Stenographer.

ster: Sterilize.

stev: Stevedore.

stg: Staging.

StgAr: Staging area.

STgt: Secondary target.

stk: Stock.

stlr: Semitrailer.

STon: Short ton.

stor: Storage.

stp: Stoppage.

str: Strength.

strag: Straggler.

StragL: Straggler line.

strat: Strategic.

strato: Stratosphere.

stu: Student.

SU: Area service unit.

subj: Subject.

subor: Subordinate.

subq: Subsequent.

subs: Subsistence.

suf: Sufficient.

sug: Suggest.

SumC: Summary court.

SumCM: Summary court-martial.

sup: Supply.

sup d: Supplementary decision.

super: Supersede or supercession.

supp: Support; Supplement.

suppl: Supplement.

SupPt: Supply point.

supr: Superior.

supt: Superintend or superintendent.

supv: Supervise or supervisor.

sur: Surface in combination only.

surf: Surface.

surg: Surgeon or surgical.

surr: Surrender.

SurTrans: (Via) first available government transportation not including air.

surv: Survive.

SUSMOP: Senior United States military observer, Palestine.

susp: Suspend.

sv: Surveyer; Survey; Service.

svc: Service.

SW: Steel worker.

SWB: Short wheelbase.

swbd: Switchboard.

SWeFCO: Special weapons ferry control office.

SWEL: Special weapons equipment list.

SWSD: Special weapons supply depot.

SWTA: Special weapons training allowance.

synop: Synopsis or synoptic.

sys: System.

T

TA. Table of allowance; Target area.

tab: Tabulate.

TAC: Tactical Air Command.

tac: Tactics or tactical used in combining abbreviations, as in tac officer; Tacometer.

TACC: Tactical air control center.

TACGru: Tactical air control group.

TACRon: Tactical air control squadron.

TAF: Tactical air force.

TAFMSD: Total active federal military service date.

TAG: The Adjutant General.

TAHq: Theater Army Headquarters.

TAT: To accompany troops. Used and written 'tat', as in tat box, tat equipment.

TATB: Theatre Air Transportation Board.

TB: Technical bulletin.

TBA: To be activated.

TBD: To be disbanded.

TBGAA: Travel by government automobile authorized.

TBI: To be inactivated.

TBMAA: Travel by military aircraft authorized.

TBS: The basic school.

TC: Trial counsel; Training circular; Transportation Corps; Training center; True course; Troop carrier.

T.C.: Tax Court Reports.

TCC: Transport control center; Tactical control center; Troop Carrier.

TCO: Test control officer.

TCP: Traffic control post.

TCS: Temporary change of station.

TD: Table of distribution; Tank destroyer; Transmitter distributor.

T.D. Treasury Decision.

TDN: Travel as directed is necessary in the military service.

TDPFO: Temporary duty pending further orders.

TDRL: Temporary disability retired list.

tdwy: Treadway.

TDY: Temporary duty.

TE: Twin engine; Task element.

tec: Technician.

tech: Technical.

telecom: Telecommunications.

telecon: Teletypewriter conference.

temp: Temporary; Temperature.

term: Terminate.

terr: Territory.

TF: Total forfeitures; Task force; Training film; Trainer-fighter; Test flight.

tfc: Traffic.

TDCSD: Total federal commissioned service date.

tg: Telegraph or telegram.

tgt: Target.

thou: Thousand.

THq: Theater headquarters.

thru: Through.

thtr: Theater.

TIG: The Inspector General.

TimIG: Time in grade.

TJA: Trial judge advocate.

TJAG: The Judge Advocate General.

TJAGC: The Judge Advocate General's Corps.

TJAGSA: The Judge Advocate General's School, United States Army.

tkr: Tanker.

tl: Truckload.

TLP: Total loss of pay.

tlr: Trailer.

tltr: Translator.

TM: Technical manual.

TMDAG: This mode of transportation has been determined to be more advantageous to the Government.

TMSD: Total military service date.

tn: Train.

tng: Training.

tnr: Trainer.

tntv: Tentative.

TO: Technical order, officially in combinations only but used alone in common practice; Theater of operations, in combinations only; Takeoff.

TOC: Technical order compliance; Theater of operations command.

TOD: Time of delivery.

TOE: Term of enlistment; Tables of organization and equipment.

TOF: Time of filing.

TOO: Time of origin.

topo: Topography.

TopSec: Top Secret.

TOR: Time of receipt.

torp: Torpedo in combinations only; torpedoman.

TOS: Term of service.

TOT: Time on target or time over target; Time of transmission; Table of organization.

tp: Telephone.

TPA: Travel by privately owned conveyance authorized.

TPSN: Troop program sequence number.

TQMG: The Quartermaster General.

TR: Transportation request; Transmit-receive.

tr: Training division; Transcript.

tra: Training in combinations only.

trac: Tractor; Tracer.

tracdr: Tractor-drawn.

tran: Transient.

trans: Transport.

TrB: Troop basis.

trcmn: Traincrewman.

trf: Transfer.

trip: Triplicate.

trk: Truck.

trmt: Treatment.

trne: Trainee.

trns: Transition.

trp: Troop.

trsy: Treasury.

TS: Transit storage; Transmittal sheet; Top Secret.

TSD: Theater shipping document.

TSG: The Surgeon General.

TSgt: Technical sergeant.

TTA: Travel time authorized.

TTAF: Technical Training Air Force.

TTE: Tentative table of equipment.

TTP: Total taxable pay.

TU: Taks unit; Technical service unit; Training unit as used in combination.

TV: Television; Test vehicle (guided missile); Terminal velocity.

tvl: Travel.

TWoT: Travel without troops.

twr: Tower.

TWT: Travel with troops.

TWX: Teletypewriter exchange (commercial).

twy: Taxiway.

TYSD: Total years service date.

U

U: Unit.

UA: Uniform allowance; Unauthorized absence.

UAM: Underwater-to-air missile.

UC: Under construction.

UCMJ: Uniform Code of Military Justice.

UCWR: Upon completion thereof will return to.

UD: Undesirable discharge.

UDT: Underwater demolition team.

UDU: Underwater demolition unit.

UE: Unit exhausted; Unit equipment.

UEAC: Unit equipment aircraft.

UEE: Unit essential equipment.

UF: Unit of fire.

UHC: Under honorable conditions.

UHF: Ultra high frequency. Also written 'uhf'.

UK: United Kingdom.

UMTS: Universal military training in service.

UN: United Nations.

UNCMAC: United Nations Command Military Armistice Commission.

unex: Unexecuted.

unfav: Unfavorable.

unif: Uniform or uniformity.

univ: Universal or university.

unilq: Unliquidated.

UnODir: Unless otherwise directed.

UNOINDC: Unless otherwise indicated.

unpd: Unpaid.

unqual: Unqualified.

unrep: Unreported.

unsat: Unsatisfactory.

unskd: Unskilled.

unsvc: Unserviceable.

UNSvM: United Nations Service Medal.

UOHC: Under other than honorable conditions.

UP: Under provisions of.

UP&T: Unit personnel and tonnage table.

UPO: Unit personnel office or unit personnel officer.

UPREAL: Unit property record and equipment authorization list.

UpRec: Upon receipt.

UPREL: Unit property record and equipment list.

UPS: Under provisions of section.

urg: Urgent.

US: United States. Often written U.S.

USA: United States Army.

USAF: United States Air Force.

USAFA: United States Air Force Academy.

USAFECI: United States Air Force Extension Course Institute.

USAFI: United States Armed Force Institute.

USAFOCS: United States Air Force Officer Candidate School.

USAFPS: United States Air Force Pilot School.

USAFSS: United States Air Force Security Service.

USAirA: United States Air Attache.

USC: Under separate cover; United States Code.

USCA: United States Code Annotated.

USCG: United States Coast Guard.

USCGA: United States Coast Guard Academy.

USCINCEur: United States Commander in Chief, Europe.

USCMA: United States Court of Military Appeals.

USDB: United States Disciplinary Barracks.

usea: Undersea.

USForAz: United States Forces in Azores.

USLant: United States Atlantic Subarea.

USLO: United States liaison officer.

USM: Underwater-to-surface missile.

USMA: United States Military Academy.

USMC: United States Marine Corps.

USMeMilComUn: United States members, UN Military Staff Committee.

USMilComUN: United States delegation, UN Military Staff Committee.

USMilLias: United States Military Liaison Office.

USMS: United States Maritime Service.

USN: United States Navy.

USNA: United States Naval Academy.

USO: United Service Organizations.

USPDO: United States Property and Disbursing Officer.

USPHS: United States Public Health Service.

USRepMilComUN: United States Representative, United Nations Military Staff Committee.

USS: United States Ship.

USSecMilComUN: The Secretary. United States Delegation, United Nations Staff Committee.

UST: United States Treaties.

ut: Utility, in combinations only.

util: Utility.

UWaTU: Underway training unit.

uwtr: Underwater.

UXB: Unexploded bomb.

V

VA: Veterans Administration.

vac: Vacant, vacate, or vacuum.

vacci: Vaccine or vaccinate.

VA Reg.: VA Regulations.

VAdm: Vice admiral.

VCP: Vehicle collecting point.

VCS: Vice Chief of Staff.

veh: Vehicle.

vel: Velocity.

ver: Verify.

vert: Vertical.

vet: Veteran or veterinary.

Vet. Reg.: Veterans' Regulations.

VFR: Visual flight rules.

VH: Very high.

VHF: Very high frequency.

vic: Vicinity.

VIP: Very important person; Very important passenger.

vis: Visual or visibility.

VLR: Very long range.

VMWW I: Victory Medal, World War I.

VMWW II: Victory Medal, World War II.

VO: Verbal orders.

VOC: Verbal orders of the commander; Vehicle out of commission.

VOCG: Verbal order commanding general.

VOCO: Verbal orders commanding officer.

VOCS: Verbal orders chief of staff.

vol: Volume or volunteer.

VOQ: Visiting officers' quarters.

VOR: VHF omnidirectional range.

vou: Voucher.

VPM: Vehicles per mile.

VTU: Volunteer training unit.

W

w: With, in combinations only; wife.

W/A: Wrongful appropriation.

WAB: When authorized by.

WAC: Women's Army Corps; World Aeronautical Chart.

WAF: Women in the Air Force.

WB: Weather Bureau; Wage Board, as used by Civil Service in job classification.

w/b: Will be.

WBI: Will be issued.

WD: When directed; Wind direction.

wd: Withdrawn.

wea: Weather.

wg: Wing.

wh: When or where.

w/h: Withholding.

whap: When or where applicable.

whs: Warehouse.

wi: Within.

WIA: Wounded in action.

wit: Witness.

wk: Week.

WMS: Women's Medical Specialist.

WMSC: Women's Medical Specialist Corps.

WNB: Will not be.

wng: Warning.

WO: Warrant officer; Warning order.

wo: Without. Often written w/o.

WOHC: Warrant officer, Hospital Corps.

WOJG: Warrant officer, junior grade.

WOQT: Warrant Officer Qualification Test.

WP: Will proceed; White phosphorus.

WPM: Words per minute.

wpn: Weapon.

WPS: With prior service.

WPWOD: Will proceed without delay.

WR: Water-rail.

WREN: Women's Royal Naval Service, British.

wrnt: Warrant.

wrtr: Writer.

WS: Water supply.

WSEG: Weapons Systems Evaluation Group.

WSP: Water supply point.

WSup: Water Supply.

wvd: Waived.

WW: World wide or World War.

WW I: World War I.

WW II: World War II.

X

X: Experimental.

xfmr: Transformer.

xmit: Transmit.

xmsn: Transmission.

xmtr: Transmitter.

XO: Executive officer.

xpd: Expedite.

xplt: Exploit.

xtal: Crystal.

Y

YOB: Year of birth.

yr: Year.

YSP: Years service for severance pay purposes.

Z

Z: Zone, in combinations only.

ZF: Zone of fire.

ZI: Zone of interior.

ZTO: Zone transportation office.

BIBLIOGRAPHY

Black, Henry Campbell, 1860-1927.
Black's Law dictionary; definitions of the terms and phrases of American and English jurisprudence, ancient and modern. 4th ed. by the publisher's editorial staff. St. Paul, West Pub. Co., 1951.

Blakiston's new Gould medical dictionary.
A modern comprehensive dictionary of the terms used in all branches of medicine and allied sciences . . . Editors: Normand L. Hoerr and Arthur Osol. With the cooperation of an editorial board and 88 contributors. 2d ed. New York, Blakiston Division, McGraw-Hill, 1956.

Bouvier, John.
Bouvier's law dictionary. Baldwin's Students ed., 1934, edited by William Edward Baldwin . . . Cleveland, Banks-Baldwin law publishing company, 1934.

Bradford, Gershom.
A glossary of sea terms, by Gershom Bradford . . . New York, Dodd, Mead & company, 1942.

Dorland, William Alexander Newman.
The American illustrated medical dictionary; a new and complete dictionary of the terms used in medicine, surgery, dentistry, pharmacy, chemistry, and the kindred branches, with their pronunciation, derivation and definition . . . Philadelphia, Saunders, 1957.

Gaynor, Frank.
The new military and naval dictionary. New York, Philosophical Library, 1951.

Kerchove, Rene de.
International maritime dictionary; an encyclopedic dictionary of useful maritime terms and phrases, together with equivalents in French and German. New York, D. Van Nostrand Co., 1948.

Kupper, William Howard, 1908-.
Dictionary of psychiatry and psychology; an illustrated condensed encyclopedia of psychiatry, neurology, and psychology. With a foreword by Douglas M. Kelley. Paterson, N. J., Colt Press, 1953.

Maloy, Bernard S. 1875-.
The simplified medical dictionary for lawyers. 2d. ed. Chicago, Calleghan, 1951. vii, 582 p. illus. 26cm.

Noel, John Vavasour.
Naval terms dictionary. New York, Van Nostrand, 1952.

Radin, Max, 1880-1950.
Law dictionary; edited by Lawrence G. Greene. ed. New York, Oceana Publication, 1955.

Schwartz, Robert J.
The complete dictionary of abbreviations. New York, Crowell, 1955.

Shumaker, Walter Adams.
The cyclopedic law dictionary defining terms and phrases of American jurisprudence, of ancient and modern common law, international law, civil law, the French and Spanish law, and other juridical systems, with an exhaustive collection of legal maxims,

by Walter A. Shumaker and George Foster Longsdorf. 3d ed., by Frank D. Moore. Chicago, Callaghan and company, 1940.

Tedrow, R. L.
Digested and Annotated Opinions of the United States Court of Military Appeals. Washington, D. C., Dept. of the Navy, 1957.

U. S. Department of the Army.
Evidence: Special Text of the Judge Advocate General's School. Charlottesville, Va., 1959.

U. S. Department of the Army.
Military Justice Handbook: The Law Officer. Washington, D. C., U. S. Army. April, 1958.

U. S. Department of the Army.
Military Terms, Abbreviations and Symbols; Dictionary of United States Army Terms. Washington, D. C., 1958.

U. S. Air University. Research Studies Institute.
The United States Air Force dictionary. Woodford Agee Heflin, editor. Maxwell Air Force Base? Ala., Air University Press, 1956.

U. S. Joint Chiefs of Staff.
Dictionary of United States military terms for joint usage. Washington, Depts. of the Army, Navy, and the Air Force, July, 1959.

Words and phrases.
Permanent ed. 1658 to date . . . All judicial constructions and definitions of words and phrases by the state and federal courts from the earliest times, alphabetically arranged and indexed. St. Paul, Minn., West publishing co., 1940.